Live Safely in a Dangerous World

How to Beat the Odds of Dying in an Accident

John C. Myre

Live Safely in a Dangerous World:
How to Beat the Odds of Dying in an Accident

Copyright © 2002 by John C. Myre

> BookMasters, Inc.
> Telephone: (800)247-6553
> Fax: (419)281-6883
> E-mail: order@bookmaster.com
> Internet: www.atlasbooks.com

Illustrations: R.J. Shay
Cover Design: Chuck Hathaway / Mendocino Graphics
Book Design: Cypress House

Publisher's Note:
Every effort has been made to ensure that the information contained in this book is complete and accurate. However, every hazardous situation presents unique issues and problems. Thus the ideas, procedures, and suggestions in this book must be viewed in context and considered in light of your own good judgment. This book is not intended as a substitute for consulting with your physician and obtaining medical supervision as to any activity, procedure, or suggestion that might affect your health or the health of your family. Accordingly, individual readers must assume responsibility for their own actions, safety, and health. Neither the author nor the publisher shall be liable or responsible for any loss, injury, or damage allegedly arising from any information or suggestion in this book.

Library of Congress Cataloging-in-Publication Data

Myre, John C., 1936-
  Live safely in a dangerous world : how to beat the odds of dying in an accident / John C. Myre.– 1st ed.
      p. cm.
  Includes index.
  ISBN 0-9720039-4-0 (alk. paper)
  1. Accidents–Prevention. 2. Safety education. I. Title.
  HV675 .M97 2002
613.6–dc21
                                                    2002006882

2 4 6 8 9 7 5 3 1

*To my wife Carole,
and children, Greg, Keith, and Elizabeth,
for their encouragement and support.*

About the Author and Contributors

John Myre is editor and publisher of *Safety Times*, and also does the research for the articles. He founded the publication in 1992. His experience includes thirty-four years as a financial and risk management executive with Southwestern Bell Corporation. A graduate of Washington University in St. Louis, Missouri, Myre is a member of the National Safety Council, and has achieved the Associate in Risk Management (ARM) designation. He has been a speaker at several safety conventions, has written articles for safety and risk management publications such as *Professional Safety* magazine and *Business Insurance* magazine, and is the author of the off-the-job safety chapter in *Safety and Health Management Planning* (Government Institutes, 1999).

John Myre can be contacted at sfttimes@swbell.net. The Web site for *Safety Times* is www.safetytimes.com.

Contributors

Writer

Tom Rami is a professional writer from Edwardsville, Illinois. After retiring from Southwestern Bell Corporation, he was the editor of *St. Louis* Magazine. He currently writes for organizations in the St. Louis area, and can be contacted at (618) 656-9375.

Illustrator

R. J. Shay is an illustrator/designer and principal with Studio X Design in St. Louis, Missouri. Its team of designers and video experts has created projects and campaigns for clients from Anheuser-Busch to Xerox. R. J. can be contacted at rj@rjshay.com, (314) 773-9989, or visit the Web site at studiox.cx.

Special thanks to Anthony Tharenos, graphic designer, and Sharon Lynn Campbell, M.A., Certified Safety Professional, whose skills and commitment help make the publication of *Safety Times* possible.

Contents

Introduction

A few years into the future, a new drug-resistant virus suddenly appears in the United States, striking indiscriminately: newborns and senior citizens are felled; it takes a particularly heavy toll on teenagers and young adults. Over 90,000 die each year, and millions more are disabled, some permanently. A person will leave home in the morning and, later in the day, a loved one will receive the terrible news that he or she has died or is seriously ill.

The disease quickly becomes headline news. There is no cure, but preventive measures are found and publicized. As these are developed, organizations create elaborate plans to inform their employees.

Still the disease rages. It is usually contracted as the result of an individual's failure to take proper precautions. Worse, many people are infected as a result of others' failure to follow the preventive guidelines.

This fictional virus would surely stir a national effort to find a cure. Yet today, something is causing widespread death and injury, and the response is surprisingly muted. I'm talking about accidents, and our apparent willingness to tolerate such a huge casualty toll year after year, when good safety habits, practiced consistently, could save thousands of lives each year.

The only acceptable grade when it comes to safety is 100 percent. For example, in your house you might have stairs that you use thousands of time a year. A grade of 99.9 percent isn't good enough, because that one fall could be fatal.

All of us have top priorities in life, but most of us do not consciously make safety a top priority. To have a better chance to fully experience and enjoy our priorities, we need to add personal and family safety to our top-priority list.

In our early years, we too often take the attitude that accidents will never happen to us. Even when we get older and presumably wiser, this attitude never entirely goes away. But if we wish to enjoy life to its fullest, safety must become part of our personal lifestyle, a twenty-four-hour commitment.

One purpose of this book is to alert you to the many hazards you and your family face in daily living — from driving the family car, to cooking, to swimming, to taking those first steps as a toddler. The goal is to help you beat the 1-in-45 odds of dying in an accident (see page [xii] for the facts).

It wasn't too long ago that children rode their bikes through the streets without wearing safety helmets. Car seats for children were flimsy contraptions that offered no protection. Potent medicines didn't have safety caps to guard against curious children rifling through the medicine cabinet, and few parents gave serious thought to childproofing their houses.

Family safety awareness has come a long way since then, yet most families still lack a systematic approach to safety. The information that is available comes to you in a variety of ways—magazines, newspapers, TV, and the School of Hard Knocks. Rather than the traditional piecemeal approach, this book will give you and your family an organized and comprehensive way to address safety issues.

Is an "Accident" Really an Accident?

A basic reason why we don't pay more attention to safety is that the word "accident" is used incorrectly. The dictionary defines accident as "an unexpected and undesirable event, something that occurs unexpectedly or unintentionally, fortune or chance." I have no quarrel with the "undesirable," but the belief that accidents are unexpected or the result of fortune or chance is misleading.

For example, is an accident unexpected when someone using a ladder reaches out too far and falls instead of taking time to reposition the ladder? Does an accident occur by fortune or chance when a person consistently tailgates and then, in a moment of inattention, slams into the driver ahead of him? Is it fate when a boater drinks too much and then collides with another boat on a lake at night?

The obvious answer is no! Most accidents can be better described as failures, failures on our part and failures on the part of others.

Personal Safety Plans

The key to a safer lifestyle is developing a Personal Safety Plan for every member of your family.

Each life is different. To make a safety program truly effective, it must be tailored to the individual. Family size and makeup, ages of family members, type of home and furnishings, domestic activities, recreational interests, and personal travel all differ.

Using this book, you can develop a Personal Safety Plan for each family member.

For the plan to really work, you must take the time to review the information periodically. For example, families that boat should review their boating safety file before each season.

The following are elements of a comprehensive Personal Safety Plan for you and your family to incorporate:

1. *Leadership*: There must be a safety leader within the family, one person who inspires and challenges the others to act safely. The leader establishes a safety policy and encourages setting standards for safe conditions and practices. The leader prompts the others and ensures that they are adequately equipped and educated. The leader also sets the example.

2. *Education*: Identify the hazards each family member faces on the road, at home, and in leisure activities. Use the table of contents and articles in this book to make a list of your family's activities and the related hazards.

Follow the outline on page [x] to develop a Personal Safety Plan tailored to each family member. After developing the initial safety plans, encourage everyone to become a leader, particularly with regard to his or her own safety. A Personal Safety Plan will not work unless each person is committed to doing things safely. This effort also involves periodic review and updates of Personal Safety Plans.

3. *Training*: Lack of knowledge or skill is the cause of many accidents. Training activities ensure that everyone acquires the knowledge needed for safety in all activities. Sometimes this occurs by formally teaching safe practices; at other times, it happens through self-study.

4. *Safety standards*: There are safety standards for homes, vehicles, and public areas. These standards were bought with someone's blood, and are the result of accident investigations. Someone must research the standards and verify that they are met. For example, be sure ground fault circuit interrupters are installed in bathrooms and the kitchen.

5. *Buying safe products*: Many tools and materials used in homes, hobbies, and other forms of recreation, have hazardous properties. Become familiar with them, tell family members about them, and buy the items that are least hazardous.

6. *Personal protective equipment*: Some hazards can be controlled with proper personal protective equipment, from clothing to protect against poisonous plants, to goggles or safety glasses to protect against chemicals or flying objects. The person involved must study the specific hazard, obtain suitable protection, and use it.

7. *Emergency preparedness*: Natural disasters and technological accidents can affect personal safety, and the effects vary from one situation to the next. As a family, consider potential disasters, make emergency plans, and hold emergency drills.

8. *Care of the injured*: First aid can prevent complications of injuries. Suitable first-aid kits need to be obtained and the family trained in first-aid techniques.

9. *Inspections*: Make periodic examinations of facilities, equipment, materials, and practices, to ensure that they continue to meet safety standards.

10. *Family meetings*: People need to be reminded about key aspects of safety and prevention of accidents. Hold family discussions quarterly, to review safety in the home and in the activities family members participate in. To assure their involvement, let the children assume some of the leadership.

Personal Safety Plan

The following is an example of a Personal Safety Plan developed using articles in this book. The plan is designed for working parents, with a three-year-old in daycare, who own a home in a Midwestern city, and enjoy outdoor activities. (Not all of the potentially applicable articles are listed in the example below.)

You can make copies of individual articles to put in a binder for each member of your family. To facilitate periodic reviews, highlight the safety tips that you find particularly helpful.

Article	When to Review	Action Items
Driving		
Around Big Trucks	Semiannually	
City Driving	Semiannually	
Defensive Driving	Semiannually	
Diverted Attention	Semiannually	
Expressway Driving	Semiannually	
Fall and Night Driving	Fall	Install new wiper blades
Long Distance Driving	Before a trip	Get car serviced
Occupant Protection	Semiannually	
Road Emergencies	Semiannually	Get annual safety inspection
Road Rage	Semiannually	
Speeding	Semiannually	
Home		
Bathroom	Semiannually	Install ground fault circuit interrupters
Carbon Monoxide	Fall	Install carbon monoxide detector
Electrical	Semiannually	
Falls	Semiannually	
Fire Detection & Response	Semiannually	Change smoke detector batteries in Oct.
Home Heating Equipment	Fall	Get furnace serviced in September

Article	When to Review	Action Items
Home (continued)		
Kitchen	Semiannually	Install safety locks on cabinets
Lawn Mower	Spring	Get mower serviced
Painting	Before painting	
Poisoning	Semiannually	Buy syrup of ipecac
Leisure and General		
Adult Sports	Spring	Meet with trainer to develop fitness plan
Back	Semiannually	
Bicycles - Adults	Spring	Inspect helmets; buy new ones if needed
Boating	Late spring	Test life jackets annually
Fitness	Semiannually	
Food Poisoning	Semiannually	
Heat Stress	Summer	
Skin Cancer	Summer	Use SPF-15 sunscreen
Swimming	Semiannually	
Child		
Babysitting Tips for Parents	Semiannually	Verify sitter has been trained
Burns	Semiannually	Reduce hot water temperature to 120° F
Car Seats & Booster Seats	Semiannually	Get installation checked by expert
Childcare	Semiannually	Review safety procedures with staff
Holidays	Semiannually	Check safety at grandparents' homes
Kitchens	Semiannually	
Playgrounds	Semiannually	
Toys	Quarterly	

Those 1-in-45 Odds of Dying in an Accident

As difficult as this may be to believe, the facts support the statement, and you need to know the facts if you're going to make safety part of your lifestyle. Rounding the numbers for the sake of clarity, here's how the number is arrived at:

Approximately 4,000,000 people are born each year. In a recent reporting period, over 97,000 people died from accidents (92,100 off the job, 5,200 on the job). The number killed in each age bracket stays relatively constant every year; that is, the number of one-year-olds killed remains about the same, as with two-year-olds, and fifty-five-year-olds.

Based on current statistics, 90,000 of the 4,000,000 people born each year will die in accidents. Dividing 4,000,000 by 90,000 gives us the 1-in-45 number. Here are recent statistics from the National Safety Council:

Cause	Number of Deaths
Motor vehicle	43,000
Falls	16,200
Poisoning by solids and liquids	11,700
Drowning	3,900
Fires and burns	3,600
Suffocation by ingested object	3,400
Firearms	600
Poisoning by gases and vapors	400
All other types*	14,500
Total	**97,300**

*Principal causes: medical and surgical complications and misadventures, machinery, air transport, water transport, mechanical suffocation, and excessive cold.

More Reasons to Have a Twenty-four-hour Safety Attitude

1. The lifetime odds of being killed in a motor-vehicle accident are about 1-in-100.

2. Accidents are the leading cause of death for people from ages one to thirty-eight.

3. Accidents rob Americans of more years of life before they reach age sixty-five than any other cause of death, including cancer, heart disease, homicide, and AIDS.

4. About 16,000,000 people suffer temporary or permanent disabling injuries from off-the-job accidents each year.

Driving
Safety
Introduction

Driving a car is one of our most routine activities, but it's also one of the most dangerous. Approximately 40,000 people are killed in motor-vehicle accidents each year. These 40,000 deaths translate into lifetime odds of 1-in-100 of dying in a motor-vehicle accident.

Another discouraging number is that 1-in-2 of us will suffer a temporary or permanent disabling injury* in a motor-vehicle accident.With odds like these, your only answer is to develop a defensive-driving attitude. As the articles in the Driving section show, you can take many steps to reduce the odds of becoming one of these statistics.

One of the most important steps is to develop an attitude to make every driving trip a "perfect trip." This includes such things as wearing seatbelts, obeying speed limits, and driving defensively under all weather and traffic conditions.

Driving a car should be one of life's pleasures, not one of life's tragedies.

The principal causes of motor-vehicle deaths, based on recent National Safety Council statistics, are:

Collision between Motor Vehicles	20,600
Collision with Fixed Object	11,200
Pedestrian Accidents	5,300
Non-collision Accidents	4,600
Collision with Pedalcycle	800
Collision with Train	400
Collision with Animal or Animal-drawn Vehicle	100
Total	**43,000**

* A disabling injury is one that disables you beyond the day of the injury.

Never Argue with a Big Truck

Ah, the dangers of overconfidence! Daryl had been an over-the-road truck driver for fifteen years. Still, on weekend highway trips in his car, he couldn't avoid the temptation to slip into the drafts of the large trucks to take advantage of their fuel-conserving tug. He felt no fear: he knew trucks; he knew what to look for, how to react, how to anticipate. His bravado nearly did him in when the rig he was tailgating suddenly braked violently to avoid a slow-moving car entering the highway. Daryl survived this incident, but his cherished 1959 Chevrolet convertible did not.

According to the National Institute for Highway Safety, about 5,000 people die annually in crashes involving large trucks. In collisions between large trucks and cars, 98 percent of people killed were in the car.

To safely manage your encounters with these behemoths:

Avoid Their Blind Spots

Because they sit so high, truck drivers appear to have total vision of the road. In fact, they have more blind spots than ordinary drivers. They are called "No Zones," because cars should avoid them. A big rig's four blind spots are:

- immediately in front, sometimes as much as twenty feet if the truck has a long hood;
- on either side of the cab. The right-side blind spot is especially dangerous, because trucks like to swing into the right lanes to avoid trouble in the road ahead.
- up to 200 feet in the rear.

◆ Remember: If you can't see the driver of a truck in his side mirror, he can't see you, either. To be seen, pull ahead or drop back.

◆ Don't cruise beside a truck for a long time, because, the driver might need to change lanes quickly, and he might not know you're there.

◆ Keep your lights on in bad weather. It helps truck drivers see you amidst the spray.

Pass With Care

◆ On two-lane roads, blink your lights to let a driver know you want to pass, whether it's day or night. If he blinks back, you can pass him safely; if he doesn't blink back, he's telling you it's not safe to pass. Wait and try again later.

◆ If a truck driver behind you blinks his lights, he wants to pass. Blink back and give him the time and room he needs.

◆ If a truck approaches quickly on a steep downhill grade, pull to the right and let him pass. He may have lost his braking power.

◆ When you pass a truck, wait until you're at least far enough ahead to see its headlights in your rearview mirror before you move back into the lane.

Proper Spacing

Even on dry surfaces, trucks need twice as much stopping distance as cars.

◆ Cooperate with truckers by allowing plenty of safety cushion for the truck. In heavy traffic, leave room for a truck to change lanes.

◆ Give trucks enough room to turn — especially on the right side, for both left and right turns.

◆ Do not tailgate a truck (or any other vehicle). If it stops suddenly, you could find yourself wrapped around its rear axle. Tailgating also blocks your view of the road ahead. **Rule of thumb**: Stay four to five seconds behind a truck.

◆ When following a truck, position your vehicle at the side of the lane, so you can be seen in the truck's mirrors.

◆ Another hazard of following a truck too closely is a tire blowout and flying debris.

◆ Be careful when you're behind a truck that has just entered the highway; it takes longer for a truck to pick up speed.

◆ If a trucker tailgates you or makes you angry, signal and get out of the way. Don't retaliate, it's a losing battle. Try to get some identification (safely) and report the incident.

City Lights

*T*o *Jack, right-turn-on-red was the greatest thing since sliced bread. He was a man in a hurry; every city intersection was just one more obstacle between him and his next appointment. Right-turn-on-red was his license to never stand still. Moving, moving, keep that car moving. Bad habits breed bad results, and right-on-red soon progressed to "rolling stop through red," and "ignore NO-right-on-red warnings." Jack finally came to his senses when he was broadsided by a city bus and spent several weeks stuck in a hospital bed.*

City driving is full of hassles and delays, but these minor inconveniences can't be avoided through reckless or rude behavior. The best advice is to maintain a calm and patient attitude.

Surviving Intersections

Nearly 50 percent of all city-driving collisions occur at intersections, usually because a driver failed to yield the right of way. A recent Insurance Institute for Highway Safety study reports that red-light runners are responsible for an estimated 260,000 crashes every year, about 750 of them fatal. Worse, the number of deaths related to red-light running is rising!

To keep intersections safe, remember these tips:

◆ The vehicle on the left always yields to the vehicle on the right.

◆ Rolling stops can be a dangerous habit. You can miss spotting a vehicle and cause a collision.

◆ As you approach a "stale green light," cover the brake with your foot and be prepared to stop. Indications of a stale light include: traffic flowing smoothly, considerable cross-traffic, blinking pedestrian signals, and people standing on the corner.

◆ When you encounter a yellow light, always stop if it is safe to do so. The purpose of a yellow light is to allow you time to clear an intersection you have already entered, not one you are approaching.

◆ When a red light turns green, check to see that traffic has stopped on the intersecting street. Look left, then right, then left again before you proceed. You invite disaster if you don't check for oncoming vehicles, pedestrians, and cyclists.

◆ Turning right on a red light is allowed only when it is legal, your vehicle has come to a complete stop, traffic is clear, and pedestrians are clear of the crosswalk. Always take the few extra moments to look for a no-turn-on-red sign.

Roadside Distractions

◆ Lack of consideration can cause trouble. Demanding the right of way can lead to a confrontation that benefits no one.

◆ Keep your eyes moving for potential problems such as children playing, cyclists, pets, and cars backing from driveways. Check your rearview mirror often.

◆ Establish a high visual horizon. You should be able to see one block ahead of you.

◆ Blind spots are everywhere. If you can't see beyond an object, slow down or change lanes to improve your vision.

◆ Don't tailgate. Maintain a three-second following distance.

◆ When waiting to make a left turn, point your wheels straight ahead. If you were hit from behind with your wheels turned to the left, you'd be forced into traffic.

◆ Whenever possible, avoid getting boxed in. Speed up or slow down as required.

◆ Don't fiddle with the radio or other nonessential equipment in heavy traffic.

◆ If a left turn is risky because of heavy traffic or poor vision, make a right and use an alternate route.

Backing Up

◆ Always check behind your car. Pedestrians and small children can be hidden from your view.

◆ Use your outside mirrors to help your vision.

◆ Do not back into busy streets, highways, and pedestrian crosswalks.

◆ Keep your foot firmly on the brake before shifting into reverse.

◆ Back slowly. Glance over each shoulder out the windows.

Defend Yourself

While we seek perfection in many things we do, the consequences of falling short are usually not significant. However, falling short of perfection in our driving habits can have grave consequences.

Your lifetime odds of being killed in an automobile accident are 1-in-100. Each year, one in nine drivers is involved in a reported motor-vehicle crash, according to the National Safety Council (NSC).

These figures should be enough to encourage you to drive and react defensively on the roadways. Here are some tips to make the routine use of your automobile less likely to end in an accident or disaster.

Expect the Unexpected

- Assume a "what if" posture; know what you'll do if a driver swerves or stops suddenly.

- Watch for drivers who are preoccupied or driving "offensively." Instead of watching out for you, they count on you to react to them.

- Be cautious at stoplights and stop signs. Look both ways before you enter a green-light intersection, or when you have the right of way.

◆ Search the roadway and off-road areas twenty to thirty seconds ahead for hazards that could affect you.

◆ Be particularly alert in school zones, at blind intersections, and around pedestrians and workers.

◆ Don't play chicken. If someone seems determined to enter your lane, yield the right of way.

◆ Use caution approaching curves and the crests of hills.

◆ Rush hour is especially challenging. Expect drivers around you to stop or change lanes abruptly, and be ready to brake at all times.

◆ If an approaching vehicle is signaling to turn, wait until it actually turns before pulling out into traffic.

Take the Initiative

◆ Try to make every trip a "perfect" trip.

◆ **Always buckle up. According to the NSC, drivers who buckle up have a 45 percent better chance of surviving a crash, and a 50 percent better chance of surviving without a moderate-to-critical injury.**

◆ Stay alert. No eating, drinking, fiddling with the radio, or distracting conversations.

◆ Pull off the road to use a cell phone.

◆ Avoid operating a vehicle if you're overly tired, drowsy from medications, ill, or extremely stressed or excited.

◆ Signal lane and turn changes.

◆ When you're in the right-hand lane of a multi-lane highway, help traffic merge smoothly by moving over a lane if traffic permits.

◆ Slow down. Observe the legal speed limits. The faster you're moving, the longer it takes you to stop safely.

◆ Proper maintenance can help you head off mechanical problems that could cause an accident. Work with your mechanic to develop a periodic inspection plan.

Create a Cushion

◆ Maintain a safe following distance by staying three to five seconds behind the car ahead. Increase your following distance as your speed increases. At higher speeds, a three-second gap won't give you enough time to take evasive action if an emergency occurs in front of you.

◆ At 40 mph, stay four seconds behind; at 50 mph and higher stay five seconds behind. Increase your distance at night, on rough roads, and in bad weather.

◆ On multi-lane roads, remember that other drivers have blind spots. Don't linger in them if you're at the rear-side of another vehicle. Move forward or back.

◆ Avoid driving next to other vehicles so you have more room to react to other drivers.

◆ Tailgaters are a dangerous nuisance. Pull over after signaling, or slow down slightly without braking, and allow them to pass.

◆ Be a loner. Avoid packs of cars on the highway.

Some people have no business on the road with you, but there they are, anyway. Look for the warning signs of drivers impaired by drugs, alcohol, medication, or fatigue: wandering from lane to lane; driving unusually slow or fast; running stoplights and signs; moving erratically or out of control; and driving with lights off at night.

◆ Stay as far away as you can. If possible, notify the police.

Fatal Distractions

*S*usie was driving home with her children after a medical appointment. Driving in the opposite direction was a contractor who was talking on his car phone to a supplier. While looking at the phone, the contractor lost control of his vehicle, crossed the center line, and hit Susie's vehicle head on. Susie and one of her children were killed, and her other children were injured, one of them seriously. The contractor suffered minor injuries.

A recent study by the Network of Employers for Traffic Safety estimates that more than twenty-five percent of the 6.5 million automobile crashes that occur each year are the result of drivers trying to do more than one thing at a time.

While the risks of talking on car phones while driving are well documented, car phones are only a part of the problem when it comes to distracted driving. The list of distractions in an automobile is long and continues to grow. The bottom line here is that we just have to pay closer attention to our number one responsibility behind the wheel: driving safely. Here are some tips to help achieve that objective.

Focus on the Task at Hand

◆ Start with the basics and drive defensively. Make it your goal to have a "perfect" trip.

◆ Don't turn your head to talk or look at scenery or another person.

◆ Don't fool with the radio or other nonessential equipment when the road is busy. When driving in unfamiliar areas, turn off the radio for maximum concentration.

◆ Personal grooming and reading are obvious no-nos.

◆ Experts say we eat one in ten restaurant meals in our automobile, often while weaving through traffic. Don't eat or drink while you drive.

◆ If you don't know exactly where you're going, get directions before you leave.

◆ If you need to look at a map or reach into your purse or briefcase, pull over. The same applies to dealing with troublesome children.

◆ Do not engage in stressful or emotional conversations, which may be distracting.

◆ Illness is a distraction. When you're sick, your reflexes are slower than normal and your senses may be fogged. Consider staying home until you're fully alert.

◆ Read the labels on medications and talk to the pharmacist. Many medications, such as antihistamines, can make you dizzy or drowsy.

◆ Use speed dialing for frequently dialed numbers.

◆ Never take notes while driving. Use a small tape recorder.

◆ Always assess the traffic situation before taking calls. Allow voice mail to answer the phone when it's unsafe to speak, e.g., in heavy traffic or bad weather.

◆ Suspend conversations during hazardous conditions or situations.

◆ The National Safety Council recommends not using a car phone at stoplights. You may notice cars moving in the next lane, but your light could still be red.

◆ Hearing-impaired drivers should pull over to use the phone. Otherwise, too much of your attention will be diverted to deciphering the sounds.

The Rolling Phone Booth

Car phones are an important tool for safety and convenience, and they're not going away. The challenge is to use them safely. The Cellular Telecommunications Industry Association offers these safety tips for car phone users:

◆ Be familiar with the use of your phone.

◆ Install your phone so you can reach it while maintaining a proper view of the road and all mirrors.

◆ For the best sound quality, have the phone installed by a dealer.

◆ Use a hands-free phone.

◆ Dial while your vehicle is stopped. If you absolutely must dial in light traffic, dial a few numbers, check traffic, and continue dialing when it's safe. Or, have a passenger dial for you.

◆ If you place a call while moving, stay in the lane reserved for slower traffic.

Drugged Drivers

Prescription and over-the-counter (OTC) medications are intended to keep us healthy. In the wrong circumstances — especially when we are behind the wheel of a vehicle — our drugs could contribute to our early demise. To be sure your medications don't abuse you, remember:

◆ It's your responsibility to know what you're taking and how it affects you. If you have a question, ask your doctor or pharmacist.

◆ Bodies are different, and not everyone will react the same to medications. Furthermore, a drug can affect a person differently in different situations.

◆ Don't mix medications, or mix any kind of drug with alcohol, until you have consulted with your doctor or pharmacist.

◆ Try to use only one pharmacy.

◆ The problem with some drugs, such as cough medicines, is that they have a high alcohol content. Read the literature you get with any drug to determine whether it contains sedatives or alcohol.

Driving Alert

> **Even at recommended doses, OTC drugs can affect driving ability as much, or in some cases, even more than, illegal drugs, prescription drugs, or alcohol.**

◆ According to the Southern California Research Institute, antihistamines are the principal culprits. They can cause drowsiness, dizziness, and blurred vision.

◆ Sleeping pills and nighttime cold medications can also impair drivers. Obviously, a medication intended to help you sleep will not make you a good driver.

◆ Ibuprofen, a commonly used pain reliever, can reduce concentration levels and cause drowsiness.

◆ If you're taking a medication for the first time, don't drive after you take that first dose. Wait to see how it affects you.

Driving Accident Facts

- For fatal motor-vehicle accidents, males have higher involvement rates than females.

    Males – 27 per billion miles driven
    Females – 16 per billion miles driven

- For all motor-vehicle accidents, females have higher involvement rates than males.

    Males – 90 per 10 million miles driven
    Females – 100 per 10 million miles driven

- About thirty percent of us will be involved in an alcohol-related motor-vehicle accident at some time in our lives.

- The following is a summary of motor-vehicle accidents, by the day of the week.

	Fatal Accidents	All Accidents
Monday	12.7%	14.2%
Tuesday	12.0%	14.3%
Wednesday	12.0%	14.5%
Thursday	13.1%	14.7%
Friday	15.5%	16.9%
Saturday	18.4%	14.0%
Sunday	16.4%	11.5%

For fatal accidents, peaks occur during afternoon rush hour on weekdays, and late night on weekends.

For all accidents, peaks occur during morning and afternoon rush hour.

Source: National Safety Council

Local Highways...
Global Hazards

All it took to turn a routine April morning commute into a ninety-eight-car nightmare of wreckage and mayhem was a little rain, sudden bright sunshine, and some careless drivers.

"This is a wreck that just didn't need to happen," said a spokesman for the Missouri Highway Patrol in St. Louis. "The real blame is on people driving too fast for the conditions, and following each other too closely in inclement weather. Vehicles were kicking up a lot of mist and causing glare. Someone looked ahead and saw traffic backed up, hit the brakes, and then started to skid. That's how this whole mess got started."

For forty people, the pileup ended in the emergency room. Amazingly, no one ended up in a morgue.

Remember, even local, familiar roads are dangerous if you take them for granted.

Master the Merge

According to the American Automobile Association, more collisions happen on or near expressway entrances and exits than on any other place on interstate highways.

To lower your risk:

◆ Stay three to four seconds behind the vehicle in front.

◆ If necessary, use the entire acceleration lane to get your vehicle up to traffic speed. Driving too slowly or stopping suddenly may cause a rear-end collision.

◆ If you can't see a gap in traffic, slow or stop only at the end of the acceleration lane or on the shoulder.

◆ Take a final look in the mirrors and check your blind spot before joining traffic.

◆ Match your speed to that of vehicles already on the road.

◆ Get in the proper lane well in advance of exiting. Be sure to signal your exit at least 500 feet before you reach the exit ramp.

◆ If you miss your exit, do not stop. Never back up on a highway.

Cruise Control

◆ Concentrate on your driving — no talking on the phone, food, drinks, or lively conversations.

◆ If you're going to an unfamiliar location, get good directions.

◆ Constantly scan twenty to thirty seconds ahead for potential problems.

◆ Maintain a safe following distance by staying three to five seconds behind the car ahead. Increase the distance as your speed increases, at night, and in bad weather.

◆ Use the left lane only for passing. On an expressway with three lanes, treat the far right lane as a slower-speed through lane, the middle lane as a faster through lane, and the far left as the passing lane.

◆ When you're in the right-hand lane, give a break to drivers who are entering the highway. Either adjust your speed or move into another lane.

◆ Check your mirrors every five seconds.

◆ When changing lanes, check your blind spots *before* making your move. Remember the three steps: look-signal-move.

◆ Do not drive in another driver's blind spot. If you find yourself in this position, drop back or accelerate safely.

◆ If you must pass another vehicle, accelerate to get the pass over as quickly and safely as possible. Before pulling back into the right lane, make sure you can clearly see the road surface in front of the vehicle you passed in your rearview mirror.

According to the National Highway Traffic Safety Administration, approximately 800 people die in work-zone crashes each year.

◆ Be aware of road construction signs, work crews, and signs requiring you to reduce speed or change lanes. Slow down. If you get caught in a lengthy delay, relax and make the best of it.

Tailgaters

◆ If you have room, let your turn signal flash five times before moving to the right.

◆ In heavy traffic, slow down slightly without braking. This will allow the tailgater to pass you, or provide more time to stop in an emergency.

Be Alert When the Light Changes

After a summer of vigorous off-road adventures, one headlight beam on Stan's SUV strayed across to the shoulder of the far lane. The other beam lit up the tree line on the right shoulder. That presented no problem in the summer, but the days were getting shorter now. Stan was doing more driving at night, but who's got time for headlight alignment? Other cars could see him coming, and Stan had enough light to see almost anything in his path... except that shadowy animal crossing the road at dusk on rain-slick pavement. After he ran off the road while dodging the animal, Stan finally took the time to get his headlights aligned.

Fall driving presents a variety of obstacles, and more drivers die from September through November than during the winter months of December through February.

Slick roads, foggy mornings, and roaming wildlife are just some of the increased hazards. You must also contend with less daylight, and morning and evening sun glare.

Driving in the Dark

Everyone sees less well at night. **In fact, you are two and one half times more likely to be involved in a fatal crash at night than during daylight hours.** Keep these tips in mind as the seasons change.

- Less light means slow down. Drive below the speed limit and increase your following distance.

- Take curves more slowly, and never overdrive your headlights. Be sure you can stop if something suddenly appears in the roadway.

◆ Use high beams as much as possible on highways and unlighted streets. Remember, though, low beams are mandatory if you're within 500 feet of another vehicle or in fog. Note: Low beams lose their efficiency at speeds above 40 mph.

◆ One of the greatest dangers of night driving is sudden light from streetlights, neon signs, wet pavement, and approaching cars. Try to look away from glare. Use the lines or the edge of the pavement on your right side to help guide you.

◆ Don't try to "out-glare" a vehicle that doesn't switch to low beams. Be the first to be courteous. Retaliation for bad manners only results in two blinded drivers.

◆ Take special care on poorly lit rural roads.

Preventive Maintenance

◆ Clean and check your headlights regularly. Headlight dirt or misalignment can reduce the distance a driver can detect objects at night by about thirty percent.

◆ Get your headlights aligned during a regular maintenance stop. If you can't get to a technician, the National Safety Council suggests the following steps:

• You'll need thirty-five to forty feet of flat or constantly sloped driveway.

• Shine your low beams on a garage door two to three feet away.

• Outline the bright spots with a soft pencil or tape.

• Back the car about twenty-five feet from the door. The top of the low beams should shine no higher than the top of the marks on the door, or lower than the center of the marked circle. If you have two headlights, the high beams are also aimed.

• If you have four headlights, aim the low beams first. Adjust the high beams until the center of the high beams is at the top of the low beams.

Seasonal Hazards

◆ To minimize glare problems at sunrise and sunset, use your visor, and wear sunglasses if necessary. Never wear sunglasses or tinted glasses at night. Also:

◆ Be wary of drivers who are driving into a glare at your back. Give yourself plenty of room to come to a controlled stop.

◆ Whenever you wonder if it's dark enough to use headlights, turn on your headlights. It will help you see and be seen.

◆ Clean your windshield inside and out, especially if you're a smoker. Smoke can cloud your windows and diffuse light.

◆ Keep paper towels or a rag handy in the interior of your car.

◆ Keep your wipers clean and new. Streaks worsen glare. Check the washing fluid often.

◆ To avoid skids in rainy weather, slow down. If you do skid, steer in the direction you want the front of the car to go.

◆ As soon as temperatures start diving into the 30s, slow down before crossing a bridge.

◆ Deer and other wildlife are active in the fall. If a collision is unavoidable, slow down to reduce the impact. Stay under control.

Arrive Alive

*P*erry couldn't control his excitement: he had just coached his son's little league team to a city championship, and his adrenaline was pumping. He went to bed but couldn't sleep. At 11 P.M. he roused his family from bed to tell them they were leaving on their Florida vacation then and there. The car was packed. Why waste time sleeping? His wife and kids grumbled as they climbed into the car and promptly fell asleep. Around three o'clock, Perry came back down to Earth. He dozed off, and the car slipped onto the shoulder. Fortunately, he hit a band of rumble strips and immediately snapped back to alertness. He pulled into a well-lighted rest area and slept soundly until sunrise. It turned out to be a wonderful vacation.

Summer brings out the little kid in all of us, but that doesn't mean we have to act irresponsibly. Before charging off on your driving vacation, consider these suggestions:

Plan Ahead

- Keep you car in tip-top shape. Have your mechanic check the cooling system, tires, and wiper blades. Carry a roadside emergency kit.

- Before leaving, explain the importance of good behavior and seatbelt use.

- Study new routes carefully.

- Stay five seconds behind the car in front to allow time to react to an emergency.

- Turn your radio off in heavy traffic or unfamiliar locations.

- Try to avoid driving at night.

- Never drive more than ten hours in a day. That's the limit for commercial drivers.

Asleep at the Wheel

The U.S. Department of Transportation estimates that sleepiness contributes to 200,000 accidents and up to 1,500 fatalities each year.

Sleepiness slows reaction times, decreases awareness, and impairs judgment. To help prevent drowsiness:

- Get a good night's sleep before you travel.

- Make planned stops every two hours or 100 miles.

- Avoid alcohol, medicines, and heavy meals, all of which can make you sleepy.

- Drive with a passenger who will sit in the front seat and stay awake.

- Keep the car cool and well ventilated.

- Dab your face with a wet cloth, or apply a cold pack to your neck.

- Shift your head often to change your focus and line of sight.

- Tune the radio to provocative talk radio or music you dislike; or sing, whistle, or talk aloud.

- Wear sunglasses to avoid glare.

- Coffee or soft drinks will not keep you awake. They can help you feel more alert, but the effects last only a short time.

- If you feel drowsy, don't push yourself. Change drivers, or find a well-lit place with plenty of people around (not the shoulder of the highway) to stop and take a brief nap. Roll down the window enough to allow fresh air in, but not a hand. Lock your doors. Turn off the engine, but keep parking lights lit.

- Before resuming travel, get out of the car, stretch, and make sure you're fully awake.

- Nighttime is not the only dangerous period. Almost everyone's biological clock is programmed to make us feel sleepy between 1 and 4 P.M.

If You Break Down

- In an emergency, turn on your flashers and steer to the right shoulder, even if a flat tire bends your rim.

- Get out of the car carefully. Stay off the road. Don't stand behind your car or between cars.

- Raise the hood, turn on the emergency flasher lights, and attach a white cloth to the door handle or radio antenna.

- To fix a flat tire, go to the next exit or a well-lit parking lot. Get away from traffic, even if driving there ruins your tire.

- If someone stops to help, politely ask him to phone the police.

- If you have a cell phone, call for help immediately. Do not work on your car alone in the dark.

Please —
Show Some Restraint!

*I*t's not that Melissa dismissed the idea of fastening her seatbelt; the thought just never entered her mind. She and her friends were eager to begin their picnic in the country, and there was more hurry than caution to her actions. Melissa lost control of her car, and it rolled over several times. Thrown from the vehicle, the vibrant, young high school cheerleader was left paralyzed from the waist down. She knows she could have avoided her tragedy with a simple, three-second procedure — hardly a cheerful thought.

Based on National Safety Council statistics, lifetime odds are 1-in-2 that you will suffer a temporary or permanently disabling injury in a traffic crash, and about 1-in-100 that you will be killed. Surprisingly, the majority of crashes causing injury or death occur within twenty-five miles of home at speeds under 40 mph.

Superior engineering is making automobiles safer, but the ultimate responsibility for safety rests with the people behind the wheel.

Seatbelts Are Mandatory

According to the National Safety Council, passenger car and light truck occupants who wear safety belts cut the risk of serious or fatal injury in collisions between 45 and 65 percent.

Ejection from a vehicle is one of the most injurious events that can happen to a person in a crash. **In fact, you are twenty-five times more likely to die when you are thrown from your vehicle.** The safest place in a crash is inside your car. Buckle up!

◆ If buckled in, you won't be:

- flung through the windshield;
- pitched into traffic, or against a telephone post or tree;
- thrown across rough, lacerating surfaces; or
- crushed by your own vehicle.

◆ For everyone's protection, backseat passengers should be buckled in. That way they won't become dangerous projectiles in the automobile cabin in the event of a crash.

And for the skeptics in the crowd, please note: drowning or incineration accounts for less than one-tenth of one percent of deaths in automobile crashes. And it's easier to escape if you're conscious.

In Vehicles with Air Bags

Air bags are a supplement to safety belts and are not intended to be a substitute for them. **According to the Insurance Institute for Highway Safety, the overall fatality-reducing effectiveness of air bags is about 14 percent over and above the benefits of using safety belts.** In vehicles with air bags:

◆ All passengers should wear safety belts.

◆ Place rear-facing child safety seats in the backseat of a vehicle with passenger-side air bags. A deploying air bag can cause serious or fatal head injury to a child.

◆ Keep your hands away from the steering wheel hub that contains the air bag. An inflating air bag could break a hand or fingers.

◆ If you have a passenger-side air bag, kids under age thirteen, or five feet three inches, should ride in the backseat.

◆ Sit as far back from the steering wheel as is comfortably possible. You should sit at least ten inches away from the wheel. If you're short, try tilting the steering wheel down and raising the seat to achieve ten inches and still drive comfortably. If this doesn't work, consider pedal extenders. The further away you are, the more efficiently the air bag will work.

Pregnant Women, Children and Pets

◆ Pregnant women should position the lap belt as low under the abdominal bulge as they can, and let the shoulder strap rest across their chest. Wearing both belts will protect both mother and fetus. In cold weather, unbutton outer clothing so the belt won't creep up.

◆ Never hold a child on your lap in a moving automobile. In a crash, the child could be crushed between you and the dashboard or windshield, or hit by a deploying air bag. The only safe place for a child is in an approved safety seat. To be sure the seat is correctly installed, go to a local organization that offers to check safety-seat installation.

◆ Whenever possible, children should ride in the center of the backseat, properly restrained.

◆ If a child must ride in the front seat, make sure the seat is all the way back, the child stays belted, and sits back in the seat.

◆ When you drive with your pet, use a pet seatbelt.

Safety Training

Well, it seemed like a good idea at the time: all Erin had to do was walk across the elevated railroad trestle, and she could trim some time from her walk home. Halfway across what she thought were unused tracks, a train appeared. Trying to run, Erin tripped on the tracks, so she lowered herself over the side of the trestle and hung on. The intense vibration shook her off, and she dropped sixty feet to the ground. Miraculously, she landed in a thick bush, narrowly averting the rocks surrounding it, and her worst injury was a swollen ankle. The "shortcut" resulted in a death-defying fall and a trip to the hospital.

Personal Warnings

In recent years, more than 500 people have been killed annually while trespassing on railroad rights of way and property.

- Do not walk, run, cycle, or operate all-terrain vehicles (ATVs) on railroad tracks and property or through tunnels. These activities are dangerous, and furthermore, they're against the law.

- Cross tracks only at designated pedestrian or roadway crossings. Observe all warning signs and signals.

- Do not hunt or fish from railroad trestles. There's only enough clearance on tracks for a train to pass — they're not meant to be sidewalks or pedestrian bridges.

- Do not attempt to hop aboard railroad equipment at any time. A slip of the foot can cost you a limb.

Vehicle Warnings

According to Operation Lifesaver, an average of ten collisions between trains and motorists occurs every day. More than 400 people are killed each year, and over 1,300 seriously injured. A motorist is forty times more likely to be killed or seriously injured in a collision with a train than in a collision with another motor vehicle.

◆ "Look, Listen, and Live" is the basic rule. Obey all highway rail-crossing signs and signals.

◆ Don't rely on warning signals, they could be broken. If you suspect a signal is malfunctioning, or if you feel vision at the crossing is restricted, e.g., by tall weeds, call the police or the railroad. You might want to find another route.

◆ Expect a train any time. Most trains don't follow set schedules.

◆ As you approach a railroad crossing: slow down when you see the **R × R** advance-warning sign; open a window; turn off the radio and fan; stop talking; look both ways; and listen for a train whistle.

◆ You must stop if red warning lights are flashing; warning bells are ringing; there's a STOP sign, or the gates are lowered. It's the law. Note: More than half of all train-vehicle crashes occur when a driver disregards flashing red lights or gates that warn of a coming train.

◆ Never race a train to a crossing — always assume you'll lose.

◆ Never stop or shift gears on a crossing. When traffic is heavy, wait until you're sure you can clear all of the tracks.

◆ If you start across the tracks and the warnings activate, continue to the other side. Don't stop or attempt to back up.

◆ Watch out for a second train when crossing multiple tracks.

◆ Its large mass makes it difficult to judge the speed and distance of an oncoming train. Be careful.

◆ Remember, trains can't stop quickly; they can take a mile or more to stop after the brakes are applied.

◆ Be doubly alert at night and in bad weather. Don't overdrive your lights. In many nighttime collisions, cars run into trains.

◆ Many rail-car collisions occur near a driver's home because people take a rail crossing for granted. Don't fall into that trap. Build possible delays into your schedule.

◆ Keep alcohol, distractions, and fatigue out of your car.

◆ If your car stalls on the tracks, get everyone out immediately and get a safe distance from the tracks. Call the police. If no train is coming, post lookouts and try to get the car off the tracks. Be ready to get away fast. If a train approaches, run toward the train to avoid flying debris.

RV Ready

America's love affair with the open road has grown to become a love affair with recreational vehicles. Today, there are over 30 million RV enthusiasts, and more on the way. With more than 16,000 publicly and privately owned campgrounds nationwide, RVs give us the freedom to roam from coast to coast, but getting safely from here to there takes planning.

◆ Check the owner's manual to find the trailer types that your vehicle can haul and the maximum load-weight it can pull. Obtain a "trailering guide" for your vehicle.

Be an Informed Buyer

Make sure your vehicle can safely tow an RV. Most full- and mid-size family cars can pull a trailer, and so can today's popular vans, 4×4s, and light-duty trucks. The Recreation Vehicle Industry Association suggests that you discuss these basic factors with your RV and auto dealers when evaluating trailer/tow-vehicle options: engine horsepower; transmission and axle capacity; cooling equipment; suspension; springs and shocks; power brakes; power steering; and battery capacity.

◆ You'll also want to follow your RV dealer's advice on the type and size of hitch and ball, tire inflation, and anti-sway devices.

◆ If you plan to tow a boat, getting the right-size trailer will minimize swaying.

◆ Make sure your trailer has the right tires. Never use automotive radial tires on a boat or other trailer. Carry a spare.

◆ If you're thinking of buying a recreational vehicle, call (888) GO-RVING.

Towing a Small Trailer

Make a thorough check of your vehicle and trailer before you use them.

- Be sure vehicle and trailer are hitched correctly.

- Connect the brakes and signal lights. Always check that the trailer's brakes, turn signals, and taillights work and are synchronized with those of the towing vehicle.

- Check tire pressure, and check lug nuts for tightness.

- Don't overload the towing vehicle or the trailer. Check the manuals. Placing a slightly higher percentage of cargo weight toward the front of the trailer will improve the connection by increasing weight on the hitch.

- Balance the load from side to side, and secure it so it won't shift.

- Once the trailer is loaded, make sure all doors are closed and secure. Be sure safety chains are attached, in good condition, and not dragging on the ground.

- On the road, steer as little as possible to avoid swaying. Try to avoid applying the brakes suddenly. It's better to release the gas pedal and slow down naturally.

- Trailer tires can get very hot while in use, especially tires on smaller trailers. Follow the manufacturer's directions for recommended maximum speeds. On hot days, travel under the speed limit.

- Check and grease your trailer's wheel bearings once a year and after each immersion in water.

Big Tow

Whether you're driving a motorized RV or towing a travel trailer, special precautions are required.

- Before leaving on a trip, sit in the driver's seat and adjust all mirrors for optimal road views. Equip a towing vehicle with large mirrors for the fenders on both sides.

- Check for leaks in propane gas bottles, heating equipment, and associated tubing. Turn off all valves.

- Load tools and emergency and foul-weather items in a readily accessible location in the towing vehicle.

- While moving, don't let anyone ride in the towed vehicle; it's dangerous and, in many states, illegal.

- Allow for your vehicle's size when turning.

- Increase your normal following distance.

- Allow more time to brake, change lanes, and enter a busy highway, since bigger vehicles take more time to accelerate and slow down.

- After passing, allow plenty of room before changing lanes again.

- Most trailering mishaps occur while going downhill, when the trailer begins pushing the towing vehicle. When descending steep hills, it's important to use a lower gear to get some braking action from the engine rather than depending solely on the brake system.

- Back up with care. Use someone outside the vehicle to assist the driver. If there's no one to help, get out and inspect the area.

- Always carry tire-changing instructions when you travel.

Send Help

We put a lot of faith in our vehicles. We expect them to transport us in safety and comfort mile after mile, year after year. Generally, they do, but, hey, anybody (or anything) can have a bad day, including the trusty family sedan.

In a recent year, the AAA alone responded to over 25 million calls for emergency road services.

There are ways to avoid that unpleasant situation, and safe ways to respond if it does occur.

Preventive Maintenance

◆ Take your vehicle in for regular professional check-ups, especially before long trips.

◆ Always carry the owner's manual in the vehicle.

◆ Change oil and other fluids as recommended.

◆ Periodically, inspect the radiator hoses for cracks or bulges and feel them for firmness. A good hose will feel similar to a garden hose. Signs of wear include a spongy or very hard hose.

◆ Make a habit of checking tire pressure and fluid levels regularly, particularly before long trips. Always check the tires at cold pressure.

◆ Never exceed the maximum pressure shown on the sides of the tires or in the owner's manual.

◆ Carry a complete emergency kit of tools for both vehicle and personal emergencies. Your kit should include: a reflective vest; an inflated spare tire; a tire jack; a one-foot-square piece of wood ($^3/_8$-1" thick) to set the jack on; a heavy-duty lug wrench, screwdrivers and pliers; penetrating oil for the lug nuts; duct tape; a flashlight with fresh batteries; reflective triangles or flares; first-aid kit; safety goggles; work rags; a jacket to protect your clothes; a SEND HELP sign; a spare fan belt; jumper cables; two one-gallon bottles of water for you and your car; cold weather gear; non-perishable food; a wire clothes hanger; and change for phones.

◆ Purchase cell-phone service, or consider renting a cell phone for long car trips or vacations.

◆ Play it safe: Join a motor club, or ask your car-insurance company about emergency service towing.

◆ Keep an outline of battery jump-start procedures in your car. Review the procedures every time you use jumper cables. Or, use lighter-to-lighter jumpers, instead.

Handling the Unexpected

A power loss or flat tire is frightening, but knowing what to do will help you through the situation.

◆ Remain calm. Grip the steering wheel at nine and three o'clock. Signal your intentions, ease off the accelerator, brake gently, and steer to the right shoulder. The farther you are from moving traffic, the better.

◆ Ideally, drive the car to the next exit or to a well-lighted parking lot. You can drive several miles on a flat tire. Drive slowly with your emergency flashers on and stay in the right lane. If the engine is overheating, stop driving.

◆ Raise the hood. Attach a white cloth to the door handle or radio antenna. Stay in the car with the doors locked and your seatbelt on.

◆ Display the SEND HELP sign, if necessary. If somebody stops to help, open the window slightly and ask him to phone the police. If you suspect danger, sound your horn.

◆ In a hazardous location, leave the car and get away from the road. Never walk along the roadway. A passing vehicle could hit you, and you are more vulnerable to crime.

◆ If there's steam coming from under the hood, pop the latch and let the engine cool. Wait thirty minutes before attempting to remove the radiator cap. Open it slowly. Use goggles and protect your hands.

◆ Don't work on your car in the dark if you're alone.

◆ In isolated areas, or at night, cautiously set out three reflector triangles — ten, 100 and 200 feet behind the vehicle. On a two-lane roadway, place another triangle 100 feet in front of the vehicle.

◆ Flares work better than triangles in foggy weather. If there's a chance of a fuel leak, do not use flares.

Rudes of the Road

*L*arry *is as macho as the next guy. He played all the sports, had a couple of rousing fistfights in his youth, and hunts and fishes on the weekends. So, when Mr. Inconsiderate rudely cut off Mr. Macho on the interstate, Larry flashed an obvious signal of disapproval. A mile or so later, he and Mr. I. sat side by side at a stoplight. Larry glanced over and saw that he was staring into the barrel of a huge handgun. He froze in fear. The driver looked at him stonily, shook his head, then lowered the pistol and drove off. As you might imagine, Larry has since become much more tolerant behind the wheel.*

The highways have always been dangerous, but increasingly, people are using their vehicles as weapons, or worse, using actual weapons to prove a point about their driving.

A recent six-year study by the American Automobile Association found more than 10,000 violent road clashes that resulted in 218 deaths and 12,000 injuries.

Hey! Who You Calling Aggressive?!

Aggressive drivers are more likely to speed, tailgate, fail to yield, weave in and out of traffic, pass on the right, make improper lane changes, run stop signs and lights, make hand and facial gestures, scream, honk, and flash their lights. To coexist with aggressive drivers:

◆ Be patient and flexible. Practice cooperative driving behavior.

◆ Don't be goaded into confrontation.

◆ Don't take other drivers' behavior personally.

◆ Do not respond by blaring your horn, following too closely, cutting people off, or tapping your brakes.

◆ Give other drivers plenty of space, especially those behaving competitively or aggressively.

◆ If you a make a driving error that upsets another driver, try to signal an apology with a smile and a wave of your hand.

◆ Drive in the right or center lanes unless passing. If you're in the left lane, even driving the speed limit, and someone wants to pass you, let him. It's common courtesy to move over if you can.

◆ Use turn signals when changing lanes or turning.

◆ Use your horn very sparingly.

◆ Dim your high beams as you approach another vehicle.

◆ When you merge, make sure you have plenty of room.

◆ If someone cuts you off, slow down and give him room to merge into your lane.

◆ Don't tailgate. Allow at least a three-second space between your car and the one ahead.

◆ If you feel you're being followed too closely, signal and pull over, or slow down slightly without braking, to allow the other driver to go by.

◆ Few things make another driver angrier than an obscene gesture. (If you don't believe us, ask Larry.) Keep your hands on the wheel. Don't even shake your head in disgust.

◆ Avoid eye contact. Looking or staring at another driver can turn an impersonal encounter between two strangers into a personal duel.

◆ Open doors carefully in parking lots.

◆ If a situation is getting out of hand, use your cell phone to call for help, or drive to a place where people are around, such as a police station or convenience store. Use your horn to attract attention. Do not get out of your car. And definitely *do not go home* if the other driver is in sight.

To Calm the Beast in You

◆ Adjust your attitude. Strive to be the most courteous person on the road; others might follow your lead.

◆ Forget winning. Driving is not a contest.

◆ If you feel like you're losing control, refocus your thoughts and take deep breaths. Think of a pleasant situation or memory.

◆ Relieve stress by allowing plenty of time to reach your destination.

◆ Listen to soothing music or a book on tape.

◆ Consider that you might know the other driver, or that he or she might have a reason for driving erratically.

◆ If you think you have a problem with anger management, seek professional help.

Dangerous Curves

*T*om pulled from the university parking lot at dusk on a crisp October Friday. It was a five-hour drive home, but he knew some short cuts through the rolling Iowa corn country. Clipping along in the dark at 70 mph, he swooped over a hill and was surprised to see the lights of a small town appear on the horizon. He didn't recall a town on this part of the road. Seconds later, the lights were almost directly in front of him, and only his youthful reflexes allowed him to swerve around the huge, lumbering combine straddling both lanes of the narrow, two-lane blacktop. When he had gathered his wits, Tom slowed down, and he approached the next town with considerable caution.

The National Safety Council reports that rural areas account for about 65 percent of traffic deaths. Further, 75 percent of all non-collision accidents (overturns, jackknifes) occur in rural areas. The allure of the countryside is obvious, but danger is all around.

Rural Hazards

Rural roads are usually not as well maintained as urban roads and major highways. Always wear your seatbelt and be especially alert for:

◆ Blind curves or intersections. Approach each curve expecting the worst, meaning slow down and stay on your side of the road.

◆ Excessive speed. Drive within the speed limit. It's based on the road's characteristics under ideal conditions, and is established for your protection. Reduce speed in heavily wooded areas and at night.

◆ Soft shoulders. They'll give way under the weight of your vehicle, and they could pull it down a slope or into a ditch.

◆ Narrow roads and one-lane bridges. Like it or not, you might have to yield to another driver. Don't be stubborn.

◆ Poorly marked intersections and railroad crossings. Approach them with caution.

◆ Woods and tall crops, which obscure curves.

◆ The possibility of head-on collisions. To avoid them:

- Always stay to the right of the centerline.

- If, for any reason, an oncoming vehicle veers into your lane, slow down right away, sound your horn, and flash your headlights. Drive to the right to get out of the way. Driving into a ditch is less dangerous than driving into a vehicle.

- If the choice is between a head-on collision and hitting a fixed object, such as a tree or utility pole, it's safer to hit the fixed object, which has no momentum of its own.

- If your tires run off the road:

  - Take your foot off the accelerator, and don't hit the brakes.

  - Keep two hands on the wheel, and coast.

  - Look for a place where you can ease the car back onto the road.

Unpredictable Weather and Animals

Weather hazards are compounded on rural roads.

- Carry a survival kit and a cell phone.

- In wet weather, try to stay in the path in the road that has been worn by traffic. The traction is better there.

- Heavy rains can cause flooding in low areas. A car can be swept away in only two feet of water. Don't try to cross rushing water.

- Wet gravel roads and fallen leaves require extra stopping distance. Slow down in the rain.

Animals are a special danger in the country. According to the National Highway Traffic Safety Administration, more than 100 people are killed and 8,000 injured each year in crashes involving animals, particularly deer. You can't predict an animal's actions, but you can prepare your response.

- Use an animal-warning device.

- If you encounter a small animal on the road, do not swerve to avoid hitting it. Stay on the roadway. The alternative could mean the loss of your life.

- Because of their size and increased numbers, deer present a special hazard:

  - Dusk and dawn are their times of peak activity.

  - If one deer crosses in front of you, stay alert — they usually travel in groups.

  - Be most alert in areas where foliage and trees extend to the road.

  - If colliding with a deer is unavoidable, slow down to reduce the impact. Never swerve left!

Beware! Farm Machinery Crossing

The National Safety Council reports that there are about 30,000 collisions each year between vehicles and farm machines.

Farm machines are usually big and ponderous. Mishaps can be avoided if drivers show restraint and patience.

- Slow down when you approach farm implements. Be prepared to stop if necessary.

- Stay calm. Your chance to pass will come eventually. Don't risk your life to save a minute or two.

- Be wary. These implements need more room to maneuver than you do. Tractors will veer to their right before they make left turns. Don't mistake this to mean the tractor is moving aside to let you pass.

A Little Sound Advice

Suzy loved her compact car. It was easy to maintain, efficient, and very maneuverable. Like her, it was small, so she could settle into the driver's seat and feel the little car almost wrap around her. She felt in total control. But when she hit an ice patch one cold morning, she lost control. The car rolled over three times, pinning Suzy to the steering wheel and inflicting fatal injuries. The strengths of her little car had become its greatest weaknesses.

There are many reasons people buy small cars. For all their advantages, however, a small car generally absorbs more force in a collision than a heavier car.

> **According to the Insurance Institute for Highway Safety, people in small cars are injured more often and more severely than are those in larger vehicles.**

Still, like Suzy, many of us maintain our love affairs with our small cars. The challenge for drivers is to make up in safety awareness what their vehicles may lack in size and weight.

See and Be Seen

In a small car, you are up to nine inches lower than the driver of a large car. Barriers, medians, curbs, guardrails, and roadway obstacles may make it harder for the drivers of small cars to see and be seen. Most accidents involving small cars actually occur because drivers of large vehicles have trouble seeing the small car. Here are a few suggestions to help you compensate for your disadvantage:

◆ Realize that because you are closer to the ground, your range of vision is limited. You will also catch more glare off the road at night and in wet weather. Be cautious and respectful of the things you can't see. If your vision is restricted in any way, *slow down*!

◆ Leave a "cushion of space" between you and other vehicles. Your purpose is to defend yourself from the dangers around you.

◆ Drive with your lights on during daylight hours, especially in inclement weather.

◆ Do not ride alongside or behind larger vehicles. You are likely to fall into their blind spots.

◆ Try to keep your car where it's visible in the rearview mirrors of cars ahead of you.

◆ Keep in mind that dark colors, such as black, dark green, or brown, are less visible than bright colors.

◆ If you think a larger vehicle doesn't see you, flash your headlights on and off, or honk your horn.

You Win with Defense

◆ When purchasing a car, pay special attention to safety features.

◆ *Always* wear your seatbelt.

According to the National Safety Council, lap and shoulder belts reduce the risk of fatal injury to front-seat passenger-car occupants by 45 percent, and reduce the risk of moderate-to-critical injury by 50 percent.

◆ Do not drive aggressively. Resist the temptation to weave or slip through tight spaces.

◆ Sudden changes of wind can greatly affect control of a small car. Such changes can occur when passing or being passed by larger vehicles, or when driving on stretches of highway open to wind gusts. Grip the steering wheel at nine and three o'clock and move to the far side of your lane, away from the larger vehicle. This applies to windy conditions as well.

◆ Use the side and rearview mirrors constantly. Know what's behind, beside, and ahead of your car at all times.

Highway Tips

Most small cars don't have the engine power of large vehicles, and most highways in the United States have been engineered for larger cars. With that in mind:

◆ Small cars must accelerate rapidly on a highway entrance ramp. Don't wait until you reach the highway.

◆ For that same reason, allow plenty of distance and time when passing a vehicle or merging.

Hey —
Not So Fast!

It's the classic story of the tortoise and the hare: You're driving responsibly, following the speed limit and doing your best to arrive safely at your destination, then, out of the blue, some vehicle comes roaring by, weaving in and out of traffic. Five miles down the road, you pull up to a stoplight, and the guy who bolted past you is one car-length ahead of you. For that one car-length, he endangered himself, his passengers, and everyone he encountered on the highway. Obviously, it wasn't worth the risk.

In fact, studies have demonstrated that increased motor-vehicle speed does not significantly reduce travel time. In heavy city traffic, high speeds require frequent, sudden braking for traffic conditions and signals. Time gains are small or nil. Even on the open highway, the driver who speeds is often forced to reduce speed for various reasons.

Yes, Speed Kills

According to the National Highway Traffic Safety Administration, speeding is a factor in 30 percent of the fatal motor-vehicle incidents in the United States, and contributes to more fatalities than any other improper driving practice. This equates to more than 12,000 deaths annually due to speeding. Before you push that pedal, remember:

Speeding reduces a driver's ability to steer safely around curves or objects in the roadway, extends the distance necessary to stop a vehicle, and increases the distance a vehicle travels while the driver reacts to a dangerous situation.

Excessive speed increases the physical forces that increase the severity of injuries. The energy of impact is so much greater at high speeds that it exceeds the life-saving capabilities of seatbelts, air bags, and roadside hardware and safety features.

The driver fatality risk in a crash sharply rises with the impact speed.

Above 50 mph, your chances of death double for every 10 mph increase in impact speed.

The safety consequences of traveling at high speeds can be counted in terms of lost lives. The Insurance Institute for Highway Safety, in a recent study of the 1995 repeal of the national maximum speed limit, estimates that fatalities on interstates and freeways have increased by 15 percent where speed limits were raised. **Institute researchers estimate 450–500 lives are lost each year because of the higher limits.**

Some Hard and Fast Safety Rules

Speeding can generally be defined as an excessive and unsafe motor-vehicle speed in regard to other current factors.

- ◆ Slow down when:
  - road conditions such as slick surfaces, hills, loose gravel, and mud may affect braking distances;
  - hills and curves obstruct your vision of the road. Heavy traffic, trees, buildings, and bill-boards can also limit visibility;
  - driving at night or in bad weather conditions;
  - you are among pedestrians and children;
  - poor lights, bulky loads, dirty windshields, and poor car design block your view;
  - visibility conditions change at sunrise and sunset;
  - you are not at your physical or mental best.

- ◆ Maintain a safe following distance by staying three to five seconds behind the car ahead. Increase your following distance as your speed increases. At higher speeds, a three-second gap won't give you enough time to take evasive action if an emergency occurs in front of you.

- ◆ At 40 mph, stay four seconds behind; at 50 mph and higher stay five seconds behind. Increase your distance at night, on rough roads, and in bad weather.

When you keep your car under control by honoring speed limits and reducing your speed under less-than-ideal driving conditions, you'll be in a better position to react to hazardous situations around you.

Remember: It's better to be late than to have people refer to you as "The late (your name)."

A Wintry Mix

Betty and Bill were thrilled to be leaving the Midwest for the winter. They'd reached that point in life where the cold weather went right through their bones, and Bill was no longer comfortable driving on snow-packed, icy roads. Florida's sunny beaches beckoned. As they crossed the Florida state line, a torrential downpour forced them off the road. When the storm had passed, Bill hit the gas to get to Tampa as soon as possible. The car struck a puddle, Bill lost control, and he and Betty made the final leg of their journey riding in a tow truck.

The road doesn't need to be icy for winter driving to be dangerous. The following tips apply year round, whether you live in northern Minnesota or southern Texas.

When the Roads Are Wet

◆ Increase your following distance by two seconds compared to the three to five seconds recommended for ideal conditions.

◆ Slow down immediately. Light rain can be more dangerous than a downpour, because it mixes with oil and grease that have accumulated on the road, making an extremely slippery surface.

◆ Turn your lights on so you can see and be seen.

◆ To prevent fogging, turn your defrosters on.

◆ As soon as it starts to rain, squirt your windows with windshield-washer fluid to avoid streaking and smearing of accumulated road film.

◆ Scan the roadway for standing water.

◆ By driving more slowly you'll also avoid hydroplaning, which occurs when a vehicle's tires lose contact with the road and ride on a layer of water. To avoid hydroplaning:

  • Reduce your speed. The faster you drive above 30 mph, the more likely you are to hydroplane.

  • Steer away from puddles. Note: Moisture from dew or fog can also cause hydroplaning.

  • Be sure your tires have good tread. Check them by putting a Lincoln penny in the groove; if you can see the top of Abe's head, replace the tire.

◆ If you start to hydroplane, remain calm, ease off the gas, but don't try to brake. Turn the steering wheel in the direction you want to go.

◆ Follow the tracks of the car in front of you.

◆ Remember, speed limits are designed for ideal conditions.

◆ Know what type of brakes you have and how to use them. Practice with antilock brakes before you need them.

Plowing Through Fog

Hundreds of people die each year as a result of fog on the highways.

If you must keep going through fog:

◆ Slow down gradually, but don't drive so slowly that you become a hazard yourself. Distances are hard to judge in fog, and low visibility decreases your reaction time. Give yourself extra time to respond to any road hazards.

◆ Don't hit your brakes in a panic. You increase your chances of being rear-ended.

◆ Turn on your wipers and defroster, and turn off your radio.

◆ Use your low beams. High beams produce too much glare in fog.

◆ Try to exit as soon as possible, and wait until visibility improves.

◆ Use the right-hand edge of the road to guide you.

◆ Roll down your windows at least partway so you can hear vehicles and other traffic noises.

◆ Honk your horn periodically to let other drivers know you're there.

◆ Avoid hunching forward to see. You'll see better if you sit normally.

◆ Never attempt to pass in fog. If someone needs to pass you, slow down and let him.

◆ As a last resort, pull off the road. Keep the motor running with the windows down, leave your headlights off, and turn on your flashers. Keep your seatbelts on.

Winterize Your Driving

Josh was cruising along on the interstate. It had been snowing for a half-hour, but he had a comfortable feel for the road. The car was heavy, he was in control, and he'd be home for dinner. But it was time to find better music on the radio. He reached for the dial and, in the process, twitched the steering wheel just enough to send the car into a tailspin across two lanes of traffic and the shallow median, and into the oncoming lanes. Only luck kept him from slamming into another vehicle. In his desire to control conditions inside the car, Josh had lost control of the ones outside.

Winter presents a special set of driving challenges that require careful preparation and extra attention. To beat the weather:

Advance Preparations

- Have your car winterized. Get a general checkup that includes fluids, belts, hoses, cables, brakes, tires, and electrical and exhaust systems. Install new wiper blades; consider using winter blades.

- Let the engine warm briefly (about a minute should do) before heading out. But *never* idle in an enclosed area, such as a garage.

- Before driving, clean all snow and ice off your windows, not just a peephole. Remove snow from the hood, roof, and grill so it won't blow back and affect your vision. Also, clean your headlights and taillights.

- Before leaving, turn on the heater first, and then the defroster. This prevents moisture from fogging the windshield.

- Turn your headlights on during the day so other drivers can see you.

- Do not put extra weight in your trunk. It may help traction, but it can also make it harder to steer and stop.

- Inflate tires to the proper level. Low pressure can affect steering.

◆ Keep your gas tank at least half full for emergencies, and to prevent gas-line freeze-up.

◆ Carry a survival kit, including: a cell phone; warm clothes; blankets; boots; food and water; snow shovel; first-aid kit; jumper cables with safety tips; splash goggles; flashlight and extra batteries; traction mats, sand, or cat litter.

Master the Elements

◆ Check weather conditions before you leave, and continue to stay informed when traveling in potentially adverse weather.

◆ Make sure someone knows your route and intended arrival time.

◆ Test the roadway and your tire grip by braking hard at a slow speed when you start out, but not in traffic.

◆ When temperatures hover near thirty-two degrees, a thin layer of water can cover ice, making it harder to stop than when temperatures are lower.

◆ Bridges, overpasses, and shady areas freeze before other roadways, and stay frozen longer. Intersections stay slick and fast, too, due to traffic stopping and starting. Be extra cautious in early-morning hours.

◆ Beware of "black ice" — ice that stays on roads not in direct sunlight.

◆ When snow is heavy, travel familiar routes to lessen the possibility of driving off the road.

◆ Apply gentle pressure on the accelerator at all times.

◆ Don't get "SUV overconfidence." While your SUV might get through some tough conditions more easily, it won't stop more quickly.

◆ Focus your attention far ahead. On slick surfaces, keep eight to ten seconds between you and the vehicle ahead.

◆ Before going down hills, slow down. Check the owner's manual for tips specific to your car.

◆ Each winter, practice skidding and recovering in a safe location.

Skid Marks

◆ You're most prone to skidding when you change directions, or accelerate or brake suddenly. Avoid braking in the middle of a curve.

◆ When you slow down or stop, reduce speed sooner than normal by removing your foot from the accelerator and not applying the brake.

◆ To brake safely without antilock brakes, apply firm, steady pressure. If the wheels lock, ease up slightly to regain steering and stopping traction.

◆ With antilock brakes, keep your foot on the pedal; don't pump it.

◆ When you encounter an unexpected icy patch, take your foot off the gas and brakes and steer your way across. **If you do start to skid**:

  • Remove your foot from the accelerator, and the brake pedal if the skid is due to hard braking.

  • Look to where you want to go, and steer the car that way.

  • When the skid is corrected, apply the brakes gently.

Home Safety

Introduction

If there's any place where we feel safe, it's in our homes. Away from traffic and daily hassles, we have the opportunity to relax and enjoy some of life's simple pleasures. However, we cannot relax our safety awareness in the home. Almost 30,000 of us die each year in and around our homes, and approximately 7 million of us suffer temporary or permanent disabling injuries in home-related incidents. In fact, more disabling injuries occur at home than in the workplace and motor-vehicle accidents combined.

Based on recent National Safety Council statistics, the principal causes of deaths at home are:

Poisonings	9,700
Falls	9,300
Fires and Burns	3,200
Suffocation	2,600
Drowning	900
Firearms	400
All Other*	3,400
Total	**29,500**

* Most important types are electric current, hot substances, corrosive liquids and steam, and explosive materials.

Cookin' with Gas

Mmm, mmm! Smells good! Somebody just broke out the gas grill, and the neighborhood is awash in the yummy smell of hamburgers, steaks, and hot dogs. Wants to make you smile, doesn't it? Or cry.

The Consumer Product Safety Commission reports that more than 15,000 people are treated in hospital emergency rooms each year due to injuries associated with gas and charcoal grills. However, there are ways to assure your grilling tears are limited to the culinary effect of slicing a thick, juicy onion.

Getting Started

- Read and follow the manufacturer's instructions for your grill. Review them each year.

- Place the grill in an open area outdoors, at least ten feet away from any building, and away from pedestrian traffic. Keep it away from shrubbery and dry vegetation.

- Resist the temptation to cook in a garage, tent, house, or any other enclosed area when the weather is bad. Opening a garage door or window or using a fan might not reduce carbon monoxide to safe levels.

- Do not use a grill on top of or under any surface that will burn, such as a porch or carport. The wooden deck attached to your house is *not* a good place to barbecue.

- Wear a heavy apron, long pants, and an oven mitt. Cover your forearms with a mitt that extends over your elbow, or wear a long-sleeved, close-fitting shirt.

- All tools should have long handles to keep your hands and clothing away from heat and flames.

- Keep children and pets away from a hot grill. Never leave a lighted grill unattended.

- Reduce grease flare-ups by trimming excess fat. Keep a spray bottle of water handy. Use baking soda, a fire extinguisher, sand, or a garden hose to control any fires.

- As soon as possible, clear away all cooking equipment. This will assure kids don't get into it.

- If you use electric starters, accessories, or a grill, be sure they're properly grounded. Never use them in wet weather.

Using Gas Grills

- Have your tank filled by a qualified dealer. Overfilling can be dangerous.

- Store the gas cylinder outside, and be sure the gas is turned off at the tank to prevent unintentional ignitions. Leave the tank upright and in a cool area.

- Never use an LP cylinder that shows any visible sign of damage.

- Never attach or disconnect a cylinder, or move or alter fittings, when the grill is in operation or hot.

- If the burner doesn't ignite quickly, turn off the gas and leave the lid open. Wait five minutes before you try to light it again.

- Check the hose(s) and connections frequently for leaks by using a soap-and-water mixture. Escaping gas will appear as bubbles. Tighten the connections, or call a professional to repair the grill.

- Clean the tubes annually with a bottlebrush or pipe cleaner.

- Clean the grill twice a year. If you use a wire brush to clean it, be sure to wipe the grill with a cloth or paper towel to remove any wire strands.

- Be especially careful at the beginning of the "barbecue season." Many incidents occur when a grill has been unused over a period of time, or after a gas container has been refilled and reattached.

- Do not attempt to repair the gas container valve or appliance yourself. See your LP gas dealer or a qualified repairperson.

Charcoal and Other Fixings

- Use the starter fluids designated for your grill. Place the capped can and matches away from the grill. Never use gasoline or kerosene.

- If the coals start to flag or are slow to catch, fan them or use dry kindling and rolled-up newspaper to give a boost. Adding liquid fuel could result in a flash fire.

- If you use instant-light briquettes, do not use lighter fluids, or electric, solid, or metal chimney-style starters. If you need to add briquettes, add regular briquettes only.

- Close nearby windows and doors when cooking outside.

- When finished, close the vents and allow the ashes to cool forty-eight hours before disposing. Wrap them in heavy-duty aluminum foil and put them in a metal container that contains no other combustible materials. Be careful. Seemingly "dead" charcoal can re-ignite hours later. Soak with water for added safety.

Rub-a-dub-dub, Be Safe in a Tub

After a hard day at work, Joan loved to luxuriate in the comfort of her tub, surrounded by flickering candles and soothed by her special "stress relief" body lotions. It was her reward to herself. She should have rewarded herself with some better, slip-resistant bathroom rugs, too. If she had, she wouldn't have lost her balance, fallen to the floor, and cracked her shoulder, which resulted in surgery. Months later, Joan still had to see a physical therapist to help regain the strength she lost as a result. Hardly relaxing.

According to the National Safety Council, more than 200,000 people have to be rushed to emergency rooms each year because of incidents in bathrooms. Hundreds of people die. The most serious injuries involve slips, falls, scalding, and electricity.

Water Hazards

Most injuries in the bathroom occur when people are climbing into and out of a tub. For that reason, install skid-resistant mats, abrasive strips, or textured surfaces in tubs and showers. Consider adding a separate shower stall.

- Also, use slip-resistant flooring or carpeting. All rugs should have rubberized, slip-resistant backing.

- Anchor grab bars securely into the wall studding with long screws. Nailing or gluing into the plaster, tile, or wallboard does not offer adequate stability. The best grab bar is one with a sure-grip, rough finish.

- To prevent scalding, reduce the temperature of your hot water to 120 degrees F.

- Install anti-scald devices that stop water flow when the temperature exceeds 115 degrees in your shower and bathtub fixtures.

- When filling a tub, add the cold water first, then follow with hot until the tub is ready.

- Always test the water temperature before entering a tub or shower. This applies especially to children or elderly persons.

- To test water temperature, place your whole hand in the tub and move it back and forth for several seconds.

- When climbing in or out of a tub, instead of stepping over the side, sit on the edge and swing your legs over the edge one at a time.

- Never leave a small child alone in a bathroom.

Don't Be Shocked

- Avoid using electrical implements in the bathroom, unless they're labeled safe to use around water. Select appliances with the Underwriters Laboratory label.

- Never touch any electrical fixture or appliance with wet hands, while standing on a damp floor, while you are in the bathtub, or while you are touching any metal object.

- Install nightlights, especially for elderly persons and children.

- No light fixture should be within reach of a person seated or standing in the tub or shower.

- If you do use electrical appliances in the bathroom, choose battery-operated models. Or, place them where they cannot possibly reach or fall into a tub, sink, or toilet.

- Install bathroom electrical outlets with ground fault circuit interrupters and childproof covers.

- Stay away from plumbing during electrical storms.

Preventive Medicine

- If you wear glasses or contact lenses, keep an extra pair handy. Many injuries occur when people can't see clearly.

- Install shatter-resistant faucets and handles with no sharp edges in the shower or tub.

- Shower and tub enclosures should be of impact-resistant safety glass or acrylic.

- It's best to have door handles that can be unlocked from both sides.

- Prescriptions and hazardous non-prescription products should be stored in a locked closet or shelf, out of reach of small children.

- Make sure medication lids are tightly closed after each use.

- Flush unneeded liquids and pills down the toilet. Wash the containers.

- Discard razor blades carefully.

- Use plastic or paper cups.

Clean Air Policies

*A*lex loved to barbecue. He had all the tools and all the recipes, so, when it started raining on daughter Kristin's birthday party, it made sense to move his grilling job indoors. It took some levelheaded action by fourteen-year-old Kristin to open the garage door and convince Alex she'd be perfectly happy with a takeout pizza. It seems Kristin had attended a carbon monoxide presentation given at her school by the local fire department, and — her father should be proud to know — she was listening.

According to the American Lung Association, carbon monoxide (CO) poisoning kills more than 500 people a year in the U.S., and causes 10,000 to become ill.

Cause for Concern

Symptoms of CO poisoning are similar to the flu, minus the fever. They include dizziness, fatigue, headache, nausea, and disorientation. Your vision may blur, your reflexes may slow, and you might experience a feeling of tightness across the chest.

If you have any of these symptoms inside your home and you feel better outside, you may have CO poisoning. See a doctor immediately.

Appliances to Be Wary Of

The most common source of dangerous CO levels in homes is an improperly maintained furnace. That's why you should have a qualified serviceperson install (and annually inspect) all fuel-burning appliances used in your home, trailer, camper, and vacation sites. This includes heating systems, water heaters, kitchen stoves, gas clothes dryers, non-vented space heaters, and fireplaces. You should also:

◆ Check all flue and vent pipes regularly for cracks, loose connections, and corrosion.

◆ Buy only appliances that display the mark of a recognized testing agency, such as the American Gas Association or the UL label.

◆ Never operate non-vented gas-burning appliances overnight, in a closed room, or in a room in which you're sleeping.

◆ Make sure burner flames on furnaces and stoves are blue, burn evenly, and have a uniform shape. Flames with yellow tips and poorly defined edges indicate incomplete combustion. Use your exhaust fan when cooking.

◆ Do not use the oven, gas range, or dryer for heating.

◆ Be sure all combustion appliances are vented directly outside.

◆ Never ignore a safety device when it shuts off an appliance.

◆ Follow manufacturer's directions for operation of all appliances.

◆ Problems suggesting improper appliance operation include:

  • decreasing hot water supply;

  • furnace unable to heat house or runs constantly;

  • rusting or water streaking on vent/chimney;

  • debris or soot falling from chimney, fireplace, or appliances;

  • loose masonry on chimney;

  • moisture on inside windows;

  • unfamiliar or burning odor. Never ignore the smell of fuel!

More to Know about CO

◆ No matter how cold it is, *never* run a car engine in a closed garage.

◆ Never use charcoal to heat or cook in a house or enclosed space.

◆ Use kerosene heaters only in well-ventilated rooms.

◆ Avoid "garage-sale specials" and antique stoves.

◆ Open a window when a fireplace or any stove is in use.

◆ CO detectors provide early warning before the gas builds to dangerous levels. Plug-in and corded models are the most effective. Battery-operated models are available for locations away from an electrical outlet, or if you heat with wood. Be sure they have the UL label.

◆ People who live in energy-efficient homes should be very wary of CO; it's easier for gas to build up in those homes.

◆ The Consumer Product Safety Commission suggests installing at least one CO detector — with an audible alarm — near the sleeping area. For more safety, put one on every level and outside each bedroom.

◆ Put detectors in rooms with fuel-burning appliances, no nearer than fifteen feet to the appliance.

Don't Choke Under Pressure

It can happen to professional football players and Rhodes scholars like Pat Haden, and it can happen to you. Fortunately for Haden, his friend Verne Lundquist was close by to save his life. Others have not been so blessed.

Choking accounts for about 3,000 deaths each year. Anyone can choke on food, and almost anyone can come to the rescue of a choking person.

If you don't already know the Heimlich maneuver, find a professional who can teach it to you. Try the YMCA or Red Cross. Remember, special procedures are needed for infants, and pregnant and obese victims.

Choking Prevention

Adults

An ounce of prevention is worth a pound of cure.

◆ Don't drink excessive alcohol before a meal.

◆ Cut food into small pieces and chew slowly, especially if you wear dentures.

◆ Do not talk or laugh with food in your mouth.

Children

◆ Children under the age of six should not blow up balloons, nor should they be alone with balloons.

◆ Teach children to never suck or chew on balloons.

◆ Keep balloons safely out of reach when it's not playtime. Safely dispose of broken balloons.

◆ Remind children how to eat properly, with small bites and thorough chewing.

◆ Don't let children run with food in their mouths.

Infants and Toddlers

In general, children under six should not eat foods that are firm and round. If not chewed properly, these foods could be inhaled into the trachea (windpipe).

◆ Avoid foods such as hot dogs, grapes, raisins, raw carrots, nuts, hard candies, popcorn, large chunks of meat, and chunks of peanut butter and hard fruit.

◆ Bread can be dangerous to toddlers. Give it in moderation.

◆ Don't offer chewing gum.

◆ Avoid toys with small parts that could disassemble and be swallowed. Use a toilet-paper tube as a size guideline. If older children have such toys, be sure they're kept away from small children.

Home Accident Facts

Home Workshop Equipment	Annual Injuries
Saws (hand or power)	97,000
Hammers	40,000
Welding & soldering equipment	18,000
Drills	18,000
Power grinders, buffers and polishers	17,000

Household Packaging and Containers	Annual Injuries
Bottles and jars	76,000
Bags	28,000
Household containers and packaging	20,000

Housewares	Annual Injuries
Knives	446,000
Tableware & flatware (excluding knives)	113,000
Drinking glasses	100,000
Cookware, bowls & canisters	31,000
Scissors	30,000
Waste containers, trash baskets, etc.	29,000

Source: National Safety Council

Staying Current on Electricity

*W*hen safety procedures are not followed, life can be a series of painful should-haves and could-haves. Such was the case for California parents who shouldn't have let their seven- and nine-year-old daughters play in a filled bathtub near a hair dryer, especially when the dryer should not have been plugged in, and the outlet should have had a ground fault circuit interrupter (GFCI). Both children died when the dryer fell into the bathtub.

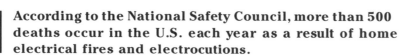

According to the National Safety Council, more than 500 deaths occur in the U.S. each year as a result of home electrical fires and electrocutions.

Here are some very important actions you *should* take to protect your family.

Get Your Home Up to Code

◆ Signs of problems include: blown fuses; tripped circuit breakers; dim or flickering lights; buzzing sounds; odors; hot switch plates; and switches or outlets that don't work. Get professional help immediately!

◆ The National Electrical Safety Foundation recommends an inspection by a licensed electrician every ten to forty years, and when you buy a house. Also consider an inspection when you add high-wattage appliances or renovate.

◆ Use a GFCI where appliances will be used near water, and in all outdoor outlets. The GFCI protects the body from shock by switching off power to a malfunctioning circuit. Test the GFCI monthly and after a major electrical storm. Use a plug-in device, e.g., a nightlight, and turn it on. Depress the TEST button. If the light turns off, the outlet is working. If the RESET button pops out but the light stays on, the GFCI is not working. Press RESET and call a licensed electrician. You can also buy a special GFCI tester.

◆ Consider installing arc fault circuit interrupters (AFCI). They can prevent fires caused by bad wiring.

An Important TO DO List

◆ Buy only electrical products — preferably double insulated — that are certified by a nationally recognized testing lab such as UL, CSA, ITS, or Met Labs.

◆ As a general rule, do not plug appliances into the same outlet if their combined wattage exceeds 1500 watts. If the wattage is not on the product, multiply the amps by 125.

◆ No more than one heat-producing appliance (microwave, toaster, coffeemaker, or waffle iron) should be plugged into an outlet.

◆ Unplug immediately any appliance that sparks or stalls.

◆ To replace a blown fuse, use the same size as the original.

◆ If a lamp's wattage isn't marked, use a sixty-watt bulb (or less).

◆ Keep electrical appliances away from water. Be sure your hands and feet are dry before you touch any plugged-in appliance.

◆ When you finish using small appliances or power tools, unplug them. They can electrocute if they fall into water — even if turned off.

◆ Despite Hollywood, never use a telephone, even a portable, in a bathtub, shower, or swimming pool.

◆ During an electrical storm, avoid bathing, touching an appliance, or using a telephone or computer.

◆ Don't tuck in or cover an electric blanket. It can overheat and catch fire.

◆ If you smell gas, do not use a phone or electrical product, including a light switch. A spark can ignite gas. Evacuate the premises immediately, and call the gas company or fire department.

◆ Use one-piece safety caps on unused wall and extension cord outlets, particularly if kids are around.

◆ Call in an expert to work around power lines.

◆ If someone is shocked, do not touch him if he is still in contact with the electrical source. Turn off the power and seek help.

Plugs and Extension Cords

◆ On a polarized plug, one blade is wider than the other. If it doesn't fit your outlet, don't try to force it; use an adapter.

◆ To avoid overloading a cord, add up the wattage of the products plugged into the cord, and compare the total to the cord's wattage rating.

◆ Never use extension cords to replace permanent wiring. The longer a cord is used, the greater the fire hazard due to heat buildup.

◆ Unplug and safely store extension cords that are not in use. In a child's mouth, the unplugged end can lead to serious injury or death.

◆ To pull a plug from an outlet, grip the plug. Don't yank the cord.

◆ Keep cords off steam pipes, heaters, and other hot surfaces.

◆ Don't run cords under rugs or furniture. Untangle twisted cords. They can overheat and start a fire.

◆ Insert plugs fully into extension cords so the prongs are not exposed.

◆ Discontinue using a cord that is hot or very warm to the touch.

◆ Only use cords outdoors that are marked for outdoor use.

◆ Avoid using extension cords with high-wattage appliances such as air conditioners, heaters, and irons. If you must, use a heavy-duty cord.

◆ Check all electrical cords at least once a year. Cracked or frayed cords are a principal cause of fires. Also, check appliances for cracks that could lead to overheating.

Balancing Act

For years, Gail kept her favorite captain's chair with its comfortable seat cushion beside her kitchen pantry. It was an attractive piece of furniture, and it was perfect to stand on for reaching objects stored high in the pantry. On a stylistic whim, she replaced the flat cushion with a thicker version. The next time Gail climbed onto the chair, the surprising thickness of the new cushion caused her to lose her balance and crash to the floor, injuring her shoulder and whacking her head.

Falls are the leading cause of preventable deaths in the home.

According to the National Safety Council, more than 9,000 people die from falls in their homes each year.

Anyone is susceptible to a fall. With forethought, however, most falls can be prevented.

On the Stairs

Stairs and steps account for over forty percent of all fatal falls in the home.

- Maintain treads, risers, and carpeting in mint condition. Be sure carpeting won't move or slide.

- *Always* keep stairs clear of obstructions. Never use them as a temporary shelf.

- Keep stairwells well lighted.

- Place a light switch at the top and bottom of the stairs.

- Install sturdy handrails on all stairways, regardless of length or frequency of use. One rail is a necessity, but one on each side is ideal.

- Always use the handrail when you're walking the steps.

- Do not carry bundles that can obstruct your vision. Make two or three trips if necessary. Use a laundry bag to carry laundry.

- Teach children the safety procedures to follow when using the stairs.

- Install safety gates at the top and bottom of stairs when small children are in the house.

- Never use throw rugs near stairs. Tape or tack them to the floor wherever you use them.

- For those with impaired vision, mark the length of each step with bright or glow-in-the-dark tape, especially the bottom step.

Avoiding Bedroom Nightmares

- Tidy the bedroom before going to sleep. Clear a path between the bed and the bathroom or doorway.

- Do not bound from bed the instant you wake up. Sit on the edge of the bed to get your bearings and your balance.

- Keep a flashlight by your bed, and a lamp, if possible.

- Keep all dresser drawers closed when they're not in use.

- Have a phone next to the bed.

All Around the House

- Never stand on a chair or box. Buy a sturdy stool or safety ladder.

- Move cautiously. Don't rush through the house to answer a telephone or doorbell.

- Arrange furniture so walkways are as wide as possible.

- Secure loose wires and cords, preferably around the edges of the room.

- Immediately pick up toys and clutter, and wipe up spills. It takes only a second for a serious incident to happen.

- Make porches and balconies off-limits to young children, and use safety gates. Make the openings small so a young child can't fall through. Never trust a railing to support your entire body weight.

- Watch out for pets in your path.

- Move chairs and furniture away from windows, so young children can't use them to reach a window. Windows in rooms used by small children should have fire-safe guards.

- Be extra-careful with bifocals. Looking through the reading portion can distort your depth perception.

- Around the house, avoid wearing high heels, clogs, and slippers with open heels. Walking in socks or stockings is risky, too. Wear shoes and slippers with nonskid soles.

- Use non-skid wax on bare floors.

- Make sure all areas are well lighted, including outside areas where you walk at night.

- If you fall, try to relax; let your arms and legs give like springs, to absorb the impact of the fall, and roll with the direction of the fall.

Early Warning, Rapid Response

A Fire Timeline

:00 A cigarette falls on a couch.

:30 Fire ignites and grows rapidly.

1:04 Fire spreads and smoke begins to fill the room.

1:35 Smoke layer descends rapidly.

1:50 Smoke alarm sounds at the foot of the stairs; still time to escape.

2:30 Temperature over couch exceeds 400° F.

2:48 Smoke pours into other rooms.

3:03 Temperature three feet above the floor in room of origin exceeds 500° F. No one could survive.

3:20 Upstairs hall filled with smoke; escape more difficult.

3:50 Second exit only way out.

4:33 Flames just now visible from the exterior of the house. Rescue may not be possible.

> **Each year, about 3,000 people die and tens of thousands are injured in home fires across the U.S.**

Often, people underestimate the speed at which fire grows. Don't be caught off guard.

Smoke Alarms

A smoke alarm cuts your chances of dying in a fire by nearly 50 percent.

◆ Install at least one smoke alarm on every level of your home, especially outside the bedrooms. Mount them on the ceiling or high on a wall.

◆ Make sure everyone can hear the alarms. Use a strobe-light version, if needed.

◆ Check the batteries monthly; replace them at least once a year.

◆ Replace a battery immediately if the alarm chirps to signal low battery power. Keep spares on hand.

◆ Never remove batteries.

◆ Do not paint over an alarm.

◆ Keep the unit clear of dust and cobwebs by cleaning it according to directions at least once a year.

◆ If a smoke alarm is plagued by false alarms, don't disable it. Relocate it, or install an exhaust fan.

◆ Replace any alarm that is more than ten years old.

◆ Don't install smoke alarms near windows, doors, or forced-air registers, where drafts could blow smoke away.

Fire Extinguishers

Keep a fire extinguisher in the kitchen and any other area where there is a risk of fire.

◆ A good choice for a fire extinguisher is a multipurpose Type A-B-C model with a UL listing. Learn how to use it.

◆ Check the pressure gauge on a fire extinguisher regularly, and replace if needed.

◆ Place the extinguisher near an exit.

◆ Fire extinguishers should be used only by adults.

Warning: Fire extinguishers are for small, contained fires only. Before you fight a fire, be sure that:

• everyone has left, or is leaving, the building;

• the fire department has been notified;

• the fire is confined to a small area and is not spreading;

• you have an unobstructed escape route if the fire cannot be quickly contained.

Remember, you are taking a risk fighting a house fire. Your best bet is to leave immediately and close off the area. Call the fire department even if you think the fire is out.

A Fast and Orderly Exit

◆ Practice using escape routes (especially from bedrooms) twice a year, including at night. Designate family members to help infants and disabled people.

◆ Always use the safest exit, but if you must escape through smoke, crawl low under it.

◆ Designate a place outside where all family members will meet. Do not re-enter the home!

◆ Have at least two exits for every room, and keep bedroom doors closed at night to keep smoke out.

◆ Place fire escape ladders in all upper-level rooms.

◆ Make sure locks and security bars feature quick-release devices that everyone can use.

◆ In apartments, check with your manager to be sure detection and alarm systems are working.

Some of this information is courtesy of The National Fire Protection Association.

Burning Issues

It was a large, noisy family gathering. The college students were back from school, and a crackling fireplace and lighted candles added to the festivities. Leslie looked forward to some home cooking, and catching up on everyone's activities. She picked up a paper plate, held a paper napkin under it, and eyed the goodies. However, she didn't keep an eye on the candle, which ignited the napkin as she reached for some food. Fortunately, Carole was on the other side of the table; seeing what was happening, she snatched the napkin from Leslie's hand and extinguished the flames.

Annual "Fire Prevention Week" is held during the Sunday through Saturday containing October 9th. That's the date of the Great Chicago Fire of 1871, and it serves as a somber reminder of the perils of fire, whether caused by a smelly cow or a scented candle.

Waxing Eloquent on Candles

From kids to college students to grandparents, candles are the rage. Unfortunately, they cause thousands of fires each year. The National Fire Protection Association offers these warnings when using candles:

◆ Keep candles away from all combustible items and flammable liquids.

◆ Place candles in sturdy, non-combustible holders that won't tip over and are big enough to collect dripping wax.

◆ Don't place lighted candles in windows. Blinds or curtains can be inadvertently closed over them.

◆ Never leave a child unattended in a room with a lighted candle, or place a candle where children or pets could knock it over.

◆ Extinguish all candles when you leave the room or go to sleep.

◆ Do not use water to extinguish a candle. The wax can splatter, or the flame could flare.

◆ Use battery-powered lights in a power outage. Keep extra batteries and bulbs on hand.

Hot Advice

Smoking is the leading cause of fatalities due to fires in the U.S., with more than 800 deaths annually.

◆ Never smoke when medicated or sleepy, after consuming alcoholic beverages, or in bed.

◆ Use deep, non-tip ashtrays and empty them frequently. Douse the ashes with water, or flush them down the toilet.

◆ Check in and around upholstery cushions for smoldering butts before leaving home or going to sleep. More fatal smoking fires begin in family rooms or living rooms than in bedrooms.

◆ When you have guests who smoke, provide plenty of ashtrays. Empty wastebaskets, lift cushions, and feel around in furniture crevices after they leave.

Some More Precautions

Playing with matches and lighters is the leading cause of fire deaths for children under age six.

◆ Teach children to respect fire as a tool, not a toy. If they play with matches or lighters and don't respond to your efforts to redirect their interests, seek professional counseling.

◆ Keep matches and lighters out of children's sight and reach, preferably in a locked cabinet. Teach children to bring them to an adult if they find them.

◆ Use only child-resistant lighters.

◆ Never let children use matches or lighters.

◆ Keep halogen lamps away from furnishings, draperies, high traffic areas, children, and pets. Only use lamps with a metal grate and a thermal protector. Use bulbs of 300 watts or less. To obtain information on a free safety kit for older models, call (800) 985-2220.

◆ When drying clothes, hang them a safe distance from stoves, heaters, and other sources of fire.

◆ Keep the clothes dryer free of lint. Vacuum the interior lint pathway and duct at least once a year. *Consumer Reports* recommends the use of metal ducts.

◆ Keep storage areas neat. Get rid of newspapers, rubbish, old clothes, oily rags, and damp waste.

Firearms Protection

It happened in Sacramento, but tragedies like it occur in homes around the country all too frequently. A mother whose husband was away on business slept in her sons' bedroom, and placed a handgun in the nightstand for protection. She failed to remove the gun the next morning, and the children, aged three and four, found it. The woman was in the kitchen when she heard the gunshot in the boys' bedroom. She arrived to find that her three-year-old son had been shot in the side by his four-year-old brother. The injured child was rushed to the hospital, where he later died.

According to the National Safety Council, about 600 people die from unintentional firearm incidents each year. The Centers for Disease Control estimate that more than 1.2 million latchkey children have access to loaded and unlocked firearms. Over 10,000 times a year, someone is shot unintentionally. Firearms are a fact of life, but one we need to live with in a safe manner.

Buying and Storing Your Weapon

◆ When purchasing a gun, ask the storeowner for instructions on how to use and handle the weapon.

◆ Take a gun-safety course.

◆ Long arms, such as rifles and shotguns, should be stored securely in locked racks or cabinets. Handguns should be stored in locked cabinets or drawers.

◆ Store your ammunition under lock and key, and in a separate room from the gun.

◆ All guns should be stored unloaded.

◆ Do not store a handgun under your pillow or mattress.

◆ Buy trigger locks for your weapons. They're available for all kinds of firearms.

◆ Carry the keys that open the locks on your key chain.

Safe Handling

In a 1998 study, the New England Journal of Medicine reported that a gun kept in the home for self-protection is twenty-two times more likely to be used to kill a family member, friend, or acquaintance than an intruder.

Most accidents at home are caused by unsafe handling while cleaning guns, while loading or unloading ammunition, by a child finding an improperly stored or unlocked gun, or by carelessness while holding a gun.

◆ *Always* point a gun in a safe direction. This is the golden rule of gun safety. A "safe" direction is one in which no one would be harmed even if the gun went off accidentally.

◆ Never handle or show guns without first carefully checking to be sure they are unloaded. Open the action and keep it open until the gun is again ready for storage. *Never assume* that a gun is not loaded.

◆ Unload a gun before taking it into your home. Guns should be loaded only in the hunting field or practice range. If you don't know how to open the action to make the gun safe, seek out an expert. Do not experiment.

◆ Always carry a handgun with the hammer down on an empty chamber.

◆ Do not put your finger on the trigger until you are ready to shoot.

◆ Do not assume the safety will make a loaded gun safe. Like any mechanical device, safeties on guns can malfunction. You are the ultimate safety device.

Kids and Guns

There are guns in nearly half the homes in the United States, so it is likely that children will come into contact with firearms.

◆ Answer your child's questions about guns openly and honestly. Don't make a gun an object of curiosity.

◆ Teach gun safety when your child acts out "gunplay," or starts asking questions about guns.

◆ Make sure your child knows the difference between a toy and a real gun, and between "pretend" on TV and real life.

◆ If you keep a gun, enroll your child in a gun-handling training course.

◆ Ask friends and relatives if they keep guns. Urge them to follow safe practices. Don't allow your child to visit unless they do.

◆ If your child sees a gun, he should follow this three-step safety measure:

1. STOP, don't touch.
2. LEAVE the room immediately.
3. TELL a trustworthy adult.

Up in Smoke

Each year, many home fatalities due to burns and fires are caused by careless use of flammable and combustible liquids, such as gasoline, kerosene, alcohol, lacquer thinner, turpentine, contact cements, paint thinner, and charcoal lighter fluid.

These staples of modern life need to be treated with respect:

◆ Always keep flammable liquids in approved cans with the Underwriters Laboratories or Factory Mutual label.

◆ Keep the containers in a shed or garage outside your home, and definitely out of reach of children.

◆ Do not use these flammable substances in areas where there is an open flame, electric motor, or other heat source.

◆ Never smoke or light a match near flammable liquids.

◆ Do not pour charcoal lighter fluid on hot charcoal.

◆ To store oily rags for a short time, place them in a covered metal container with a tight-fitting cover.

Warning: Gasoline

◆ Gasoline should not be used to clean anything.

◆ When fueling your lawn mower or other gas-powered equipment, turn off the equipment and allow it to cool before adding fuel. Always refuel outdoors and far from ignition sources.

◆ Wipe up spills immediately. Move the equipment at least ten feet away from the fueling area before you start the engine.

◆ When filling a portable gasoline container, put the container on the ground, which will eliminate the danger of spills inside your vehicle and avoid a possible static-electricity spark.

◆ Transport the can in the trunk with the trunk lid partially open. Drive directly to the nearest gas station and back home.

◆ Do not leave containers of gasoline or other flammable liquids open in any room or confined space where vapors can accumulate.

Home Accident Facts

Home Structures and Construction Materials	Annual Injuries
Stairs or steps	1,029,000
Floors or flooring materials	1,024,000
Other doors (excludes glass doors and garage doors)	331,000
Ceilings and walls	259,000
Household cabinets, racks and shelves	241,000
Nails, screws, tacks, or bolts	163,000
Porches, balconies, open-side floors	139,000
Windows	129,000
Fences or fence posts	117,000
House repair and construction materials	74,000
Door sills or frames	43,000
Handrails, railings or banisters	40,000
Glass doors	39,000
Counters or countertops	39,000
Poles	37,000
Fireplaces	19,000
Cabinets or door hardware	18,000
Ramps or landings	17,000

Source: National Safety Council

The Unvarnished Truth About Refinishing

*A*lice bought the end table at a country auction, and was saving it for the perfect miserable day in February. She gathered her refinishing materials and headed to the basement. It was warm and comfortable, at first, but she soon became lightheaded and nearly fainted as she stumbled to the stairs. She managed to climb into the clean air of her kitchen. There wasn't a gas leak in her basement — Alice had fallen victim to the fumes from the paint thinner she was using.

As Alice learned, a simple task like woodworking can be hazardous to one's health. Most solvents evaporate quickly, filling a room with fumes. The result can be acute, though temporary, intoxication, drowsiness, and headache.

Pregnant women and people with heart or lung disease should avoid products that contain solvents. According to *Consumer Reports*, the Consumer Product Safety Commission received reports of fifty-five injuries and ten deaths linked to the accidental inhalation of fumes from cleaning, painting, and home-repair products in a two-and-a-half-year period — and those figures are probably undercounts.

Because winter is when many of us tackle refinishing projects, please keep the following in mind.

Ventilation is a Must

The chemicals used for refinishing work are powerful.

◆ When possible, work outside.

◆ Indoors, you must have adequate ventilation. To create proper airflow, make sure there's good cross-ventilation. Many indoor spaces, particularly basements, have very poor air-movement qualities.

◆ Make sure that at least two windows or doors can be opened to produce proper airflow.

◆ Use a fan or other forced-air device to increase air movement.

Careful: Some solvents are extremely flammable and should not be used around fans, appliances, and heating equipment, which can produce friction and sparks that may lead to fires. Read the labels!

Know the Materials

◆ Follow the label directions. All stores are required to have safety data sheets on their products. Ask the salesperson to provide you with the appropriate data sheet for the product you're buying. Additional information can be obtained from the manufacturer.

◆ If you're not willing to educate yourself, skip the project, or leave it to a professional.

◆ Is the solvent ingredient necessary? Often, a product with little or no solvent can substitute for a higher-solvent product.

◆ Don't use more than one solvent product at a time, and don't use one right after another.

◆ Store leftover solvents, cleaners, and paints in labeled and sealed containers.

◆ Dispose of used products according to the manufacturer's guidelines, or call your local hazardous waste organization.

Proper Precautions

The dust created by sanding wood can trigger allergic reactions, and cause such diseases as dermatitis, bronchitis, and asthma.

◆ Wear pants, socks, shoes, head covering, and a long-sleeved shirt when sanding or stripping paint.

◆ Gather the necessary personal protective equipment before starting.

◆ Some chemicals can irritate or damage your eyes or skin; this means you need the proper gloves, goggles, or an apron or protective suit when you use them.

◆ Choose chemical-resistant gloves that are unlined and made of neoprene or butyl. If there's a hole or tear in a glove, discard it.

◆ Do not use regular household gloves, which can tear easily.

◆ Wear the appropriate mask to reduce dust and solvent exposure. Note: A mask without a filtering mechanism does not protect against chemical exposure.

◆ Fumes from some chemicals sink. If you're bent over while working, you may inhale more vapors than when standing.

◆ Don't drink alcoholic beverages on the day you use solvents. Alcohol can heighten toxic effects.

◆ If you take medication, ask your doctor about adverse interactions.

◆ If storing solvent products, lock them up. Keep them out of children's reach, and keep children and pets out of any room containing solvent fumes. A dose that doesn't affect you could be fatal to them.

Growing Concerns

*P*eggy knew everything about gardening: which plants need sun and which need shade, when to prune, and when to fertilize. She read all the books, attended all the lectures, and watched all the TV shows intended to help her master her aromatic domain. The only thing she didn't learn was when to quit; Peggy's love of gardening resulted in heat exhaustion.

Gardening can be strenuous on a body not accustomed to manual labor. As you head into the garden for the spring season, here are some fertile ideas for staying fit.

Spring Training

◆ Wear clothes that are comfortable and fit well, including long-sleeved shirts, pants instead of shorts, and a wide-brimmed hat. Wear sturdy, heavy-soled shoes to protect your feet when you push a spade or step on a nail or broken glass. Work gloves protect your hands from scratches, cuts, blisters, and irritation from harsh chemicals. You might also want to invest in a gardening stool, and cushioned pads to protect your knees.

◆ Avoid the 10 A.M.–2 P.M. time period when the sun's rays are the strongest.

◆ About fifteen minutes before going out, apply sunscreen with at least a 15-SPF to exposed skin.

◆ Before digging in, warm up and loosen up. Walk around the yard, and follow with gentle stretching exercises, particularly of the muscles in the lower back, legs, and arms.

◆ When lifting, keep your spine straight and bend your knees. Hold the load close and push upward with your legs. Avoid twisting your body. Instead, swivel on your feet and face the direction the material is going.

◆ Alternate or use both arms when you can.

◆ Work below shoulder level whenever possible. If you must work above shoulder level, perform the task for five minutes or less.

◆ Pace yourself. Don't try to do everything in one afternoon.

◆ Switch off your chores every fifteen to twenty minutes to activities that use different muscle groups.

◆ Use a sheet or lightweight tarp to collect raked-up debris so it can be dragged instead of carried.

◆ On warm days, keep water handy and drink plenty to remain hydrated.

◆ Keep a cordless phone nearby.

◆ For heavy work, hire a professional, or get someone to help you.

◆ Garden dirt and compost are rife with bacteria. Wash your hands thoroughly after gardening.

◆ Before digging in a new area, arrange to have all underground utilities marked.

Let the Tools Do the Work

◆ Buy tools with handles appropriate to your height, so you won't have to bend unnecessarily. Be sure the handles are smooth and sturdy.

◆ Use tools with a comfortable weight. Heavy tools can cause strain. Also, look for adaptive tools to reduce the strain on your body.

◆ Tighten loose handles. If they can't be tightened, replace them. Flying tool-heads are dangerous.

◆ When temporarily not in use, stand tools on end and lean them against a tree or building, with the metal blades facing inward. Do not leave them lying where they can be tripped over or stepped on.

◆ Keep tools in good condition, clean, and with sharp cutting edges. Oil wooden handles and metal blades to maintain their strength and prevent rusting.

◆ Store tools in a dry place where they will not rust and become weakened by the elements.

◆ When hanging tools on a rack, point the metal blades toward the wall.

Pesticide Warning

◆ Identify the specific pest to determine the proper treatment. Buy the least toxic pesticide needed.

◆ Read *all* statements on a label carefully before using any pesticide. Follow directions to the letter.

◆ Wear the correct protective equipment. This may include goggles, impermeable gloves, long sleeves, long pants, a painter's mask, and boots.

◆ Avoid breathing spray mists.

◆ Don't use pesticides near kids.

◆ Don't spray on windy days.

◆ Substitute non-poisonous insecticides whenever possible, such as soapsuds, talcum powder, or red-pepper spray.

◆ Do not smoke.

◆ Mix sprays outdoors.

◆ After using a pesticide, and before eating or drinking, always wash your face and hands with soap and water. Wash immediately if you spill a pesticide on your skin.

◆ Store pesticides in their original containers, out of children's reach.

Basic Rules for Hand Tools

You know Uncle Will — the poster boy for Yankee ingenuity, the guy who can solve any household problem with little more than a hammer and screwdriver. One day, he used a screwdriver instead of a pry bar to rip boards off an old deck. When the screwdriver snapped under the strain, Will fell and broke his two front teeth. That's genius?

There's a right way and a wrong way to use hand tools, but a lot of people don't seem to know it.

According to the U.S. Consumer Product Safety Commission, each year, more than 100,000 injuries require hospital treatment due to misuse of hand tools.

First Steps to a Quality Job

◆ Buy the best tool you can afford. Cheap tools are harder to use and more likely to break. Buy several versions or sizes of the same tool to assure you have the right tool for the right job.

◆ Use a hand tool for the job it was manufactured to perform.

◆ Inspect tools for cracks, chips, mushrooming, and wear. Discard damaged tools promptly.

◆ Be sure handles are fixed firmly into a tool's working end.

◆ Plan your job before you start.

◆ Check for hidden hazards, e.g., electric wires in a wall.

◆ Shut off the current when working near electricity.

◆ Organize your tools in a toolbox.

◆ Position your body securely while working with any tool. Wear eye protection.

◆ No matter how trivial the task seems, concentrate!

Striking and Struck Tools

◆ Wear safety goggles any time you're using one of these tools.

◆ A hammer head should be at least 3/8" larger in diameter than the striking surface of a chisel, punch, wedge, or other struck tools.

◆ Strike a hammer with the face parallel to the surface being struck. Glancing, off-center blows can throw dangerous splinters into the air. Aim the blow away from your body.

◆ Use the right hammer for the job.

◆ Do not use one hammer to strike another hammer or a hatchet.

- Never use a striking tool with a loose or damaged handle.

- Pull nails or pry wood away from your face.

- Sharpen struck tools before use. Aim the blow or cut away from your body.

Screwdrivers

- The blade tip should fit a slotted screw, without hanging over.

- For many jobs, you'll need to drill a pilot hole first.

- Do not strike a screwdriver handle with a hammer. It could splinter and shatter.

- Never use the handle as a striking tool.

- Do not use a screwdriver as a pry bar, scraper, lid remover, punch, or chisel.

- Don't hold work in one hand while using a screwdriver in the other. If the blade slips, you could get hurt.

- Screws are designed to be driven with the proper type of screwdriver. If you don't take the time to match the screw with the screwdriver, the tool blade can slip out of the screw slot, resulting in injury.

- Use insulated screwdrivers when working around electricity, but also turn off the power.

Wrenches

- For better control, pull the wrench toward you; don't push it away from you. On high-torque jobs, stand firmly.

- Replace wrenches when the teeth become marred or worn.

- Do not substitute pliers for work a wrench should do.

- Never hammer with a wrench.

- Never put your face or head level with a wrench handle.

- Never use a handle extender while turning a wrench. Switch to a wrench with a longer handle or one designed to withstand more force. Homemade handle extenders can slip off and break.

- Use a box-end or socket wrench to free a tight or frozen nut.

- Make sure the wrench fits a nut or bolt exactly. Limit your use of adjustable wrenches.

Cordless Tools

- Read and thoroughly understand the instruction manual.

- Do not operate cordless tools in or near flammable liquids, or in explosive atmospheres.

- Keep the tool and the recharging unit in an area not accessible to children.

- Remove batteries, or lock the switch in its OFF position, before changing accessories, adjusting, or cleaning the tool.

- When cutting, drilling, or driving into walls, floors, or wherever live electrical wires may be encountered, hold the tool only by its insulated gripping surfaces.

- Do not touch the drill bit, blade, or cutter immediately after operation. It may be extremely hot.

Open Me First!

For most of us, during the holidays there just aren't enough hours in the day. However, if we don't slow down and take some time for safety, what should be a joyous time can become a season of regrets. Here's a collection of suggestions to help keep you safe for the holidays.

Fresh Trees and Safe Lights

◆ Buy a fresh tree that smells like pine. Be sure its needles are hard to pull from the branches. Otherwise, it may be too dry and a fire risk.

◆ Keep the tree outside with the trunk in water, snow, wet dirt, or sand until you're ready to use it.

◆ Place your tree at least five feet from heat sources that can dry it out.

◆ Saw about two inches off the trunk. Keep water in the stand.

◆ Check the water in the stand daily.

◆ If a tree begins dropping its needles, put it out-doors at once.

◆ Use only strings of lights that have the UL mark. Don't use strings that are frayed or have broken wires.

◆ Unplug electrical decorations when making adjust-ments or repairs, and when leaving the house or going to bed.

◆ Don't run extension cords under the carpet, through doorways, or near heaters. Be sure cords are not pinched behind or under furniture.

◆ Secure all electrical cords, so no one will trip over them.

◆ Use no more than three standard sets of lights per outlet.

◆ Plug lights into multiple-outlet surge protectors.

◆ Never use light strings marked FOR INDOOR USE out-doors.

◆ Power for all outdoor lighting should be supplied by permanent weatherproof wiring, and be installed by a professional electrician.

◆ When stringing outdoor lights, work with a helper, not alone.

Candles, Fireplaces, and Potpourri

◆ Decorate with flame-retardant or noncombustible materials.

◆ Read labels before you use special holiday materials.

◆ Put candles in stable holders.

◆ Keep lighted candles away from decorations, trees, draperies, and other flammable materials. Never put them in windows or near exits.

◆ Do not burn wrapping paper in the fireplace. A flash fire may result, as wrappings ignite suddenly.

◆ If you build a fire, use a fireplace screen, and do not leave young children unattended.

◆ Always keep a fire extinguisher handy. Know how to use it.

◆ Wear gloves while decorating with spun glass "angel hair" to avoid irritation to eyes and skin.

◆ Use a sturdy ladder or stepstool to reach high places.

◆ Keep kids' safety in mind when decorating and when buying holiday treats. Carefully supervise youngsters during holiday activities, including while visiting relatives or friends.

Adults Just Want to Have Fun

Children aren't the only ones who want to have fun this holiday season. If you plan to host or attend a holiday party, keep these safety stocking-stuffers in mind:

◆ If you have guests, be sure walkways and steps are well lighted. Clear any ice or snow thoroughly.

◆ Avoid leaving perishable foods at room temperature for more than two hours.

◆ Provide smokers with large, deep ashtrays, and pay special attention to any smoker who's drinking. Empty ashtrays often, wetting their contents before dumping them.

◆ After the party, check on and under cushions for cigarette butts.

◆ If you plan on drinking, use a designated driver or call a cab.

◆ Eat before and while you're drinking alcohol. Food in your stomach slows the absorption of alcohol.

◆ Make your first drink a large glass of water, juice, or soda to quench your thirst. Never drink alcohol because you're thirsty.

◆ Stand away from the bar. Dance, mingle and talk to the guests.

◆ Space drinks to a maximum of one an hour. Alternate between alcoholic and non-alcoholic beverages.

◆ Stop drinking alcohol ninety minutes before the party is over. There is no other way to sober up.

Appliance Controls

When home appliances were carpet sweepers, churns, and washboards, there was little to fear. Today's appliances save us time and energy, but they can turn against us in a second. Until "smart" appliances eliminate the hazards, we've got to control the power of our appliances.

Keep Your Appliances User-friendly

♦ Look for safety features when you buy, such as an automatic shut-off switch for your iron.

♦ Buy only appliances certified by a nationally recognized testing lab such as UL, CSA, ITS or Met Labs.

♦ Read and follow instructions.

♦ Place small appliances on solid, dry, stable counters or tables.

♦ Unplug appliances not in use.

♦ Inspect your appliances periodically for damage, wear, or loose parts. If there's a problem, have it checked by a qualified service center before using the appliance again.

♦ Use the appliance only for its intended purpose. For example, an oven is not a furnace.

♦ If any appliance sparks or stalls, unplug it immediately.

♦ Try to avoid using extension cords. If you must, use a heavy-duty cord.

♦ If a fire starts in a microwave oven, unplug the unit immediately. Do not open the microwave door until the fire goes out by itself.

♦ Have your gas-burning equipment inspected annually by a professional. Replace any flexible gas appliance connectors that are more than ten years old.

♦ If you smell a faint gas odor near a heating appliance, the pilot light may need re-lighting. If the odor is strong or you hear a hissing noise, leave the house immediately. Leave the door open behind you for ventilation. Don't use anything that can create a spark — even the telephone. Go to a neighbor's house to make the emergency call.

♦ Clean your dryer's lint trap before every load.

Appliances and Kids

While most home appliances are purchased for adult use, many of us share our homes with children or grandchildren. Children would love to play with those "toys" they see us using so industriously. Our job is to see that they don't.

◆ Keep small appliances as far away from prying hands as possible.

◆ On major appliances, use latches designed to lock out youngsters.

◆ Use the back burners of the range as much as possible. Install a range guard, and turn pot and skillet handles away from the edge.

◆ Always keep the dishwasher closed and locked. Store knives and sharp utensils with the pointed edge facing down.

◆ Garbage disposals that work by a wall switch should have a safety-lock switch installed.

◆ Trash compactors should only work with a key, and it should be kept away from children.

◆ Keep your deep freezer locked, and the key well hidden.

Respect Electricity

◆ Be sure your hands and feet are dry before you touch any plugged-in appliance.

◆ If possible, remove all electrical appliances from the bathroom. This includes radios, hair dryers, hair curlers, toothbrushes, and electrical heaters. Try to use appliances that are battery powered.

◆ If you must use electrical appliances in the bathroom, keep them well away from sinks, toilets, and tubs.

◆ Have an electrician install ground fault circuit interrupters (GFCIs) in outlets in bathrooms, kitchen, basement, outdoor circuits, and garage, or buy portable GFCIs.

◆ If an appliance cord falls into water, turn off the appliance and unplug it before pulling the cord out of the water. Wait for the cord to be completely dry before using.

◆ As a general rule, don't plug appliances into the same circuit if their combined wattage exceeds 1500 watts.

◆ When replacing a light bulb, turn off the switch and unplug the lamp. Never touch the metal base while inserting or removing a bulb.

House Warming Hints

Home heating equipment that provides warmth and comfort on a cool day also brings deadly risks if used incorrectly.

According to recent statistics from the National Fire Protection Association, home heating equipment results in approximately 50,000 fires and 375 fatalities across America each year.

Here are a few tips to keep your house cozy and safe.

Start with the Basics

- Have your heating systems inspected by a professional before the start of each heating season.

- Install smoke detectors on every level of your home, including the basement, outside sleeping areas, and in rooms with space heaters. Put carbon monoxide detectors outside sleeping areas, and in rooms with a fireplace or stove, unvented gas or liquid heaters, or a furnace.

- Keep flammable items at least three feet from a heater, fireplace, chimney, stove, or chimney pipe. This includes papers, wallpaper, curtains, clothing, and bedding.

- Keep a fire extinguisher handy, and know how to use it.

Be Cautious with Portable Heaters

◆ Buy a heater that's approved by a nationally recognized independent testing lab and has automatic shut-off safety features.

◆ Always turn heaters off when leaving a room or going to bed.

◆ Never use a heater in a room where children or incapacitated adults are unsupervised.

◆ If you have an electric heater:

• Do not curl the cord and do not bury it under carpeting. The heat from the cord could start a fire.

• If the cord overheats, stop using the heater and have it serviced.

• Don't use an extension cord. If you must use one temporarily, be sure it's marked with a power rating at least equal to the heater's rating.

• Check periodically for fraying or splitting wires. Do not try to repair a broken heater yourself. Take it to a qualified service center.

◆ Avoid using kerosene heaters. They are illegal in many areas. If you must use one, make sure you use the correct fuel, follow manufacturer's directions exactly, never refill the heater when it is hot, and never fill it indoors.

Hot Tips for Fireplaces and Stoves

◆ Have your chimney inspected by a certified sweep at the start of each heating season. If you regularly use the fireplace or stove more than four times a week, or use soft or green woods, have it inspected more often.

◆ Never leave small children unattended near a fireplace or stove.

◆ Block out animals and sparks with a mesh screen spark arrester on the chimney, and keep the roof clear of leaves, pine needles, overhanging branches, and other debris.

◆ Never use flammable liquids to light or stoke a fire.

◆ Do not burn paper, boxes, trash, or pine boughs. The particles can float out onto the roof.

◆ To reduce creosote, use hardwoods seasoned for at least a year.

◆ Don't burn preservative-treated wood. The ash will contain chemicals that are a hazardous waste.

◆ Remove ashes only in a metal container with a tight-fitting lid. Put the ashes outside, away from combustible materials.

◆ Don't overload a fireplace. A roaring fire can overheat your walls or roof and lead to an inferno. Also:

• Read the instructions before lighting an artificial log. These logs can burn unevenly and release abnormal levels of carbon monoxide.

• Be sure the fire is out before you go to bed or leave the house.

• To avoid flying sparks, use a sturdy screen made of metal or heat-tempered glass.

◆ If you purchase a stove, buy one that bears a label from a reputable testing lab, and have it installed by a certified company. Also:

• Frequently check and clean flues for creosote.

• Keep a window ajar to avoid a buildup of combustion products.

◆ If there's a roaring noise inside the house from the chimney area, or sparks and/or flames are shooting from the chimney top, call the fire department immediately. If the chimney cracks, or if heat radiates through it, the house may catch fire.

Home Work Requirements

Carl thought working from home would be a piece of cake. He was good at his job, had clearly defined objectives, and had a budget to purchase the resources he needed. What he didn't realize — until several harrowing and painful incidents later — was that besides being an efficient investment manager, he also needed to be to an electrician, carpenter, fireman, nurse, ergonomics expert, physical therapist, and fitness instructor. Carl learned a lot about managing risk while working at home, and much of his education had nothing to do with financial management.

An estimated 55 million Americans now do some office work from their homes.

While neck, back, and arm injuries from chairs or keyboards are the most obvious dangers when working at home, problems like strained power outlets, bad lighting that can lead to eye damage, high shelves overloaded with supplies, and unsecured file cabinets also pose risk.

Create a Safe Environment

◆ Don't run extension cords across the floor. Keep cords out of foot traffic, but don't put them under rugs or the feet of furniture. Use cord covers.

◆ Replace extension cords with power strips that have surge protectors. Heavy power users, such as air-conditioning units, need their own circuits.

◆ To remove stray cords, move desks closer to power outlets and phone jacks. You can also install new outlets.

◆ Tape or tack down floor coverings and carpeting that present tripping hazards.

◆ Avoid fires by not using cooking devices, space heaters, or candles. Don't smoke.

◆ Keep an "ABC" fire extinguisher handy, and know how to use it.

◆ Don't stack cabinets with binders and heavy books.

◆ Close any drawers not in use, and open only one drawer at a time. You're asking for trouble by opening the top drawer of a file cabinet all the way.

◆ Working at home you may have pets and children's toys lying around. Put all toys away when they're not in use.

At the Work Station

◆ The Prevent Blindness America organization recommends positioning the monitor twenty to twenty-six inches from your eyes. The top of the monitor should be at least fifteen degrees below eye level with a backward tilt. This eases strain on the neck and reduces the exposed surface area of your eyes.

◆ Use a screen that swivels or tilts, and has contrast and brightness controls. Modify the lighting or screen location to eliminate glare or harsh reflections.

◆ Use safe and correct posture when sitting down.

◆ Get an adjustable chair that allows you to make all adjustments while seated, including seat height, seat tension, chair back, and moveable armrests. This allows you to position yourself at a proper angle and distance from the screen.

◆ A proper chair should allow you to place your feet firmly on a support surface to provide stability for the seated posture and adequate lower leg support. If your feet aren't planted firmly on the floor, use a footrest.

◆ The most important area for back support is the lower back. If you don't feel your chair gives you the necessary support in that area, try to position a pillow or a rolled-up towel in the curve of your lower back.

◆ Look for a chair with a five-prong base, since chairs with four-prong bases tend to tip over more.

◆ When using a keyboard, your elbow angle should be at ninety degrees, and your wrists should be flat.

◆ Place the mouse close to your body to minimize the motion of reaching out and away.

◆ Consider buying special glasses for monitor work.

Maintain Your Personal Resources

◆ Vary your routine. Try to take a few minutes every hour or so to organize materials, file, or do some different task.

◆ If you use a keyboard constantly, frequent breaks to stretch, stand up, and rest your eyes are important. For example, take a thirty-second break after each ten minutes of intense typing. Periodic breaks of ten or fifteen minutes also keep you fresh.

◆ Change positions often, so your hands and wrists aren't kept in the same place for long periods.

◆ If you have to lift heavy boxes or file cabinets, get help or use a hand-held cart. Also, don't store heavy boxes in high places.

◆ When typing or working from notes, put documents or books at eye level close to the screen.

◆ Headsets are superior to hand-held receivers. If you don't have a headset, avoid straining your neck to keep the handset balanced on your shoulder.

Fiddler on the Roof

As a graphic artist, Tony knew a lot about perspective, so he was pretty sure there was nothing to fear in climbing the twenty feet to the roof of his house. Funny how twenty feet suddenly looked like a hundred feet when Tony was standing on the roof looking down. He froze at the thought of climbing back onto the ladder and nearly panicked. Firemen rescuing terrified cats from trees was one thing; escorting foolish men from a roof was quite another. Tony barely summoned the courage to climb back down, and once on solid ground he had a whole new perspective on how high twenty feet really was.

Experts advise against tackling projects that involve wiring, plumbing, heating, or climbing — even when you've had some training in those areas.

They're complicated, dangerous jobs, and a mis-cue could lead to disaster. However, there are many jobs the average do-it-yourselfer can tackle around the house, as long as he or she uses good judgment and proven safety practices.

Dress for Success

The minimum safety equipment for all do-it-yourself projects includes:

- *Safety glasses* with impact-resistant lenses and frames for work that could produce flying particles; and *safety goggles* for work with liquids that could splatter. Do not rely on regular reading glasses for protection. Safety goggles should have a sturdy head strap and many ventilation holes on the sides, which make them more comfortable in warm weather and prevent fogging.

- *Dust masks* to filter common dusts, such as fiberglass insulation particles and sanding dust. Some toxic materials, such as lead paint and asbestos, require special respirator masks with cartridge-type filters.

- *Rubber gloves* to protect your hands from skin damage when using paints or strong solvents. Leather or cloth gloves will provide protection for other types of work.

- *Hearing protectors* worn during prolonged exposure to loud noises produced by equipment such as drills and power saws.

- *Head protection* in close quarters and low ceiling areas, especially with nails sticking down. Use an old bike helmet or buy a hard hat.

- *Sturdy, heavy-soled shoes with steel toes.*

- Get expert advice for the purchase and use of safety equipment.

Planning and Performance

- Think small. Don't overdo it by taking on more challenge than you can handle. If you're going to need help, get it early in your project.

- Plan the job before starting. Look for potential hazards.

- Allow enough time to do the job without hurrying or cutting corners. Work during "your" most productive hours.

- Have all the needed tools on hand before starting. Don't improvise. For example, don't extend the length of a wrench with a hollow pipe.

- Alternate heavy and light work to avoid fatigue. Take breaks often.

- When carrying tools or supplies, make sure the route is clear. Put pets out of the way.

- When lifting, clutch a heavy load to your body and lift straight up. Let your legs do the work, not your back.

- Know your limits.

- Keep the area clean of debris.

- Never saw into walls without knowing the exact layout of electrical wires, plumbing, gas pipes, asbestos insulation, and studs. To help yourself, use a stud sensor, and run a shower to listen for running water in pipes in the wall.

Tools of the Trade

- Review all instructions for your equipment. Understand the equipment before you use it.

- When renting an unfamiliar piece of machinery, ask the dealer to explain how to operate it. Take the time to get to know a new tool.

- Use the correct guard, shield, or safety mechanism that came with the equipment. Do not remove them!

- Stay alert, especially when you're teamed with another person on a machine. Communicate clearly.

- Keep equipment in good working condition.

- If the tool requires two hands, hold on with both hands.

- If a wood saw does not cut well with little pressure, it probably needs sharpening.

- If a power tool sparks, stalls, or overheats, do not use it. Have it repaired professionally.

- Use the proper ladder for the job. Keep it in good repair. Put it on a surface that's firm, level, and not slippery. Keep your body within the side rails.

Keep in mind that any house or apartment built before 1978 may contain lead-based paint. Lead-based paint can be harmful to children and pregnant women. Before you disturb a surface with old paint:

- Call your local health department for guidance on testing.

- If lead-based paint is present, have the repair or renovation done by a professional. If you must do it yourself, get instructions from your health department.

Chemical Reactions

Jim was going to show Suzy this time. He'd been complaining for weeks that the sink in the mudroom was getting too stained. She insisted there was nothing she could do about it. Jim knew better — it just required some manly elbow grease and an extra special application of powerful cleanser. He got out the ammonia and the chlorine bleach, mixed them into his secret weapon, and set to work. The only smart thing Jim did that afternoon was to leave the windows open. Instead of killing himself with the toxic fumes, he just made himself violently ill. As for the stains, well, Suzy ordered a new sink.

Each year, thousands of people are poisoned, blinded, burned, and killed by common household products.

We can protect our health and environment from these products by taking some preventive steps.

Preliminary Precautions

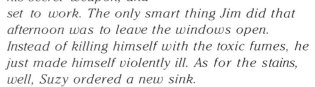

- If you have to use hazardous materials, always buy the least toxic product available that will get the job done. Get any needed personal protection equipment (PPE) at that time.

- Try to avoid products with labels containing these words: caustic, corrosive, explosive, danger, flammable, poison, volatile, toxic, or warning.

- Buy only the amount of product you will need. When hazardous products can no longer be used, they become hazardous waste.

- Read the labels on the products you buy, and follow the directions carefully.

- Never mix any household chemicals. Formulations often change.

- Never mix chlorine bleach with toilet bowl cleaner, ammonia, lye, rust remover, vinegar, or oven cleaner. It could create a toxic gas — just ask Jim.

- Dilute cleaning agents. Many products do not need to be used at full strength. Check the label for instructions on dilution.

- While not as powerful, some household food-grade products can replace commercial cleaners. Check reputable Web sites, libraries, or bookstores for examples.

- If you make up a homemade cleaner, always list the exact ingredients on the container.

◆ Gather PPE before you start, and use it.

◆ Always make sure you have the right protection for mist-producing chemicals such as insecticides and spray paints.

◆ Post the phone number of your local poison control center.

Handle With Care

◆ Use the recommended amounts. More is not necessarily better, and may even be hazardous to your health or safety.

◆ Do one product-related cleaning task at a time.

◆ Do not use hazardous materials if you are pregnant.

◆ Never sniff a chemical to identify what it is.

◆ Do not drink alcoholic beverages or use judgment-altering drugs on the day you use solvents. Alcohol can heighten the toxic effects. If you are on medication, ask your doctor about dangerous effects.

◆ Do not smoke when using household chemicals. Many toxic products are flammable.

◆ Open doors and windows when you use chemicals, or go outside. Use a fan when working with most toxic solvents.

◆ If the air smells bad and hurts your lungs, get far away and stay there until the air clears.

◆ If a commercial drain opener doesn't work, don't follow with sulfuric acid. The chemical reaction could splatter you.

◆ To protect your hands, use rubber gloves that won't tear easily. Discard worn or damaged gloves.

Safe Storage and Disposal

◆ Keep hazardous materials on cool, dry, well-ventilated shelves, beyond the reach of children and animals. If possible, lock them up.

◆ Place all hazardous products away from food, heat, and flames.

◆ Store all products in their original containers with their labels intact.

◆ Keep all products tightly closed.

◆ Flammables, corrosives, and poisons should be stored away from one another.

◆ If you end up with more than you need, give away the excess.

◆ Do not reuse containers for other purposes.

◆ Dispose of hazardous materials properly. They can poison the environment, and the grounds and waters where children play. Local government agencies, public health offices, authorized waste disposal companies, and the product manufacturers can answer your questions about proper disposal.

Kitchen Cautions

Ray was a good cook who had all the right utensils, from the best pots and pans to the finest cutlery. He took his prized set of carving knives to every family cookout and even on summer vacation. He kept the blades sharp and clean and wielded them with an artist's skill. Unfortunately, Ray's wit was as sharp as his knives. While preparing his favorite chicken dish one evening, he also engaged in a heated discussion with his guests. Good-natured disagreement led to raised voices and soon a howl from Ray, who, having taken his eye off his work, inadvertently took a slice off his thumb.

The kitchen is often the center of activity in a home, and no other room contains as many potential hazards. Here are a few precautions to protect yourself from menaces lurking in the cozy kitchen.

For Starters

A safe kitchen requires three essentials: safe planning, safe equipment, and safe habits.

- Clear counters of unnecessary items before cooking.

- Focus on the meal. Keep toddlers, guests, and pets out of the kitchen during the busiest times of meal preparation. Haste and distractions can make you careless.

- Make sure there's ample light.

- Clean up spilled water, grease, or food peelings immediately.

- Use a sturdy stool or ladder with treaded steps to reach high shelves. Never stand on a chair.

- Keep doors and drawers closed.

Now You're Cooking

Cooking is the primary cause of residential fires in the U.S., killing more than 200 people annually.

- Wear short or tight-fitting sleeves when cooking. Floor-length robes and floppy slippers are hazardous in the kitchen.

- Always watch food being heated. The leading cause of home cooking fires and injuries is unattended cooking.

- Use the proper size burner. The exposed part of a larger burner could ignite your clothing.

- Do not pick up a hot pan unless you have an insulated spot where you can put it easily.

- Always keep dry potholders or mitts handy to hold hot objects. Wet holders carry the heat to your hand.

- Use potholders or mitts, not towels, to handle food in the oven, and to remove items from the stove or microwave.

- Do not place potholders, plastic utensils, towels, or unnecessary items near the stove.

- When lifting a lid from a pan, tilt the far side up first so the steam will be directed away from your face and hands.

- Keep a pot lid near the stove. If a grease fire starts on the stove, use the lid as a shield and slide it over the fire. If a grease fire starts in the oven, close the oven door. Be sure to turn off the heat.

- Keep a fire extinguisher handy. An "ABC" type is most practical for home use. Check its pressure gauge regularly. Know how to use it.

- After cooking, make sure all knobs are turned completely off.

- Use microwave-safe containers for microwave cooking.

Getting Right to the Point

Fires and burns may cause more serious injuries, but cuts are the most common kitchen injury.

More than 400,000 emergency room visits occur each year in the U.S. due to injuries associated with knives.

- There's no such thing as an "all-purpose" knife. Buy a size and style of knife appropriate to the kind of cutting you intend to do.

- Always use a sharp knife and a cutting board that provides a clean, flat surface. A dull knife requires a lot of pressure, so it's more likely to slip and cut someone.

- Angle knives downward when you cut, and always cut away from your fingers.

- Hold food down with your knuckles to prevent cutting a finger.

- Have a special rack or compartment for storing knives.

- Wash and dry knives and put them away immediately. Don't leave knives to soak in soapy water — you may find them the hard way.

Ladder Tips
(Climber Falls!)

Man, what a great day to patch that loose shingle at the base of the chimney: sun's out, not a cloud in the sky, light breeze, high of eighty-seven degrees. Mick took the ladder from the garage, removed his shirt, and sent Carol shopping. Five minutes after she'd left he inadvertently knocked the ladder to the ground. Let's see — the wife and kids are gone, the neighbors are away on vacation, and Mick lives on a street where there's little traffic. Mick sat on the roof for four hours, which gave him plenty of time to fix the shingle — and get so badly blistered from the sun that he missed two days' work.

Annually, there are approximately 150,000 injuries associated with ladders.

Most ladder incidents are caused by a loss of balance, or by a ladder's being placed on a slippery surface. Others are caused by sheer foolishness. Almost all of them could be avoided.

Before You Climb

◆ For any project involving a straight ladder, consider hiring a professional.

◆ Choose the proper ladder for the job. Wood and fiberglass ladders are best for working around electrical sources, although any type of ladder can conduct electricity if wet.

◆ Before climbing a ladder, check it thoroughly to be sure it's safe. Look for missing, damaged, or loose parts. Be sure the non-slip feet aren't worn. If there's a problem, get a new ladder. Repairing a damaged ladder is taking a risk.

◆ Verify the weight capacity, and include tools you carry in your calculation.

◆ Whether working indoors or outside, place the ladder on a firm, solid surface. If you must put it on a soft surface, place a board under the ladder's feet to provide firm footing.

◆ Always have someone steady the ladder on windy days, or if there's a question about the ladder's stability.

◆ When using an extension ladder outside, place the ladder about one-fourth the length of the ladder away from the wall. For a quick estimate, place your toes against the ladder feet. Stand erect and extend your arms straight out. The palms of your hands should rest on the base section rung nearest to shoulder level.

◆ Wear clean, dry, slip-resistant shoes, and be sure the rungs of the ladder are dry.

◆ If you use a ladder in front of a door, lock the door and barricade the other side.

◆ Never use a folded-up stepladder as a straight ladder. The feet won't rest squarely on the ground, and the ladder may slip.

◆ Never lean a ladder against a window pane or other unstable surface.

◆ Do not climb a ladder if you have been using alcohol, have balance problems, are subject to fainting spells, are using medication, or are physically handicapped.

◆ Do not paint a wood ladder.

◆ Arrange for someone to check on you periodically.

Avoiding a Crash Landing

◆ Never climb with equipment in your hands. Use your pockets, an equipment belt, a tool pouch, or raise heavy objects with a hand line.

◆ For added stability, tie the top of the ladder to a support, or use special devices available from your hardware store.

◆ To climb or descend, face the ladder and grip the rungs firmly with both hands.

◆ Keep your body between the rails at all times, and never reach or lean too far to the side. Rule of thumb: Your belt buckle should never extend outside the ladder rail.

◆ Hold on to the ladder with one hand. If you must use both hands, put one leg around a rung.

◆ If you need to shift to a new position, climb down and reposition the ladder. Don't try to change the ladder's position while standing on it.

◆ On a straight or extension ladder, don't climb higher than the fourth rung from the top. On a stepladder, don't climb higher than the second rung from the top.

◆ When climbing onto a roof, be sure the ladder extends three to five feet above the edge. This added length is needed to step safely onto the roof. Do not climb the ladder above the rooftop.

◆ When moving a metal ladder, lower it to avoid touching a power line. Better yet, never place a ladder where it could slide into power lines. Give them a wide berth.

◆ Descend immediately if high winds or rain begin.

Mower Sound Advice

Here's the irony: Tom owned a nursery that offered lawn maintenance service. His company would cut your lawn, trim your shrubs, and leave your yard looking immaculate. Every morning, Tom would caution his crews about the use of their power tools and check each employee for steel-toed work shoes. He was a real stickler for those shoes... for everybody but himself. One evening, rushing to cut his own yard before dark, Tom slipped on a hillside, and his power mower chopped two toes off his right foot, which was protected only by thin tennis shoes. That was a hard one for Tom to explain to himself and his employees.

Operating Instructions

Each year, more than 70,000 people with lawn mower-related injuries end up in emergency rooms, including over 7,000 children under fifteen.

To protect everyone:

◆ Buy only a mower with a control that stops the mower when you let go of the handle.

◆ Each year, thoroughly review and follow the operating and maintenance instructions in your operator's manual.

◆ Get your mower professionally serviced before each cutting season.

◆ Leave all safety features intact.

◆ Know how to start and stop the machine safely.

◆ Invest in good safety glasses, especially when using side-discharge mowers and lawn trimmers.

◆ Do not operate a lawn mower when you're tired or under the influence of alcohol or medication.

◆ Wear hearing protection, but do not listen to music or the radio.

◆ Fill the tank outdoors. To avoid refueling, put in just enough gasoline to perform the job.

◆ Use extra care when refueling:

- If you have to refuel, take a break and let the engine cool.

- Don't spill when you fill. Remove any spilled gasoline before starting the engine.

◆ Put children and pets in the house until you finish.

◆ The Outdoor Power Equipment Institute recommends that children not operate a lawn mower. If you allow a mature teenager to mow grass, be sure he understands the operator's manual, will exercise caution, and is strong enough to manage the mower. Supervise several jobs before allowing him to do the job on his own, and spot-monitor unannounced later.

When Walking Behind a Mower

◆ Mow only in dry conditions and daylight.

◆ Before starting, pick up any rocks, sticks, cans, wires, or toys in your path.

◆ Wear close-fitting long pants and heavy-duty shoes with non-slip soles and steel toe protection. For mowing terraces, consider shoes with cleats.

◆ Cut the difficult or hilly areas first, while you're fresh and your concentration is at its peak.

◆ Never leave the mower unattended while the engine is running.

◆ Stop when a person — especially a child — or a pet is in the area.

◆ Never cross driveways or paths with the blade rotating. The blade can pick up and throw rocks.

◆ To clear a clogged discharge chute, turn off the engine, and then use only a stick.

◆ If the blade strikes an object, turn off the engine and examine the mower thoroughly for damage. Before checking the blade, remove the spark plug wire, if accessible.

◆ Mow across inclines.

◆ Keep the mower flat.

◆ Push the mower; pulling it increases the risk of slipping and pulling it over your foot.

Special Tips for Riding Mowers

◆ Don't carry passengers on a riding mower, especially small children.

About fifteen children are killed each year in riding mower incidents, usually from falling off the mower and being run over.

◆ When backing up, look behind and down for children and pets.

◆ Always start the machine from the operator's seat.

◆ Slow down at corners, blind spots, and when descending hills.

◆ Watch for holes, ruts, or bumps obscured by grass.

◆ Do not mow in reverse. If you must back up, disengage the blade and proceed with caution.

◆ To avoid tipping, mow up and down on gentle slopes, never across.

◆ If there's doubt about tipping or losing control of the riding mower, stay off the slope.

◆ If the tires slip on a slope, it's too steep. Disengage the blade and go slowly, straight down the slope.

◆ Inspect your riding mower each time before you start it.

Senior Safety

Anita, sixty-five, lived alone. One autumn day she decided to put up her storm windows to prepare for winter. She had done this by herself many times, so she saw no need to get help. This time, however, the kitchen storm window wasn't going on properly due to paint residue in the hooks. Anita was already several steps up the ladder when she decided to climb another step to gain better leverage. Struggling to hold on to the window, she climbed to the next step, lost her balance, and fell, shattering her kneecap. It took hours of surgery and several months of rehabilitation before Anita could walk again, and she will never have full mobility.

Poor eyesight and hearing, arthritis, mobility impairments, and the side effects of medication can make older people more prone to injuries. The following tips should make life safer.

Stay on Your Feet

Falls are the most common injury in the home.

> **About 8,000 people sixty-five and older die from falls at home each year.**

To prevent falls:

- Being physically fit reduces the chances of falling. See a health professional for a fitness program.

- Make sure you know the effects of your medicines. According to the *Johns Hopkins Medical Letter*, if you take four or more prescriptions you are more likely to fall, largely due to drug interactions or side effects such as weakness or dizziness.

- Don't walk around the house in worn-out, loose-fitting slippers or stocking feet. Wear shoes that fit well, fasten securely, and have thin, nonskid soles.

- Keep exits clear of obstructions. Remove all objects from floors and stairways.

- Stair carpet must be firmly attached to the steps. Put nonskid treads on stairs without carpeting.

- Place sturdy handrails on all stairs, preferably on both sides.

- Remove throw rugs. Securely fasten doormats and area rugs.

- Place electrical and telephone cords where they cannot be walked on or tripped over.

- Don't rush to answer the phone or doorbell.

- Paint the edges of outdoor steps white so they can be more easily seen.

- Put non-slip mats around areas likely to get wet.

- Use a solid stepladder with high railings to hold on to.

◆ Get help for difficult jobs, including snow shoveling.

◆ Hip protectors may be appropriate. Ask your doctor.

Go Heavy on the Light

◆ To see adequately, older adults may need three times more light than younger people do.

◆ Provide good, easily accessible lighting throughout the home, especially on the stairways.

◆ Place light switches (or a good flashlight) at both the top and bottom of stairwells.

◆ Install "glow-light" or remote control switches to avoid groping in the dark for wall switches.

◆ Consider putting a light-sensitive plug-in nightlight in every room.

◆ Reduce dangerous glare by using frosted bulbs, indirect lighting, shades, or globes on light fixtures. Use adjustable blinds or window covering to reduce the sun's glare.

◆ Provide plenty of bright outdoor lighting at night, too.

All Around the House

◆ Develop a plan for each type of emergency that could occur. Contact your fire department to let them know of someone with special needs.

◆ Add a bath mat or nonskid abrasive strips or decals to the bottom of the tub or shower stall.

◆ Place a small corner shelf or easy-to-reach holder in the tub for bath supplies. This will prevent dangerous standing or reaching.

◆ Keep lotions and shampoos in unbreakable plastic containers.

◆ Lower the setting on your hot water heater to LOW or 120 degrees Fahrenheit.

◆ Add a bath bench, if needed.

◆ Add grab bars on the bathroom walls, especially near the toilet and in the tub. To assure a steady base, anchor the bar into the wall studding with long screws.

◆ Adjust the height of the bed so it's easy to get into and out of.

◆ Store everyday items in easy-to-reach locations. Use a long-handled "reacher" for lightweight items on high shelves.

◆ Place a lamp so it can be easily reached without leaving the bed, or use a "Clapper" device.

◆ Provide a telephone and a clock with large numbers beside the bed. Place emergency numbers printed in large letters there, too.

◆ Sit up for a moment before getting out of bed. Stand and get your balance before walking.

◆ Provide a firm chair with arms to sit and dress.

◆ Do not place anything over an electric blanket. Don't tuck it in, either. That can cause excessive heat build-up and start a fire.

◆ Write down your prescriptions and give them to a friend or relative. This could help in an emergency.

◆ Use a daily pill organizer to take medicines.

A Second Coat of Safety

Betty was standing on a stool to paint the ceiling. The treadmill in the corner was too heavy to move, so Betty placed the stool on it. As she stepped back onto the stool, one of the legs pushed through a gap in the treadmill's frame. She fell, shattering her shoulder and breaking her arm.

Painting can be fun and therapeutic. However, it has its dangers. Next time you consider picking up a brush, keep these things in mind.

◆ Evaluate the job. Are you comfortable doing it? Consider hiring a professional.

◆ Get the proper equipment and ladders. Review ladder safety.

◆ Allow sufficient time to move the furniture and do the job right. Don't rush into an accident.

◆ If the label says the paint product is flammable or combustible, take the following precautions:

• Open all windows and doors to create ventilation and minimize vapor accumulation.

• Eliminate all sources of flame, sparks, and ignition. Put out pilot lights by turning off the gas, and do not re-light them until the room is free of fumes.

• Do not smoke.

• Don't use electrical equipment that may spark. This includes most electrical fans.

• Keep cans closed when not in use, and away from children.

◆ Never heat a can of paint on a stove. Instead, warm it by placing the opened can in a pan of previously heated water.

◆ To prevent spontaneous combustion, paint rags should be hung outside to dry for four days, put in a closed metal container, or disposed of in an outdoor, covered trash can.

◆ If you clean brushes with paint thinner or turpentine, keep them away from ignition sources.

◆ Call your local waste authority for guidance on paint disposal.

Protect Yourself

◆ Avoid direct physical contact with paints and solvents. When painting, wear:

• a long-sleeve shirt and long pants;

• butyl rubber gloves. Not only will this protect the skin, it will make cleanup much easier;

• splash goggles;

• a respirator for spray painting.

◆ If your eyes water, or you feel dizzy or nauseated, leave the work area and get plenty of fresh air. If the discomfort persists, see a doctor.

Home Accident Facts

General Household Appliances	Annual Injuries
Refrigerators	28,000
Ranges	27,000
Irons	16,000

Home Communication and Entertainment Equipment	Annual Injuries
Televisions	41,000
Sound recording and reproducing equipment	21,000
Telephones or telephone accessories	17,000

Personal Use Items	Annual Injuries
Jewelry	65,000
Razors and shavers	38,000
Coins	30,000
Daywear	28,000
Hair grooming equipment and accessories	23,000
Other clothing	20,000
Luggage	16,000

Source: National Safety Council

Security Begins at Home

Since the events of September 11, 2001, there has been heightened emphasis on "homeland security." We're all taking a more serious look at what is necessary to protect our nation, our families, and ourselves. The first realization we need to reach is that homeland security begins at home.

Develop a Safety Plan

Whether the hazard is an enemy power, the power of blind circumstance, or the forces of Nature, each of us should develop a personal/family safety plan. To do that:

◆ Determine the hazards you're likely to experience in your daily and recreational activities.

◆ Keep up-to-date folders with safety tips on the hazards your family might face. Clip articles from publications, jot down comments from TV and radio, and call organizations that focus on your particular activities and places. Also, contact local police and fire departments.

◆ Make a list of the safety tips by activity, and review them periodically. For example, at the start of each boating season, review tips for water hazards you might encounter.

◆ Hold regular family safety meetings. To assure their involvement, let the kids assume some of the leadership.

◆ Make a house tour, and be sure every family member knows how to shut off electricity, gas, and water. Keep needed tools at each site.

- Establish "safe spots" in and around your home for storms and earthquakes.

- Post emergency and important phone numbers at all telephones, including work, doctors, and the poison control center.

- Take courses and refreshers in first aid and CPR.

- Purchase and use appropriate safety equipment.

Know When to Leave

- Do some research on natural disasters likely to strike your area, particularly when you move to a new location. Contact your local emergency management office for help.

- Draw up a floor plan of your home. Make sure everyone knows at least two ways out of each room.

- Practice your escape plan as a family at least twice a year. Have formal plans for evacuating very young or disabled family members.

- In the event of an evacuation emergency, decide on a meeting place outside where all household members will meet. One location should be near your home; the other outside your neighborhood, in case you can't return.

- Ask an out-of-state person to be your family contact in a disaster. It's often easier to call long-distance than to call inside the disaster area.

- Know where nearby official storm shelters are located, and alternative evacuation routes. Childcare providers should also know this.

- Learn to recognize your community's disaster warning signals, and what to do when you hear them.

- Assemble a disaster-supply kit, which you can take with you if you have to evacuate your home. Periodically, check and replace any outdated items in it. A good kit includes: a three-day supply of water (one gallon per person per day) and food that won't spoil; cups, plates and utensils; first-aid supplies; prescription and non-prescription drugs; bedding, a change of clothing, and footwear, all in airtight plastic bags; raingear; flashlight; portable radio; extra batteries; sanitary supplies; special items for infants, seniors, and people with disabilities; a non-electric can opener; and pet supplies.

- A more detailed list of items to include in the kit is available at www.fema.gov/pte/diskit.htm.

- Make plans for your pets.

Some "New" Safety Concerns

- In public places, don't ignore safety. Avoid events with lax security, and notify law enforcement of any suspicious activities or persons.

- If you receive suspicious mail:
  - Don't handle it.
  - Wash your hands thoroughly.
  - Notify local law enforcement and public health organizations.

- If bio-terrorism concerns you, some experts suggest fiber masks and goggles, but not gas masks.

Poison Control

According to the American Association of Poison Control Centers, there are more than 2 million human poisoning exposures a year in the United States, and approximately 900 deaths. Additional thousands of adults and older children die due to drug overdoses.

These are frightening statistics and unnecessarily high. The first and best antidote is caution.

Good Advice and Bad Medicine

◆ Keep these telephone numbers by your phones: poison control center, doctor, and hospital.

◆ Always follow label directions. Poisoning can occur by eating, drinking, or inhaling a substance, or getting it on the skin or in the eyes.

◆ Always read the label on any medication before you take it.

◆ Discard drugs that are past their expiration date, or look or smell unusual. Flush them down the toilet.

◆ Never take a medicine prescribed for another person. There might be side effects you don't know about, or an interaction with your medicine.

◆ Don't take drugs in the dark.

◆ To avoid overdoses, use a daily pill organizer.

◆ People with poor eyesight and failing memory are at greater risk for unintentional drug misuse.

This Isn't Kid Stuff

More than one million unintentional poisoning exposures among children under six are reported to U.S. poison control centers each year. Nearly 90 percent of these incidents occur in homes and involve common household items.

◆ Lock up all medicines and keep medicines in child-resistant containers. However, don't rely solely on these containers; they are *child-resistant* not *childproof*.

◆ If you're interrupted while using a product, take it or your child with you, or lock up the product.

◆ Never leave open medications out of your sight.

◆ If you must keep medicine by the bed when kids are around, use a lockable tackle box.

◆ Grandparents: Put away and secure poisonous items before kids arrive. A disproportionately high number of childhood poisonings involve grandparents' drugs.

◆ Place purses, bags, and suitcases out of reach.

◆ Teach children not to eat or drink anything not given to them by an adult whom they know.

◆ Never refer to any kind of medication as "candy," even when trying to coax children to take it.

◆ Avoid taking medications in front of children. They will want to copy your actions.

◆ Child exposures often occur in late afternoon or early evening, when supervision may not be as strict.

◆ Poisonings increase during periods when the household is disrupted (e.g. children visiting, holidays, personal crisis, moving).

◆ Be alert for repeat poisonings. Children who swallow a poison are likely to try again within a year.

◆ Only use syrup of ipecac on the advice of the poison control center. Replace it by the expiration date.

◆ If you suspect a child has been exposed to a poisonous substance:

  • Remain calm, and keep the child calm.

  • Look in the child's mouth. Remove any remaining pills, pieces of plant, etc.

  • Take the child and the poison to the phone. Call the poison control center or your doctor. Be prepared to give your child's age, weight, the product name on the label, when it was eaten, the amount swallowed, and the child's condition.

Note: Most parents can identify the top three drugs used by children: alcohol, tobacco and marijuana. Few parents realize that inhalants are the fourth most commonly abused drug group. And remember: tobacco is often the "gateway" to other drugs.

◆ If you suspect your child is using illegal drugs or abusing prescription drugs, seek professional help immediately.

The Toxic Household

◆ Do not store household and cleaning products in the same place you store food.

◆ Keep all products in their original containers.

◆ Contact a local nursery or poison control center to find nontoxic plants to buy. More than 700 species of plants are harmful to humans. Ingestion of houseplants is a leading cause of calls to poison control centers.

◆ Store cleaning supplies or other poisonous products in cabinets with childproof locks, or in closets that require a key to open.

◆ Never mix a "home-brewed" cleaning product without first checking the poison control center.

Common Household Hazards

Alcohol
Tobacco
Detergents
Drugs and pills
Plants

Kitchen

Ammonia
Carpet cleaners
Drain cleaners
Furniture polish
Metal cleaners
Oven cleaner
Plants
Rust remover
Scouring powders
Upholstery cleaners

Bedroom or Purse

Cosmetics
Jewelry cleaner
Perfume

Laundry

Bleaches
Disinfectant
Dyes
Stain remover

Storage Places

Batteries
Moth balls and sprays
Rat and insect poisons

Bathroom

Bath oil
Boric acid
Creams
Deodorants
Deodorizers
Drain cleaners
Hair remover
Hand, shaving and sun lotions
Mouthwash
Nail polish and remover
Rubbing alcohol
Shampoo, wave lotion and sprays
Toilet bowl cleaners

Basement or Garage

Antifreeze
Bug killers
Fertilizers
Gasoline and oil
Kerosene
Lighter fluids
Lime
Lye
Paint
Paint remover and thinner
Tree and lawn sprays
Turpentine
Weed killers
Windshield cleaner

Workshop Woes

Craig is a skilled and experienced woodworker. More than a hobby for him, it's his passion. And sometimes our passions get the best of us, like that Saturday when Craig wanted to make one more cut near the end of a long day. In a moment of rare inattention, the saw blade snagged in the wood and his hand flew toward the blade. Thanks to a skilled surgeon, Craig did not lose part of his thumb that day. They say, "Let the tools do the work," but tools can't do the thinking, too. Craig learned an important lesson. Now he turns off the machines and doesn't overdo it.

According to the U.S. Consumer Product Safety Commission, more than 120,000 people each year suffer injuries that require emergency room treatment from using home power tools. The table saw is involved in more serious injuries than any other woodworking device. Most table-saw injuries occur during ripping operations.

Proper Preparation

- ◆ Take the time to read all instructions on the proper use of your power tools. If you don't use a tool frequently, review the safety instructions before each use. Follow the maintenance schedule suggested by the manufacturer.

- ◆ Plan power tool projects. Think through the moves your hands will make before you make them.

- ◆ Select the proper tool for the job, and use only the accessories built specifically for that tool.

◆ Do not force a small tool or attachment to do the job of a heavy-duty tool. Makeshift tools can cause accidents.

◆ Keep all safety guards in place and in proper working condition.

◆ Allow ample space in the workshop to work safely.

◆ Keep the area free of clutter.

◆ Keep the area well lighted. Eliminate all shadows.

◆ Keep children and onlookers out of your work area.

◆ Wear safety apparel, including goggles or safety glasses with side shields. Never wear loose clothing or jewelry around power equipment. Use gloves that are job-rated for the kind of work you are doing.

◆ To prevent slippage, clean your hands before using tools.

◆ Never work when you're tired, distracted, or angry.

◆ If your hands are sore, arthritic, or injured, don't use power tools.

◆ Don't use any tool that is worn or broken.

◆ Keep your workshop well ventilated.

◆ Keep idle tools stored and out of the reach of children.

In the Heat of the Action

◆ Avoid overconfidence and repetitious operations that lull you into carelessness. Pause periodically and refocus.

◆ Maintain good balance and footing. Don't overreach, or reach over or behind a moving saw blade.

◆ Do not force tools. Let them do the work.

◆ When cutting, use sticks or blocks to keep your hands away from moving blades.

◆ Use clamps and vises to secure the object you're working on.

◆ Do not touch a bit or blade after cutting or drilling. They can be painfully hot.

◆ Do not try to catch falling objects. The sudden movement can disrupt your safety equilibrium.

◆ Never leave a machine with the motor "coasting."

◆ Never hurry a job.

◆ Sweep up all sawdust promptly.

◆ Don't drink alcohol or smoke when working.

Respect the Power

◆ Always use a ground fault circuit interrupter (GFCI).

◆ Ground all your power tools, unless they are clearly marked DOUBLE-INSULATED.

◆ Do not use power tools in wet or damp places. Rubber-soled shoes and heavy rubber mats are good precautions in any conditions.

◆ Don't use tools with damaged cords or improper extension cords.

◆ Never carry a portable tool by its cord or yank the tool or extension cords from the receptacle.

◆ Be certain the switch is on OFF when plugging in a tool. Do not carry a plugged-in tool with your finger on the switch.

◆ Unplug tools when they're not in use, or when you're adjusting them or installing accessories.

Let it Melt

A beautiful new snow should be a wonder to behold. Sadly, in many instances, it leads to tragedy as people die or injure themselves while trying to shovel it. The fact is, some men and women have no business even reaching for a shovel. Among them are:

- the elderly;
- those with heart disease, or who have a high risk of heart disease (smokers, or those who are overweight or have high blood pressure.)

Shoveling heavy snow requires as much energy as vigorous running; however, most people should be able to do it safely. To protect yourself:

◆ Wear a scarf over your nose and mouth to avoid breathing the cold air, which makes your heart work harder. Wear a hat to retain body heat.

◆ Dress in layers. You want to be able to shed clothing as you get warmer. Overheating puts extra strain on your heart.

◆ Wear shoes with good traction to avoid falling.

◆ To avoid excessive strain on the heart, warm up before shoveling by doing some slow, light exercise.

◆ Do not shovel snow after smoking, eating a heavy meal, or drinking alcohol or caffeinated beverages. These activities can place an added burden on your cardiovascular system once you begin shoveling.

◆ Pace yourself by taking frequent rest breaks. What will hurrying really accomplish at a time like this, anyway?

◆ Bend your legs at the knee. Let your thigh muscles do most of the pushing and lifting work. And remember to keep your back straight. This method reduces the strain on your heart and your back.

◆ Use a shovel with a small blade to keep your loads small and light.

Home Accident Facts

Home Furnishings, Fixtures & Accessories	Annual Injuries
Beds	455,000
Tables	305,000
Chairs	292,000
Bathtubs and showers	195,000
Ladders	163,000
Sofas, chairs, davenports, etc.	121,000
Rugs and carpets	117,000
Other furniture	74,000
Toilets	56,000
Benches	24,000
Electric lighting equipment	24,000
Sinks	23,000
Mirrors or mirror glass	21,000

Source: National Safety Council

Spring Forward...
(With Caution)

Deb was not a particularly demanding or impatient wife, but this was the Saturday that she was determined to organize their cluttered garage and prepare it for her spring passions, gardening and biking. Bob had other plans for the day. Rather than wait for his help, Deb impetuously threw herself into her work, and in the process threw out her back shoving fifty-pound bags of fertilizer around the garage and lifting her ten-speed bike off its wall mounts. That was the spring that Bob planted the garden while Deb recuperated in the easy chair.

Like any physical activity, spring housecleaning has potential hazards, most of which are easily avoided with planning and common sense.

General Housekeeping

◆ Pace yourself. Injuries are more likely to happen when you're tired. Take frequent breaks.

◆ Alternate light and heavy work. Get help for heavy or difficult jobs.

◆ Wear the right clothes for the work you'll be doing, including sturdy shoes and work gloves.

- Wear safety goggles for tasks that might threaten your eyes, e.g., using cleaning supplies or bleach.

- As you start the heavy cleaning, keep traffic lanes in the house open and uncluttered. Keep kids and pets away from work areas.

- Clear your steps and stairways. Check treads, risers, and carpeting, indoors and out.

- Inspect all patios, porches, and driveways for cracks and holes. Repair these hazards.

- This kind of work generally involves some climbing. A chair is not a suitable replacement for a ladder. Choose the proper ladder for the job. Check all ladders for damage before you set foot on one.

- Read the label before using any household chemical product. Look for alternatives to harsh chemicals. Never mix cleaning products before checking with the poison control center.

- Keep cleansers and tools out of the reach of kids and pets.

- Wear hearing protection when operating noisy tools or appliances.

Storage Areas

You've had several months to accumulate a lot of needless clutter in storage areas. Let's get organized:

- Childproof your storage area as you would your home. Keep all chemicals, sharp objects, and powerful equipment out of sight, out of reach, and under lock and key.

- Install wall hooks, and hang your hoses, extension cords, shovels, and rakes. It's bad enough the puppy is at your feet, your ax shouldn't be there, too.

- Hang pegboards for your tools. They'll be away from inquisitive hands, and you can find them easily.

- Look for newer, safer hooks and pegboards.

- Keep anything that hangs away from traffic areas.

- Don't hang bikes or sports gear at eye level or near doors.

- Hang tools with sharp points facing down, out of a child's reach.

- Lock up power tools. If a tool has a key, store it separately.

- Keep antifreeze and windshield-wiper solvents off the floor where they can't tempt kids or pets.

- Dump all those solvents and empty cans you've accumulated. Your city hall can probably tell you about hazardous waste collections.

- Discard old papers, magazines, clothing, and furniture. They can provide fuel for an unwanted fire.

- Throw out oily rags and anything else that can catch fire.

- While cleaning, never use the same rag with different chemicals.

Keep the Spiders Away

While fatalities from spider bites are rare, consequences can range from minor to severe.

- Sanitation should be the first step in control. With a vacuum cleaner, clean away all webbing, spiders, and eggs.

- Keep undisturbed areas of your home as free as possible of clutter. Periodically, move stored materials around and vacuum these areas.

- Caulk cracks and crevices on the outside of the house.

- Hire a certified pest-control operator for a recurring problem.

Shear Terror!

Clackety, clackety, clank! Small rocks and gravel from Dave's driveway were slapping against his house and lawn furniture. Clackety, clackety, bing! Bouncing off his garage windows and automobiles. Dave was oblivious. He'd wanted one of these gas-powered weed trimmers for years, and now, broadleaf, watch out! Clackety clackety, yipe! King, the beloved dog, sprang from his sleeping spot in the grass, looking for the culprit that'd smacked him in the back of the head, leaving a wound that required five stitches by the local veterinarian. Dave vows to be less zealous next time, and to make sure no men, women, children, or pets are in the line of fire.

Power tools can be a boon to the amateur landscape architect, but they can quickly turn into a backyard adversary when used carelessly.

More than 30,000 people start out working in their yards and end up in hospital emergency rooms each year from mishandling pruning, trimming, and edging equipment.

Rooted in the Basics

No matter what tool you're using, some basics apply:

◆ Read all operating instructions carefully before turning on the motor.

◆ Follow maintenance instructions in the manual.

◆ Use a machine only for jobs for which it was intended.

◆ Do not remove or disable protective guards or other safety devices on the tool.

◆ Fill the gas tank only when the engine is cold.

◆ Know how to stop the machine quickly.

◆ Take the tool to an experienced dealer every year for servicing.

◆ Keep all tools high on the wall, on a high shelf, or locked up.

◆ Cover lawn and garden equipment with a heavy tarp, and hide the ignition keys.

◆ With electric equipment, remember:

  • Look for the UL sticker or label to be sure the equipment has been tested to meet nationally recognized safety standards.

  • Be careful not to cut over a power cord if you are using an electric motor.

  • Check and replace damaged cords. Use only grounded extension cords marked FOR OUT-DOOR USE. For extra protection use a ground fault circuit interrupter.

  • Never use an electric-powered implement near water or in wet conditions of any kind.

  • Unplug the tool before making any adjustments.

People, Places, and Things

◆ Operate the machine only where you have firm footing and good balance. Do not operate in areas where you would need your hands to prevent a fall.

◆ Keep bystanders away from the area where you're working, especially in front of the tool.

◆ Clear loose rocks and debris from the area where you'll be working with a power tool.

◆ Stand and walk directly in back of the tool to prevent being hit by flying objects its force may kick up.

◆ Work only when you have good light and you're not rushed or tired.

◆ Never place your hands or feet near or under rotating parts while the engine is running.

◆ Hold the handles firmly with both hands. If you strike a foreign object or if your machine vibrates abnormally, stop the engine. If the motor is gas driven, disconnect and secure the spark plug wire. Then inspect and repair the damage before you continue working.

◆ Stop the engine when crossing gravel drives, walks, or roads, or under any conditions where thrown objects might be a hazard.

◆ Always use safety glasses with side shields, and hearing protection.

◆ Wear long pants, close-fitting clothes, and sturdy shoes or boots. Do not wear jewelry.

◆ Do not allow others to use the power tool unless they are responsible, have read and understand the instructions, and are schooled in its operation.

◆ Always unplug electric tools when not in use. Never allow children to use these devices.

◆ Before each use, inspect an electric tool for frayed cords and cracked or damaged casing. If it's damaged, don't use it. Have it repaired by a qualified repair shop.

Leisure and General Safety

Introduction

When we engage in leisure activities, safety too often is not a top priority. We are usually doing something that is enjoyable, and our focus is getting the most out of our free time.

However, unless you keep your twenty-four-hour safety switch on, what started out as a day of fun can end up being a day of regrets.

The principal causes of leisure and other deaths, based on recent National Safety Council statistics, are:

Falls	6,100
Drowning	2,600
Air Transport	500
Water Transport	500
Railroad	500
Other Transport	300
Firearms	200
Fires and Burns	200
All Other*	11,100
Total	**22,000**

*Principal causes: medical and surgical complications and misadventures, suffocation by ingestion, poisoning by solids and liquids, and excessive heat or cold.

Drive Safely

There are some serious hazards associated with the game of golf that have nothing to do with water and sand. You've got lightning. And the intoxicated fool in the runaway golf cart. And the screaming slice bearing down on you like a heat-seeking missile. However, the hazard most likely to strike you is a serious back injury. Swinging a golf club puts tremendous strain on the back. As a result, golfers injure their backs more than any other part of their body.

The scorecard shows that back injuries constitute up to 50 percent of all injuries sustained by male golfers.

That goes for the professionals, too. In the 1980s, Jack Nicklaus' career almost ended because of back problems.

Injuries don't have to be par for the course for golfers or other sports enthusiasts. Too many people take up a sport to get in shape; they'd be much better off getting in shape before they take up a sport.

First Rule: Get in Shape

◆ Choose a sport that's right for you. Consult a physician before you begin a new sport, especially if you're over thirty-five, overweight, easily fatigued, smoke heavily, have a history of family or personal health problems, or take medication.

◆ Take time to visit an exercise professional to develop a personal training and stretching program. Be sure you know how to stretch just before and after engaging in the activity, and how to warm up. Professional athletes take the time to stretch and warm up properly, so why should you cut corners?

◆ Take lessons. Learn from a qualified/certified instructor.

◆ Stay hydrated. Drink water or sports drinks before, during, and right after playing.

◆ If you're injured or sore, stop the activity and give the muscles time to heal. Stretching can make them worse.

Be FOREwarned

According to the National Safety Council, about 50,000 golfers require emergency room treatment each year, including more than 8,000 from golf cart incidents.

◆ Learn the proper swing and body mechanics from a pro.

◆ Always warm up before you play. Spend a few minutes swinging both the irons and the woods.

◆ Protect your back. Don't bend from the waist; use your legs. Squat, and get help lifting heavy objects, like golf bags, from the trunk of your car.

◆ Don't hang your feet out of carts; drive at a moderate speed; avoid inclines; and never drive drunk.

On the course, golf etiquette and safety go together.

◆ Before any practice swing or shot, be sure no one is close by or in a position to be hit by the club, the ball, or any stones or twigs that could be moved by your swing.

◆ Never hit a golf ball if others are in range. If you're hitting to an area you can't see, take time to be sure the area is clear.

◆ Warn others if you're making a shot from a bad lie.

◆ Heed lightning warnings. Get inside a building as quickly as possible. If no shelter is available, move toward low ground and avoid lone trees. Do not hold golf clubs.

◆ To avoid insect stings and tick bites, don't walk through woods and thick grass.

◆ Wear a hat and apply sunscreen with a 30-SPF.

◆ Call the U.S. Golf Association at (800) 345-USGA for a free video on golf course etiquette and safety.

Weeknight / Weekend Warrior Tips

◆ **Nearly 75 percent of softball injuries involve sliding.**

◆ If possible, avoid sliding. If you do slide on occasion, practice the proper technique. Encourage your league to use breakaway bases, since almost all sliding injuries involve fixed bases.

◆ **Each year, hospital emergency rooms treat nearly 40,000 people for sports-related eye injuries.** Wear sports eye-guards when participating in activities that could injure your eyes.

◆ Buy quality equipment and maintain it properly. Be sure it fits your size and shape.

Alcohol Content

Ole was having a heck of time. With a captive audience at the restaurant, the World War II fighter pilot was in rare form. The stories became bigger than life, and Ole kept ordering his favorite gin and tonics. After dinner, everyone at the table knew Ole shouldn't drive — everyone except Ole. But he was the war hero, the group's elder statesman, and it was his car. As they approached the dangerous curve in the country road, his five passengers knew he was going too fast and they sat glued to their seats, terrified. The Oldsmobile careened off the road, crashed through a barbed-wire fence, and mired in deep mud. There were two broken legs, a concussion, and nine cracked ribs. Miraculously, the six lived to tell how they almost went down in flames at the hands of the inebriated flying ace ... and how careless they'd been to let him drive.

Holiday or No Holiday

It's possible to stay sober and have a good time. It's also possible to have a few drinks and stay safe. Here are some suggestions for taming the party spirits.

- Eat at least fifteen minutes before the first drink, and continue to consume food while you're drinking.

- Make your first drink a large glass of water, juice, or soda to quench your thirst.

- Always drink slowly. Never drink alcohol because you're thirsty. You'll drink too much, too fast.

- Alternate between alcoholic and non-alcoholic beverages.

- Limit your consumption to one ounce of alcohol per hour. That equates to about one twelve-ounce beer, one four-ounce glass of wine, or one mixed drink.

- Stop drinking alcohol ninety minutes before the party is over. There is no other way to sober up.

Black coffee won't do it; neither will the mythical "cold shower" treatment, or other so-called quick-fix remedies. Only time will make you sober enough to walk, drive, or ride a bike safely.

◆ Don't drink punch or eggnog without first asking if they contain liquor.

◆ Avoid alcohol even in moderation when your energy level is low.

◆ If friends tell you that you shouldn't drive, listen to them.

If You Are the Host

◆ Serve alcohol-free drinks such as soft drinks and coffee.

◆ Serve foods, especially those rich in proteins. Eating slows the rate at which the body absorbs alcohol. You don't want your guests drinking on an empty stomach.

◆ Don't serve salty foods, which make people thirsty.

◆ Measure mixed drinks with a shot glass to avoid over-pouring.

◆ Do not allow guests to pour their own drinks. It sounds generous, but it's defeating. It's best to choose a reliable bartender who'll keep track of the size and number of drinks people consume.

◆ Carbonated water and mixers speed up alcohol's effects. It's best to add iced or non-carbonated water to dilute an alcoholic drink.

◆ Do not push drinks on guests.

◆ Stop pouring alcohol for someone who is obviously intoxicated.

◆ If the event is lunch or dinner, make the cocktail portion of the event short.

◆ Establish designated drivers in advance of the party, and offer a variety of non-alcoholic beverages. Designated drivers should drink no alcoholic beverages; even one or two drinks can impair a person's ability to drive safely.

◆ Stop serving alcoholic beverages at least ninety minutes before the party breaks up. Serve a dessert treat.

◆ Never serve alcohol to someone under the legal drinking age, and never ask children to serve alcohol at parties.

◆ If someone does drink too much, drive him home, arrange a ride with another guest who is sober, call a taxi, or invite him to stay over.

Some Personal Concerns

◆ A person's metabolism and physical makeup change with aging, so a single drink packs a much stronger wallop in a sixty-year-old than in a twenty-year-old — something senior citizen Ole forgot.

◆ Usually, the less you weigh, the faster your Blood Alcohol Concentration level will increase with the same amount of alcohol.

◆ If you wake up with a hangover, wait at least three hours after you wake to get behind the wheel of a vehicle. If you can't wait, catch a ride with a co-worker.

◆ Alcohol consumption during pregnancy is one of the major preventable causes of birth defects and childhood disabilities. The advice here is simple and humane: Do not drink when you're pregnant or planning a pregnancy.

◆ With some medications, including many over-the-counter drugs, adverse reactions can occur when alcohol is consumed. Talk to your doctor, and read labels carefully.

An ATV Is Not a Toy

Hank knew better, but his little grandson, Steven, was persuasive, and even though he was only eight years old, he was darned good at driving an ATV. What harm could there be in letting the little rascal drive himself and his sister two miles back to the barn while Hank followed in the pickup? It was a remote road, and Steven promised to drive slowly. It would have worked out perfectly, except that Steven was too small to see over the rise as he approached the intersection. He never saw the car that struck the ATV, sending him and his sister to the hospital. No one died in that collision, but Hank "died a thousand deaths" as he watched it happen.

More than 7 million people ride ATVs for work and pleasure in the U.S.

Each year, over 75,000 injuries requiring emergency room treatment happen to people riding ATVs. And in a recent fifteen-year period, 1,100 children under sixteen were killed and 372,000 injured on ATVs.

Riding Tips

ATVs are good for sport and work, but they are used on terrain that can be unforgiving, like tree roots and rocks. Here are a few tips to keep you safe:

- Before taking your first ride, enroll in a sanctioned rider-training course. Call the ATV Safety Institute at (800) 887-2887 for details.

- Read and follow the owner's manual and warning labels.

- Inspect the mechanical condition of the ATV before riding.

- Practice in a safe area before driving on more difficult terrain.

- ATVs are intended for off-road use only. Never operate one on public roads or paved surfaces.

- Do not carry passengers.

- Never ride when tired, or under the influence of alcohol or drugs, prescription or otherwise.

- Use existing trails if possible.

- Do not operate the ATV at excessive speeds.

- Never ride beyond the limit of your visibility.

- Be alert for hidden wires.

- If a hill looks too steep to climb, it probably is.

- Ride only where you have permission to ride.

- Avoid three-wheeled ATVs, which are not made anymore.

Dress the Part

To ride safely, you should dress safely. Anytime you jump on your ATV, you should be wearing:

- a motorcycle helmet approved by the Department of Transportation. This is your most important piece of protective gear.
- goggles or face shield;
- over-the-calf-style boots, with low heels to keep your feet from slipping off the footrests;
- off-highway-style gloves that are padded over the knuckles;
- long pants;
- a long-sleeved shirt or jacket.

Young Riders

Young people have a natural affinity for ATVs. They're small, fast, and look like great fun. When used properly, they're safe. At which age children should begin riding them depends on training and judgment. Before turning a young person loose on an ATV:

- Ask yourself if your child is *strong enough* and *mature enough* to operate an ATV.

- If the answer to both is yes, you must match your child to the proper size ATV. Kids under the age of sixteen should not operate an adult-sized ATV. Discuss this with your dealer. As a basic rule, kids aged:
  - six to twelve years should drive an engine under 70 cc;
  - twelve to sixteen years, 70–90 cc.

- Enroll your child in a special, hands-on training course, and take the course yourself. Call the 800 number above for details.

- To be an effective coach and overseer, you must be familiar with the ATV. Your best source of information is the owner's manual. Review it with your children.

- To be sure your children know the workings of their ATV:
  - Have them show you the *location* of the parking brake, brakes, throttle control lever, engine stop switch, and shift lever (if equipped).
  - Have them show you how the controls *work*.
  - Ask them to operate the controls as if they are riding — and do it without looking at the controls.
  - In short, be convinced your children can safely operate the ATV!

- Supervise your children's operation of the ATV at all times.

Lumbar Support

It was Tom's day to start painting the house. When he stepped from the garage, he found his son playing basketball in the driveway with the neighborhood kids. Tom pitched his paintbrushes to the ground, and raced onto the court. As he flew across the lane for one of his patented fall-away jump shots, he felt a violent twinge in his back, and he tumbled to the cement in intense pain. He hobbled off the court, but had to crawl into the house, where his wife helped him into a hot bath, and from there to bed, where he stayed for two days. That weekend, Tom realized his body had to be as warmed to a task as his brain was.

Approximately 80 percent of us will experience lower back injuries during our lifetime.

To stay one step ahead of your back, remember these tips:

Your Lifestyle is Important

◆ Stay fit, and watch your weight. Extra weight on the stomach adds extra strain on the back.

◆ Exercise and stretch regularly to keep the muscles that support your back strong and flexible. Consult a doctor to develop a fitness program.

◆ Work on good posture. Stand straight. Maintain the natural "arch" in your lower back, whether you are standing or sitting.

◆ Sleep on a firm mattress.

◆ Avoid sleeping on your stomach. It's better to sleep on your side with knees bent, and a pillow between them.

◆ If you must sleep on your back, place a pillow under your knees and a rolled-up towel under the small of your back to relieve pressure.

◆ Back injuries happen often in the morning, when you're still stiff with sleep. Don't bend at the waist to put on your socks and shoes. Pull your feet toward you.

◆ Minimize time spent wearing high heels. Keep heels to a half-inch maximum, including Western boots.

- When sitting, keep your feet flat on the floor or use a footstool.

- If you catch yourself slumping forward or slouching, correct your position by pushing the small of your back into the back of your chair. Consider using a lumbar support or pillow for extra support. (This applies in the car, too.)

- Shift your sitting position frequently. Stand and walk around to stretch your muscles at least once each hour.

- Stand up straight for dishes and ironing. Put one foot on a small stool a few inches high.

- Look for products ergonomically designed to reduce back strain.

It's All in the Technique

- Before lifting a load, stretch by reaching upward several times, followed by simple back and side bends.

- If the load is too heavy or awkward, get help.

- Bend your knees and hips and squat as close to the load as possible, with your feet about shoulders' width apart. Never bend from your waist!

- Get a good grip. Lift the load using your thigh muscles. Arch your back inward by pulling your shoulders back and sticking your chest out. Keep your chin up.

- Keep the load close to your body. The closer it is, the less pressure it puts on your back.

- Lift slowly and smoothly. Don't jerk. Keep your back straight.

- Don't twist from the waist to lift something. Instead, turn your whole body in the direction you want to reach or look.

- To set the load down, squat, bending again at the hips and knees. Keep your lower back arched in.

- For one-arm loads, bend at the knee and waist, and keep your back straight. Lift with your legs.

More Back-saving Suggestions

- Whenever possible, push, don't pull. Keep your back straight and knees bent.

- Move *to* an object; don't reach *for* it.

- If the load is above you, test its weight by pushing up on it. Then, be sure you have firm footing and a solid grasp before moving it.

- Squat down or kneel to reach low objects. Bend at the knees to lift children.

- When working in a stooped position, stand and stretch regularly.

- To unload the trunk of your car, brace one knee against the rear bumper, pull your stomach in, and unload one package at a time.

- Take short rest breaks during highly repetitive or sustained work.

- For chores that could keep you bent over for a long time, get down on one or both knees to work.

To Bee or Not to Bee

Let's clear up the buzz about the so-called "killer bee."

Yes, the "killer honeybee" does exist, mostly in South America and Mexico. Some have become established in the southern U.S. No, they do not pose an immediate threat to your life. Yes, if threatened, they are more aggressive than the domestic honeybee flitting around your backyard, and they have killed people and animals. No, they will not hunt you down and sting you for the sport of it.

While the "killer bee" invasion is more myth than fact, stinging insects can inflict pain on all of us, and endanger the lives of some of us. What's a person to do?

Avoidance is a Good Rule

◆ Africanized ("killer") bees and domestic honeybees look the same, so stay away from all bees.

◆ Bees usually don't sting unless disturbed. Stinging is their defense.

◆ When you might be exposed to stinging insects, wear long pants, a lightweight, long-sleeve shirt, and a hat.

◆ Do not wear bright- or dark-colored clothing, flowery prints, or shiny jewelry. Dull white, khaki, and solid light colors are good choices.

◆ Avoid floral-scented shampoos, soaps, powders, and perfumes.

◆ Don't walk barefoot in the grass.

◆ Avoid the types of places bees and other stinging insects congregate, such as gardens when flowers are in bloom, garbage areas, stagnant pools, seldom-used buildings, and junk piles.

◆ If you see bees flying in and out of a small opening, there is probably a nest inside. Leave it alone and call an expert.

◆ Don't reach into a space you haven't looked into.

◆ Keep your yard clean. Empty the water from barrels, old tires, cans, and wading pools. And keep the lawn mowed.

◆ Bees will respond to vibrations and exhaust from mowers and other equipment. Check for bees before using mowers, trimmers, and chain saws.

◆ Fill in potential nesting sites such as tree cavities and cracks in walls.

◆ Place screen over weep-holes in houses and on top of rainspouts and chimneys.

◆ Seal food scraps in a plastic bag, and dispose of it in a tightly closed garbage can that's lined with a garbage bag.

◆ Don't rely on insect repellents. They're effective on biting insects such as flies and mosquitoes, but do not repel stinging insects, such as bees.

◆ When drinking sweetened beverages outside, use a plastic cover and a straw.

◆ If you encounter bees during outdoor activities, leave the area immediately.

When They're in Your Midst

◆ When bees are nearby, avoid rapid movements, which may look like attacks.

◆ If a stinging insect lights on your body, brush it away. Do not slap it against your body. That will trap it and give it the chance to sting.

◆ If you stumble on a nest, move away slowly.

◆ If you are attacked by bees:
  • Run away.
  • Try to get inside a car, building, or heavy brush. Jumping into water won't help — they'll probably be waiting when you come up for air.
  • If possible, wrap your head with clothing or other material. Leave an opening for your eyes.

Watch for Allergic Reactions

◆ In case of a sting, don't leave the stinger in your skin, because it can continue to pump venom into your body for up to ten minutes.

◆ Remove the stinger by gently scraping it out with a fingernail, credit card, or the edge of a sterilized knife. Do not pinch it out — that squeezes venom into the wound.

◆ Use ice packs and sting-kill ointment to reduce swelling and pain.

◆ More than 2 million Americans are allergic to insect bites and have serious reactions. If you have any of these symptoms after an insect bite, see your doctor at once:
  • wheezing or trouble breathing;
  • fainting or dizziness;
  • hives or skin rash;
  • abdominal pain, nausea, or cramps;
  • rapid pulse;
  • diarrhea;
  • chills;
  • facial swelling, or swelling that extends beyond two joints.

◆ Anyone who has had serious reactions to bee stings should carry an insect-sting first-aid kit. Your doctor can give you the details.

Some Balanced Advice

Bicycles are as popular as ever. You'll find them in parks, city streets, residential areas, and even in the mountains. They're great for touring, exercise, and socialization. They get you out of the house and into the fresh air. However, they can also get you into the hospital emergency room, or worse.

In fact, more than 500,000 people annually require emergency room treatment due to bicycle crashes, and about 800 people die. Approximately 75 percent of the deaths result from head injury.

These following simple guidelines will keep the pleasure in biking.

Know the Basics

Each year, thousands of bicyclists suffer serious head injuries. Many never recover. The proper helmet can reduce head injuries by about 85 percent.

- Always wear a helmet with a label stating that it meets the Consumer Product Safety Commission standard. Select a helmet that fits snugly and sits flat on your head.

- Discard a helmet after it sustains a blow. Even a slight blow can affect the impact-absorbing foam.

- Take a safety course. One organization offering courses for all ages is the League of American Bicyclists, at (202) 822-1333, or www.bikeleague.org.

- Ride a bicycle that "fits" your body and riding needs. You should be able to stand over the top tube, with the tube one or two inches below your crotch. Find a qualified salesperson to help you determine which bicycle, safety features, and accessories are best for you.

◆ Before riding, make sure all bike parts are secure and working.

◆ Check your brakes before getting on your bicycle, and keep them properly adjusted.

Pedal Pushers

◆ Find a safe place to ride. Many cities and bicycle clubs offer maps of recommended routes.

◆ Cycle defensively by looking out for the other guy. More than 70 percent of car-bicycle accidents occur at driveways or other intersections. Expect a car to pull out from the side street or turn left in front of you.

◆ If traffic is heavy, walk your bike across intersections.

◆ Focus on drivers' eyes. Make eye contact and signal your intentions.

◆ Wear bright or fluorescent clothing during the day. You may want to fly an orange flag from the back of your bike.

◆ Cycle with the flow of traffic, and never against it.

◆ In a group, it's best to ride single file, unless you're off the road, or on quiet secondary roads.

◆ Don't carry passengers or items that interfere with your control.

◆ Stay alert at all times. Look out for hazardous surfaces or obstacles in your path, such as potholes, loose gravel, manhole covers, cracks, railroad tracks, or wet leaves.

◆ Leave at least three feet of distance when passing parked cars to avoid doors being opened.

◆ Be predictable. Maintain a straight line when you're cruising.

◆ Never wear headphones.

◆ Stay at least three feet to the right of cars if you can. If there's a wide clean shoulder, use it.

◆ Watch for pedestrians, especially children, or animals that might dart in front of you. If a dog chases you, and you can't safely get away, stop, dismount, and use your bike as a shield.

◆ Use a rearview mirror.

◆ Before turning, look back, check all directions for traffic, and use hand signals.

◆ Know and obey traffic regulations, signs, signals, and markings.

◆ Avoid provocative actions that might irritate drivers.

◆ When in danger, shout!

◆ The bike will be less stable with a child in a seat. A cart towed by a bike is far safer. Plan to go slower and take turns gently. Avoid busy streets.

◆ Carry loads at the rear of the bike, in cases designed for bicycles.

Night Riders

The best advice is, avoid biking at night. It's much more dangerous than riding during the day.

Remember that most bicycles need to be adapted for nighttime use.

◆ Add the brightest lights and largest reflectors you can find to the front and rear of your bicycle.

◆ Wear retro-reflective clothing or material, especially on your ankles, wrists, back, and helmet. White and fluorescent are not good enough.

◆ Ride only in areas you are familiar with. Streets with bright lighting are best.

◆ Always assume that a driver does not see you.

Staying Afloat

The proud owner of a new 175-horsepower bass boat, Stacy asked Brian to come along to try it out. On that chilly October morning, the boat's power and the breeze in their faces were exhilarating. As they neared the dam at high speed, Stacy lost control and both men were thrown out. Stacy was hit by the circling boat and drowned. A brave fisherman dived into the cold water and towed the struggling Brian to safety.

In a recent year, more than 600 people died in 8,000 recreational boating accidents.

About 25 percent of the deaths involved alcohol. The marine environment accelerates impairment. According to the U.S. Coast Guard, tests have shown that only one-third the amount of alcohol that makes a person legally impaired on the road is enough to make him or her equally impaired on the water.

Be Seaworthy

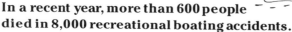

- Take a boating-safety class to learn basic seamanship skills.

Nearly 85 percent of boating fatalities involve an operator who didn't complete such a course. To take a class, contact a local safe-boating organization, or the U.S. Coast Guard Information Line, (800) 368-5647, or visit www.uscgboating.org.

- Know the rules and regulations of the area you will be navigating.

- Get a free vessel safety check from the Coast Guard Auxiliary or U.S. Power Squadron.

- Get a list of recommended safety equipment from the Coast Guard. Be sure all items are on board and work.

- The operator of the boat must assure that the vessel is in top operating condition, with no tripping hazards, exposed sharp edges, or fire hazards.

- Maintain fuel and ventilation systems as directed in the owner's manual and state and federal requirements.

- Check the fuel system for leaks or signs of deterioration. Immediately replace a corroded fuel tank or hoses that feel cracked, brittle, swollen, damp, or mushy.

- Before you cast off, be sure you're carrying the tools you might need to make repairs.

- Heed regulations concerning fire extinguishers, and keep extinguishers in good condition.

- No alcohol while boating is safest. If someone does drink, use a designated driver. *Stay sober!*

Before Shoving Off

Nearly 85 percent of the people drowned in boating-related incidents were not wearing life jackets.

◆ You and all your passengers should have a Coast Guard-approved life jacket. Make sure life jackets are selected and fitted for each passenger. Choose jackets that are comfortable so they will be worn when on board. Also, consider the water conditions you encounter, your type of boat, and your boating activity.

◆ Don't sit on a life jacket when it is not in use. The weight could damage the protective shell.

◆ Inspect all life jackets annually, and test them in a swimming pool.

◆ Children and non-swimmers should wear a life jacket on any small boat or near water.

◆ Leave your itinerary with someone. Tell them whom you'll be with, how long you'll be gone, and where you plan to go. Never go boating alone.

◆ Close hatches and openings before fueling. Turn off electrical gear and appliances. Don't smoke!

◆ Fill tanks 90–95 percent full to allow for expansion. Fill portable fuel tanks off the boat.

◆ After fueling, wipe up all spills. Open all hatches. For inboard engines, run the bilge blower for at least four minutes before starting up.

◆ Never start the engine until all traces of vapors are eliminated. Your nose is your best detector.

◆ Check for power lines in your path before launching.

On the Waves

Capsizing and falling overboard cause more than 50 percent of all boating fatalities.

Most such accidents result from overloading, improper weight distribution, high-speed maneuvers, leaning over the edge, and operator error.

◆ Be especially careful the first few trips of the season. Your skills might be rusty.

◆ On small boats, most capsizes occur because of sudden weight shifts. Move carefully and cautiously. Everyone should remain seated while the boat is in motion.

◆ If you must stand up in a small boat for *any* reason, wear a life jacket.

◆ Many accidents are collisions with other boats or with objects in the water, such as rocks, pilings, or debris. Stay alert. Keep your eyes open, and employ the same defensive measures you use behind the wheel of a car.

◆ Travel at safe speeds. Avoid sudden and sharp high-speed turns.

◆ Give swimmers, skiers, and divers plenty of distance. Be especially alert near boat docks. Shut off your engines when approaching swimmers.

◆ Before heading out, check the latest local weather forecast.

◆ Head for shore when the weather turns bad. Everybody should don a life jacket immediately. Sudden wind shifts and choppy water can mean a storm is brewing.

◆ Carry a portable radio for weather reports. A cell phone and a marine radio when venturing far from shore are good additions.

◆ If your boat capsizes, don't panic. Stay with the boat.

◆ Wear your life jacket. It floats... you don't.

Don't Be Bowled Over

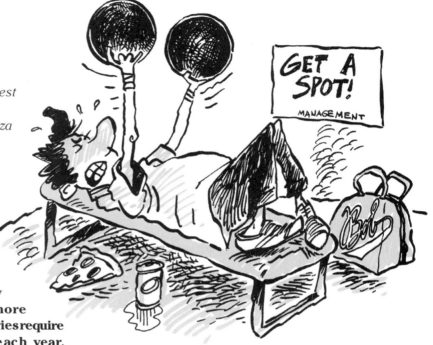

Tom had just played one of the best games of his high school football career; now for the post-game pizza and a little bowling to relax sore muscles. Although Tom hadn't fumbled during the football game, he accidentally dropped the sixteen-pound bowling ball on his foot and missed the next ball game with a broken toe.

As unlikely as it seems, the U.S. Consumer Product Safety Commission estimates that more than 20,000 bowling-related injuries require emergency room treatment each year.

Most are caused by carelessness, resulting in slips and falls, sprains, balls dropped on toes, or fingers smashed between balls.

Bowling can also result in "overuse" injuries, like tendonitis and carpal tunnel syndrome of the hand, wrist, elbow, and shoulder, caused by repetition and cumulative stress. The factors that contribute to overuse injuries include lack of a pre-bowling warm-up, lack of strength, poor physical condition, improper bowling technique, and inadequate or inappropriate equipment.

Some Precautions

- Complete a five-minute warm-up session before you bowl. Stretch all of your body parts to improve the oxygen flow to your muscles. When stretching, there should be no bouncing or jerky motions.

- Pay particular attention to the wrist, elbow, shoulder, back, hamstrings, and quadriceps. Visit your medical professional to learn about proper stretching exercises.

- Take up weight training to strengthen your biceps and triceps if you bowl regularly.

- Squeeze a tennis ball to strengthen your grip to avoid wrist tendonitis.

- Take lessons. Good bowling technique is critical. Keep your back erect, bend with your legs, and maintain a smooth approach.

- Annoying aches and pains, twinges, and tender areas are signs of possible injury. Seek medical attention before the situation becomes serious.

- Check with a pro to get a ball that's the right weight for you and fits your hand.

- Before throwing the first ball, be sure your shoes are dry, so your foot will slide at the approach line.

- Encourage your league president to disseminate safety tips to all bowlers.

Sports Accident Facts (All Ages)

Sport	Participants	Annual Injuries*
Archery	4,900,000	3,500
Baseball & softball	31,000,000	340,000
Basketball	29,600,000	597,000
Bicycle riding	42,400,000	596,000
Billiards, pool	32,100,000	5,100
Bowling	41,600,000	22,600
Boxing	1,300,000	8,900
Exercise	(data not available)	160,100
Fishing	46,700,000	70,500
Football (touch and tackle)	19,800,000	372,400
Golf	27,000,000	56,600
Gymnastics	5,000,000	32,700
Hockey (ice, street, roller, and field)	(data not available)	71,600
Horseback riding	(data not available)	72,800
Horseshoe pitching	(data not available)	2,500
Ice skating	7,700,000	30,200
In-line and roller skating	32,300,000	140,400
Martial arts	5,100,000	25,000
Mountain climbing	(data not available)	3,100
Racquetball, squash & paddleball	32,000,000	9,400
Rugby	(data not available)	8,900
Scooters	(data not available)	40,500
Scuba diving	2,300,000	1,500
Skateboarding	7,000,000	60,000
Snow skiing/snowboarding	10,000,000	165,000
Snowmobiling	3,400,000	14,100
Soccer	13,200,000	175,300
Swimming	57,900,000	99,700
Tennis	10,900,000	25,200
Track & field	(data not available)	14,900
Trampolines	(data not available)	100,000
Volleyball	11,700,000	64,200
Water skiing	6,600,000	12,600
Weight lifting	(data not available)	65,300
Wrestling	3,800,000	51,200

* Injuries treated in hospital emergency departments — all ages. Source: National Safety Council

Campfire Wisdom

We go camping to escape the rat race, to relax, and to learn about the natural world. Tragically, Nature teaches some of her cruelest lessons when we are trying to become better acquainted with her — as we are reminded whenever people drown in a flash flood while on a camping trip. Like any other human endeavor, successful and safe camping adventures require planning and cautious forethought.

Before Leaving

♦ Pack a first-aid book and a well-stocked kit. For possible bad weather, bring raingear and warm clothing that can be layered.

♦ A short list of necessities: cooking utensils, insect repellents, lanterns, toolkit, sunscreen, matches in a waterproof container, toilet paper, soap, hooded sweatshirt for children, a hat, and a compass.

♦ Bring bottled water for drinking and for mixing with food. Always assume stream and river water is not safe to drink.

♦ Learn as much as you can about the area's weather patterns and hazards before you leave home. Plan accordingly. Take a radio to get weather updates.

♦ Have a fire extinguisher or pail of water available at all times.

♦ Teach and practice the *Stop, Drop, and Roll* method of putting out a clothing fire.

♦ Take foods that don't require refrigeration or careful packing, e.g., peanut butter and canned foods.

♦ Bring emergency phone numbers and a cell phone, or know where the nearest phone is located.

♦ Read the labels before buying a tent. Only buy a tent that is flame resistant.

Setting up Camp

◆ Arrive well before sundown to select a suitable campsite.

◆ Camp on high ground. Do not camp on gravel bars or near a river or creek bank, no matter how dry it appears.

◆ Beware of trees with dead branches, and of low areas that could become muddy in heavy rain.

◆ Inspect the area for poisonous plants, nests, and other dangers.

◆ Clear away any rocks, roots, or debris that might present hazards.

◆ Pitch your tent at least fifteen feet upwind of grills and fireplaces.

◆ Leave at least a three-foot area clear of leaves, dry grass, and pine needles around grills, fireplaces, and tents.

◆ Store flammable liquids only in safety cans, at a safe distance from your tent, camper, or any source of heat or open flame.

◆ Apply insect repellent as recommended by your doctor.

At Your Temporary Home

◆ In stormy weather, avoid solitary tree lines or small groupings of trees. Go into the deeper forest.

◆ If lightning gets close, crouch down with your feet close together, which minimizes the surface area that ground current might be able to flow through. If you have a dry sleeping pad, stand on it to further protect yourself. Do not lie flat or sit down. Stay as far away from any metal as you can.

◆ Use only flashlights or battery-powered lanterns inside a tent.

◆ Develop a fire escape plan with your family.

◆ Use a funnel to pour flammable liquids. Wipe up spills.

◆ Fill lanterns and stoves a safe distance downwind from heat sources.

◆ Do not use a flammable liquid to start a fire.

◆ Don't wear loose-fitting clothing around fire.

◆ Build a campfire where it cannot spread. Never leave a fire unattended. Put it out with water and soil. Be extra-careful on windy days.

◆ Don't pour fire starter on a smoldering fire.

◆ Do not dump hot charcoal on the ground where someone can accidentally step on it. Place coals in designated ash cans.

◆ Wash your hands well before handling food. Use disposable wipes if safe water is limited, or use antibacterial liquid cleaner.

◆ Never barbecue inside a tent, camper, or vehicle.

◆ Store food in coolers or in your vehicle, where animals can't smell or reach them. Don't encourage wild animals into your campsite by offering food.

◆ Teach children not to disturb or provoke any animals.

◆ Shake out all clothing before putting it on.

A Few Good Tips on Canoeing

There is a sublime tranquillity to canoeing. No boat motors roaring, no sails flapping, and no oarlocks creaking; just a man or woman slicing a wooden paddle through the water's surface. Unfortunately, the silence is too often interrupted by the splash of that same man or woman tumbling into the water because of a careless act.

Each year, millions of Americans pick up a paddle, and studies show that more than fifty of them drown while canoeing.

As with most recreational accidents, drowning usually results from poor judgment and inadequate preparation.

On the Shore

◆ Know your personal skill level and physical condition. Don't overestimate your capabilities.

◆ A frequent source of wet paddlers — and injuries — is the simple act of putting a canoe into the water and getting into it or getting ashore.

◆ As little as one hour of competent instruction significantly reduces your chance of a serious accident. Courses are available from the American Red Cross, the American Canoe Association, the American Whitewater organization, and others.

◆ A canoeing course is especially important if you plan to tackle a river.

◆ Be a competent swimmer. Just because you start out in a canoe doesn't mean you'll stay there. Swimming could save your life.

◆ Wear appropriate clothing:

  • Avoid bulky clothing that could affect your ability to swim.

  • A dry-suit or wetsuit is recommended in rough waters, especially when the water is colder than seventy degrees. Exposure to cold water can cause hypothermia, which can be fatal.

  • Wear a broad-brimmed hat to protect yourself from the sun and rain.

  • Carry a complete change of clothing in a waterproof bag.

  • Always wear shoes. Canvas is good because it dries fast.

◆ Do not load a canoe so heavily that you have less than six inches of "side" between the water line and the top of the gunwales.

◆ Get an accurate local weather forecast. Some forecasts are broadcast fifty miles from the water you will be traveling.

The Ultimate Safety Equipment

As strange as it may seem, most canoeing accidents do not occur in raging whitewater, but in calm lakes and rivers. Why? People feel no threat in quieter waters, and forget to take proper precautions. The solution is simple:

◆ Wear a life jacket! A snug-fitting vest-type jacket will protect your back and shoulders. Find one that's Coast Guard approved.

Scouting the Waterway

◆ Know the waterways you will be traveling.

◆ On an unfamiliar waterway, go with an experienced leader, or walk the bank first. Look for hazards such as rapids, waterfalls, fallen logs, and heavy boating traffic.

◆ Always avoid:

  • water that is exceptionally cold;

  • remote areas;

  • the areas around dams;

  • rising rivers. *Never* canoe in a flooded river!

◆ Carry a canoe around a rapid that is beyond your capability.

◆ Write your state's Department of Natural Resources for a map of waterways that you can canoe.

General Safety Instructions

◆ Never canoe alone

◆ Keep weight low in a canoe. Avoid sudden movements, and shift your weight slowly and carefully.

◆ Drinking and canoeing do not mix. Coast Guard studies show that alcohol is involved in more than twenty-five percent of all boating accidents.

◆ Pack an emergency kit that contains a flashlight, rescue bag (throw rope), medical kit, knife, whistle, and waterproof matches, especially when you are canoeing on a river. Other recommended items include: an extra paddle, a radio, smoke flares, a bailing container and a sponge, and a thermos of water.

◆ If your canoe is upset for any reason, stay with your canoe! It should have enough flotation built into it to support any occupants who hang onto it until help arrives.

Dangerous Chain Reaction

There's a famous sports story about a college football team that went out the night before their Saturday game and saw the movie, The Texas Chainsaw Massacre. The next day, an opponent they were expected to easily beat humiliated them. When asked what happened, the players said they couldn't concentrate on the game, because all they could think about was the horrors they'd seen in the movie the night before.

The lesson here is, leave the massacres to the Hollywood special-effects people. Unlike the football players, you'll lose more than your composure if you're not careful using a chainsaw.

According to the Consumer Product Safety Commission, more than 25,000 chainsaw injuries require emergency room treatment each year.

Before you begin cutting your fireplace wood, remember these tips.

Dress for the Job

To work safely you'll need:

- leather gloves. They absorb some of the vibration, and protect your hands from abrasions.

- safety goggles or safety glasses with side shields. Regular prescription glasses or sunglasses will not protect you.

- a pair of protective work boots, or shoes with safety top caps, metatarsal guards, and slip-resistant soles. No tennis shoes!

- snug-fitting long pants and a long-sleeved shirt to protect you from exhaust burns.
- earmuffs or insert-type earplugs to protect against high noise levels.
- a hard hat to protect against falling objects and possible kickback.

Even Before You Start

♦ Read and understand all operating instructions, parts, and settings. Practice using the chainsaw with someone who knows how.

♦ Keep other people and animals out of your work area.

♦ Keep your work area clear of branches and other objects that could cause kickback.

♦ Be sure the chain blade is sharp and at the proper tension. A properly sharpened saw won't vibrate as much or be as tiring to operate.

♦ Clean dirt, spilled fuel, and sawdust from your saw.

♦ Stand on the uphill side of a log when cutting, because the log might roll downhill.

♦ Be sure your body is clear of the natural path the saw will follow after you complete the cut.

♦ Check that handles are clean and dry.

♦ Call a professional for jobs off the ground.

♦ Don't work alone. When chainsaw accidents occur, they are usually serious.

♦ Review safety tips the first time you use the saw each year.

When the Blade is Running

Typically, kickback results when the tip of the saw comes in contact with a solid object or tough piece of wood. It can also happen when the saw tip touches the bottom or side of the cut. Stay alert!

♦ Start the chainsaw only on clear, level ground, not on your leg.

♦ Use a well-balanced stance.

♦ To support and guide the saw, hold it with one hand on the rear handle and one on the top handle.

♦ Never carry a saw while it's running. When it's not running, carry it below your waist, with the guide bar pointed down.

♦ Cut with the part of the saw closest to the motor, not the tip.

♦ Let the chain do the work. Don't try to force the saw through the cut.

♦ Start all cuts at top speed (full throttle) and continue to cut at top speed.

♦ Take your hand off the trigger between cuts.

♦ Be sure the chain does not rotate when the controls are in the IDLE position.

♦ Watch the moving chain until it comes to a full stop before moving the saw near your body.

♦ Turn off the saw and make sure the chain has stopped before making any adjustments or repairs.

♦ Inspect the blade for cracks at least once an hour during use. If you find any, replace the blade.

♦ Refill the tank only when the engine is cold and the saw is not running.

♦ If you feel tired, rest. Fatigue can lead to accidents.

Head Up! Hands Out!

*Y*ou couldn't even call it a dive; it was more like a lunge. Mary had been standing at the shallow end of the pool, enjoying her drink and talking to a friend, when Dave sneaked up behind her and pushed her into the water. Instead of jumping in feet-first, Mary instinctively dived, throwing her drink in the air and screaming good-naturedly. In the midst of the fun, she banged her head on the bottom of the pool, severing her spinal cord. What began as a playful prank ended in tragedy — a lifetime of paralysis.

According to an estimate by the National Spinal Cord Injury Association, each year, diving accidents cause 1,000 spinal-cord injuries that result in some type of paralysis. The most likely victim of these incidents is a young man between the ages of thirteen and thirty, and alcohol is involved in about half the cases. Before you take your next plunge:

Look Before You Leap

◆ Plan your dive. Check the depth of the water and make sure there is sufficient room to dive. There should be at least twenty-five feet of clear dive path in front of you.

◆ Never dive headfirst into six feet of water or less; that's where most diving injuries occur.

◆ Check the area you're about to dive into for obstacles above and beneath the water. If you're not certain what the conditions are underwater, do not dive.

◆ Never assume you know the depth of a familiar piece of water. Droughts, tides, and shifting sediment may cause the depth to change.

◆ Always jump feet-first on your first plunge, even if you think it's safe to dive.

◆ Don't dive through objects such as inner tubes.

◆ Never dive or swim alone.

◆ Consider taking diving lessons from a qualified instructor.

◆ Alcohol and water do not mix. Don't swim or dive if you've been using alcohol or drugs. Diving requires clear thinking before and during the dive. Even half a drink, or some medicines, can impair a diver's judgment and control.

Rules for Pools

Many diving injuries occur in swimming pools, particularly backyard pools. To protect yourself and others, follow these basic rules:

◆ Never dive or slide headfirst into shallow above-ground pools.

◆ In an in-ground pool:

  • Do not dive off the sides of diving boards, slides or other pool equipment.

  • Never dive or slide headfirst in the shallow end.

  • Test a diving board to gauge its spring before using it.

◆ Always jump directly forward from the edge of the pool or diving board.

◆ For night diving, be sure the lighting is good.

◆ Never run or engage in horseplay.

◆ There are only two proper ways to use a pool slide: sitting, going down feet first; or, lying flat on your belly, headfirst. All other methods present a risk of serious injury. If headfirst slides are to be attempted, the pool slide must exit into deep water.

Survive Your Dive

◆ Keep your dives simple. Don't attempt dives with a straight vertical entry. They take a long time to slow down, and should be done only after careful training and in pools designed for competitive diving.

◆ Don't run and dive. That can give you the same impact as a dive from a board.

◆ Plan a shallow dive.

◆ During the dive, keep your head up, arms extended, and hands flat and tipped up. Your extended arms and hands help you to steer up to the surface, and protect your head.

◆ When you dive, be ready immediately to steer up and away from the bottom. Arch your back.

Managing the Unthinkable

If you think a spinal injury has occurred:

  • Do not try to move the victim unless his or her life is in danger.

  • Float the person face-up until help arrives. Do not pull him from the water.

  • Get trained help.

  • Avoid unnecessary movements. Proceed slowly and gently.

  • Immobilize the neck by making a vise with your hands and arms.

  • If there is a spinal cord injury, call the National Spinal Cord Injury Association for assistance at (800) 962-9629.

It's 20/20 Hindsight

John was in a hurry. The birthday party was starting in thirty minutes, and he found a rough edge on the wooden pencil holder he'd made for his wife. He dashed into his workshop, turned on his small power sander, and got to work. It would only take a second — he didn't need his goggles. When a wood chip landed in his eye, John's next mad dash was to the hospital emergency room.

Each year, more than 200,000 Americans are treated in emergency rooms for eye injuries, and nearly a million people have permanently lost some degree of eyesight due to injury.

Almost all of these mishaps could have been avoided. You can take measures to protect your vision:

At Home and at Play

◆ Wear chemical safety goggles when handling household cleaning products that can spill or splash into your face or eyes. Doing so will also set a good example for your children to follow.

◆ Also, always wear safety glasses or goggles when using power tools, lawn equipment, fertilizers, and pesticides.

◆ If people need to enter your work area, insist that they wear proper eye protection.

◆ Wear eye protection when jump-starting your car. Follow directions provided with the cables.

◆ For maximum eyewear protection, look for the ANSI Z87 logo. While all lenses must meet minimal government standards for impact resistance, not all provide protection for many strenuous impact hazards. Polycarbonate lenses are more impact resistant than other lenses.

◆ Goggles that fit over glasses are available in most hardware, department, and hobby stores.

◆ Wear sunglasses that block 99-100 percent of the sun's harmful UVA and UVB rays.

◆ The best colors for the lenses of sunglasses are gray, green, or brown. Other colors may distort color perception.

◆ In bright sunlight, wear a wide-brimmed hat. It will block about fifty percent of the ultraviolet radiation that might enter the eye around sunglasses.

- For the sports-minded:
  - Wear polycarbonate sports eye-guards for basketball and racquet sports.
  - Be sure the lenses in your sports eye-guards stay in place.
  - Wear goggles to swim.
  - Consider paying extra for glasses with poly-carbonate lenses.
- For more information on eye protection, ask your eye care professional, or call Prevent Blindness America at (800) 331-2020.

To Protect the Kids

- Pad or cushion sharp corners and edges of furniture and fixtures. Remove items that cannot be protected. This also applies at grandma's and other people's homes your child visits.
- Do not buy toys with sharp points, shafts, spikes, rods, or sharp edges.
- Keep toys for older children away from young children.
- Keep nails, glue, and tools away from children's reach.
- Young athletes and beginners are more prone to injuries than older people. Consider protective eye equipment when your child is playing sports involving contact, balls, bats, sticks, and racquets.
- Do not allow children to play with darts, BB guns, and games or toys with projectiles.
- Teach children not to run with pointed scissors, pencils, or other sharp objects. Keep the pointy end pointed toward the ground.
- Do not let children throw pointed objects, rocks, sand, or dirt.
- And they definitely should not play with firecrackers, matches, or flammable materials.

- Store cleaning products in a locked, secure area.
- Kids need sun protection, too. Children's sunglasses should also block 99-100 percent of UVA and UVB rays, and should have unbreakable polycarbonate lenses.

Cosmetic Concerns

- Always wash your hands thoroughly before applying eye cosmetics. Bacteria on your hands can cause infection.
- Keep all applicators clean and in good condition.
- Keep cosmetics away from excessive heat and cold, which can break down preservatives and allow bacteria to grow.
- Use and discard mascara and eyeliner within three or four months. Preservatives lose their effectiveness over time.
- Do not save brushes or use old applicators with new containers.
- Do not use saliva, and do not add water to your makeup unless the instructions call for it; water promotes bacteria growth.
- Never share makeup.
- Keep makeup containers free of dust and dirt.
- Contact lens wearers must take extra precautions, as specified by your doctor.

Hooked on Fishing

Pete had been fishing with the new bass lure he had seen advertised on television. It was a good-looking plug, and it cost a pretty penny. When he met total resistance on his fifth cast, he was sure he had landed a trophy fish. A minute later, he knew he had snagged a log. He fought to free the expensive lure, but it wouldn't budge. For added leverage, he stood in his boat and yanked with all his strength. When the lure broke free, it rocketed from the water and he lost his balance. The plug lodged in his cheek as he toppled backward into the lake. A doctor had to remove the treble hooks from his face. Knowing he had narrowly escaped being blinded and drowned, Pete called it a day and headed for the golf course, where there would be no talk of "the one that got away."

Approximately 80,000 fishing injuries require emergency room treatment annually. Fishing hooks cause most of these injuries, while most fishing-related fatalities result from drowning.

To fish safely:

In a Boat

- Always wear a Coast Guard-approved life jacket.

- Never overload your boat.

- Load properly, keeping the heaviest items in the middle and bottom of the boat.

- Before taking out any boat, make sure it's equipped with an extra oar or paddle, a bailing can, an anchor and line, and, if motorized, a full gas can.

- Change positions only on shore, or cautiously in shallow water.

- In a storm, lie low in the boat. To avoid being tipped, point the bow of the boat into the waves.

- If you must stand up in s small boat for *any* reason, wear a life jacket.

- Exercise special caution around dams. The falling water creates a back-current that can pull a small boat into its turbulence and cause it to capsize.

- At night, slow down and use running and marker lights.

- If the boat capsizes, stay with it until help arrives. Do not remove your clothing or boots; they will keep you afloat by holding air, and they will keep you warm.

- Avoid alcohol use.

In a Stream

- Never wade alone, and wear your life jacket.

- Wear cleated or felt-soled waders or boots for maximum traction on the slippery rocks underfoot.

- Unseen holes and drop-offs are dangerous. Test each step carefully in advance by taking a tentative shuffle. Better yet, use a wading staff to measure the depth of the water before each step.

In Any Event

- Carry a radio for weather information, and a cell phone for emergencies.

- Dress with the weather in mind, preferably in layers. Pack a wind- and waterproof outer shell.

- Wear properly fitted eye protection that covers the eye socket to guard against hooks and glare. Polycarbonate lenses are recommended for their strength and protective capabilities.

- Do not cast over a companion's head. Always look around before making a cast.

- Carry sharp pliers and disinfectant in your first-aid kit.

- When landing a fish, work from the rear of the boat. Use a net.

- Ease a fish out of the water. Yanking it into the boat can release the fish and create a dangerous slingshot effect.

- To remove the hook, wait until the fish is exhausted. Use a special gripping glove, and know the technique for each species.

- Be especially careful dislodging lures and hooks from submerged branches or roots. Invest in a "lure retriever" to do the work.

- If your own hook snags you, do not try to back it out. Instead, push it through the skin until the point and the barb are exposed. Snip them off; snip off the eyelet, too. Now pull the smooth hook through your skin, following its natural arc. Cleanse the wound and apply disinfectant. Watch for infection.

- Look out for overhead electrical lines, especially around the dock and in unfamiliar stretches of water. Carry your rod parallel to the ground whenever possible.

- Don't fish from railroad trestles — you're the one who might be caught.

Exercise Your (Health) Options

New Year's is the traditional time to launch into a fitness regimen, and why not resolve to live a more healthy, vigorous life? Unless, like Kathy, you're just not ready for the sudden strain exercise can place on an unprepared body. Kathy reached for the gold, when she wasn't even ready for the bronze: by overexerting herself ten minutes into her first exercise routine, she seriously injured her back.

Yes, we need to stay healthy, but not destroy ourselves in the process. Physical fitness plans can take many directions, but whichever path you pursue, there are some basic things to remember.

Think Before You Exert

See your doctor for a physical examination before you begin an exercise program, especially if you are: pregnant; older than thirty-five; overweight; easily fatigued; a heavy smoker; physically inactive; have a history of personal or family health problems; or take medication.

◆ Talk with an exercise professional to develop warm-up and cool-down routines, and an injury prevention plan specific to your activities.

◆ When you stretch, do it slowly and smoothly. Hold a stretch for at least fifteen seconds.

◆ As a general rule, do not increase the intensity, frequency, or duration of your exercise sessions by more than 10 percent per week.

◆ Drink plenty of fluids before, during, and right after your sessions.

Selecting the Right Trainer

A personal trainer can be good, but you have to be careful. Here are some guidelines:

• Does the gym where he or she works have an emergency plan?

• Does the trainer know CPR (cardiopulmonary resuscitation)?

• Check on certification credentials, training, and liability insurance. The *Wall Street Journal* lists these organizations among the most widely respected certification programs: American College of Sports Medicine; American Council on Exercise; Cooper Institute for Aerobics Research; National Strength and Conditioning Association; and Aerobics and Fitness Association of America.

• Don't be misled by an overzealous trainer.

• Seek good chemistry. You're entrusting your body to a stranger.

• Demand professionalism.

Some Weighty Considerations

Weight training can benefit all genders and ages. In fact, the older we get, the more good it might do.

◆ Whether you train at a gym or at home, get careful instruction in weight-training equipment and exercises before you start. Review your planned routines with a medical professional.

Other tips:

◆ Warm up by marching in place, swinging your arms back and forth, and rolling your shoulders for a minute or two. After the workout, stretch.

◆ Bend and lift with the knees, not the back.

◆ Exhale during the exertion part of the exercise, and inhale while returning to the starting position. Do not hold your breath.

◆ Use slow, controlled motions when you work with free weights or exercise machines.

◆ Move only the part of your body being exercised. Don't wiggle, squirm, or rock; and do not lean forward or backward, particularly by arching or rounding your back.

◆ Don't overdo it! If exercise causes pain, stop immediately.

◆ Wait ninety minutes after a meal before exercising vigorously.

◆ Consider the benefits of cross-training, where you blend aerobic-style exercises, strength/weight training, and flexibility exercises. Because it works muscles in different ways, cross-training is also safer and better for you.

WARNING: Stop exercising immediately if you experience signs of pressure or pain in your chest, shoulder, neck, jaw, arms, or upper back; or, light-headedness, faintness, or unusual fatigue or shortness of breath; palpitations or erratic heartbeat, nausea, or upset stomach. Seek emergency treatment immediately.

Watch Out, Fella — That's Salmonella!

Eating has become a thoughtful proposition. Instead of focusing on how food tastes, we're concerned with counting calories or cholesterol, fats or sugars, salts, or carbohydrates. And just when you thought it was safe to sit down at the dinner table, another scourge rears its ugly head: food poisoning.

According to the U.S. Department of Agriculture, several thousand Americans die from food poisoning each year, and millions suffer from symptoms.

The news isn't all bad: food poisoning can be avoided on the hottest or coldest days of the year by taking some basic precautions.

Food Preparation and Storage

◆ Before preparing food, and before handling a different food, wash your hands with hot soapy water. Dry with a paper towel.

◆ Clean the area where you'll be preparing foods with hot water and antibacterial soap, then rinse.

◆ Wash preparation surfaces and utensils with hot soapy water after preparing raw meat, fish, poultry, eggs, fruit, and vegetables.

- Don't put cooked foods, vegetables, or fruit on the same unwashed plate that held raw meat or poultry.

- It's best to use separate cutting boards for raw meats, vegetables, and fruit. Plastic cutting boards that can be put in the dishwasher are best.

- Use clean utensils for food preparation, cooking, and serving.

- Thaw or marinate meats in the refrigerator. Use a dish on the lowest shelf so juices won't drip.

- Set your refrigerator at 35–40° Fahrenheit (F), and your freezer at 0° F or lower.

- Use a clean dishcloth or towel every day.

- Replace dish sponges every few weeks. Soak in mild bleach between uses. (Some experts recommend avoiding sponges.)

- Never partially cook meats or casseroles one day and finish cooking them later.

- As a general rule, keep food clean, cold, and covered.

Picnics

- Keep food in a cooler as much as possible to avoid spoilage.

- Use one cooler for beverages and another for perishable foods (use cold packs and keep it closed).

- Keep leftovers only if there's enough ice in your cooler to keep them cold for the ride home.

What to Eat, and When

- Harmful bacteria are most prominent in high-protein foods that are usually considered perishable, such as eggs, milk, meat, fish, sauces, mayonnaise-based dishes, poultry products, and potato salad.

- Cook red meat to 160° F, and poultry to 180° F.

- For maximum safety, juices in cooked meat should be clear, and the meat should not be pink.

- Fish should flake easily when poked with a fork, and the thickest part should be opaque.

- Heat leftover sauces, soups, and gravies to a rolling boil for several minutes before serving. Heat other leftovers to 165° F. Discard leftovers within four days.

- Refrigerate mayonnaise, salad dressings, condiments, preserves, and canned foods after opening:

- Never leave perishable foods out at room temperature for more than two hours.

- Do not eat raw cookie dough or taste any meat, poultry, fish, or egg dish while it's partly cooked.

Food Shopping

- Make food shopping the last errand you perform. Buy refrigerated foods last.

- Do not buy food in packages that are torn, cans that bulge or leak, or any foods that have exceeded their "sell by" or "use by" dates.

- If a frozen food is not frozen solid, don't buy it.

- Pack poultry and raw meat in plastic bags, separate from groceries.

- Avoid frozen foods kept above a storage-chest freeze line in the grocery store. These foods might have partially thawed.

- In hot weather, transport perishable foods in an insulated cooler.

- Freeze fresh meat, poultry, and fish immediately if you don't plan to use it in one to two days.

Global Warning

United States residents take more than fifty million trips abroad each year. Unfortunately, many of them do not make the return trip, and 6,000 Americans die on foreign soil each year.

There are far more serious issues than not being able to locate a restroom in an emergency. To help assure that you put your return ticket to use, here are some things to consider.

Before You Go

Although we think of food and diseases as the main culprits, highway travel is the biggest threat to the safety of the overseas traveler. This is especially true in developing countries, where accident rates are between twenty and fifty times as high as in developed countries.

◆ Plan itineraries with safety as your primary consideration. As much as possible, reduce the amount of highway travel required to see various sites.

◆ Talk to your doctor about your trip. Get vaccinated. Ideally, this should be done four to six weeks prior to travel.

◆ Pack extra dosages of all your medications — they might be unavailable at your destination. Carry them with you on the plane.

◆ Bring a brief summary of your medical history.

◆ Bring a medical kit appropriate to your destination. Include medications and related supplies, such as a water-purifying chemical or device.

◆ Your physician or travel agent can help you identify a good doctor and hospital at your destination. If you haven't done your planning and find you need a doctor, ask at the front desk of a luxury hotel, or check with U.S. facilities or the embassy.

◆ Call the Centers for Disease Control and Prevention at (888) 232-3299 for health precautions at a variety of destinations, or visit www.cdc.gov.

◆ For information on safety, contact the State Department at (202) 647-5225 or www.travel.state.gov.

But I'm Hungry!

◆ Pay careful attention to safe food and water guidelines for the country you are visiting.

◆ You may need to avoid ice cubes, iced drinks, and non-carbonated bottled fluids made from water of uncertain quality. Boiling water is the most reliable way to make water safe to drink.

◆ Foods of particular concern include salads, milk products, raw meat, and shellfish.

◆ Only eat meat, poultry, and seafood that have been thoroughly cooked.

◆ Vegetables should be freshly cooked. Peel fresh fruits yourself.

◆ Brush your teeth with bottled water.

Travel Hazards

◆ On the plane, move your feet and legs every fifteen minutes. A few travelers experience blood clots on long flights.

◆ If you drive, familiarize yourself with the car, local driving rules, habits, and road signs *before* leaving.

◆ Drive defensively, and never think you know what the other driver is going to do. Drivers in other countries do not follow the same rules that we do.

◆ Don't get bitten. Many diseases are not preventable by vaccines or drugs. In buggy regions, keep your arms and legs covered, use a strong insect repellent, and avoid scented cosmetics.

Mountain sickness afflicts one-fourth of visitors to altitudes above 6,000 feet. The symptoms include headaches, fatigue, and shortness of breath, followed by appetite loss, nausea, and sleeplessness. Untreated, it can be highly dangerous. Here are some tips for avoiding or minimizing altitude sickness:

◆ Ascend gradually. If possible, spend a night or two at 5,000 feet before going higher.

◆ Take it easy. Don't jog, ski, or perform vigorous exercise the first day. Ease into physical activities on the second day.

◆ Drink a lot of water. And *don't* drink alcohol.

◆ Eat carbohydrates. They require less oxygen to metabolize than fats.

Ear Plugs

John didn't know why Alice couldn't just act her age, but no, she had to drag him to some rock-and-roll revival band at a local charity fundraiser. He'd never liked rock-and-roll, and now that he was seventy-five, he hated it. And why did they have to play it so loud that the volume made his teeth hurt? So, while Alice and her friends toe-tapped and watched the youngsters dance, John sulked in a corner and stuffed cotton in his ears. That might have eased the insult to his musical sensibilities, but it didn't help his hearing. When he complained that the band had permanently damaged his hearing, he was probably right.

With each exposure to continuous excessive noise or sudden loud noise, some of the 15–20 thousand sensory hair cells lining the cochlea in your inner ear are destroyed. When these delicate hair cells are damaged, the nerve fibers leading from them begin to deteriorate and hearing loss begins. The damage is cumulative — and irreversible.

Sound Management

- As a general rule, a noise may be harmful if you have to shout over it to be heard, if the noise hurts your ears or makes your ears ring, or if you're slightly deaf for several hours after the noise stops.

- Alternate a noisy activity with a period of quiet. Set aside a place in the house that can serve as a quiet escape.

- To block loud noises from entering your home, use storm windows, weather stripping, double panes of glass, and heavy drapes.

- When buying appliances such as dishwashers, blenders, vacuum cleaners, and waste disposals, shop for the quieter-running models.

- Place vibration mounts under large appliances, and foam pads under small appliances.

- Close doors in areas where large appliances are running.

- Set limits on television and stereo sound levels.

- If the sound coming from headphones can be heard by passersby, the level is at least 100 decibels (dB). At that level, permanent hearing loss occurs after two hours.

- Many experts agree that continuous exposure to noises of more than 85 dB can be dangerous. Heavy traffic and lawn mowers produce about this level of noise.

Sound Advice

- Wear hearing protection when you operate loud machinery, such as lawn mowers, leaf blowers, power tools, speedboats, motorcycles, snowmobiles, Jet-skis, firearms, and some home appliances. Use noise-resistant earmuffs or earplugs with at least a twenty-dB rating. When noise is extremely loud, use plugs and muffs together.

- Plan ahead. Aerobic dance classes, music presentations, and wedding receptions are often quite loud. Bring hearing protection devices (HPDs).

- Never sit next to the speakers at a concert — the damage could be severe and irreversible.

- Limit periods of exposure to noise. For example, if you're at a rock concert, walk out for a while to give your ears a break from the extreme sound.

- The most popular HPDs are earmuffs, canal caps, and earplugs. Which is the best one for you depends on a variety of factors, including:
  - the amount of noise reduction you want to achieve;
  - your personal comfort;
  - whether the hearing protection works properly with other equipment you might wear, such as head, eye, and breathing protection.

- Do not share your earplugs with anyone else. You could contract an ear infection that way.

- Throw away disposable plugs.

- Keep reusable earplugs clean. Wash them each day with soap and water.

- Use molded earplugs to keep your ears dry when swimming. Pool or lake water can cause infections.

- Consider potential noise damage when purchasing toys.

- Using cotton in your ears is *not* protection against loud noise.

Sound Maintenance

- Earwax usually comes out on its own; don't try to pry it out with cotton swabs, pins, or chemicals such as peroxide.

- If you must fly with a head cold, call your doctor for advice.

- Use dry-out drops after swimming, showering, or shampooing if your ears itch. Drops are available at pharmacies.

- Have your hearing tested regularly, including a word-recognition test, by an audiologist. A hearing test is simple and doesn't take long.

- See your doctor if you suffer from dizziness, loss of balance, or ringing in your ears. Also, if you can't hear words or phrases, if you understand people only when they are facing you, or if you have ear pain or discharge.

- If others often suggest that you get your hearing checked, do it.

Why, That Burns Me Up!

If the summer sun is leaving its mark on you, you're asking for trouble. The sun should provide warmth and the emotional lift that comes from a healthy relationship with nature, but you can get too much of a good thing.

In a typical year, more than 350 Americans die from the summer heat.

So, while it's important to spend time outdoors, protect yourself from the dangers of sun and heat by taking some basic precautions.

Combating Heat Stress

The first warning signs of heat stress are sluggishness and a foggy feeling. Other symptoms include headaches, dizziness, weakness, rapid heartbeat, muscle cramps, nausea, and light-headedness. Learn the difference between heat cramps, heat exhaustion, and heat stroke, and how to treat them.

♦ Slow down. Reduce strenuous activity. Get plenty of sleep.

♦ Avoid exposure to the sun, particularly between 10 A.M. and 4 P.M.

♦ Dress for summer.

- Lightweight, light-colored clothing reflects heat and sunlight.

- Loose-fitting cotton clothing allows the skin to breathe and absorb sweat.

- Wide-brimmed hats protect you from direct sunlight.

♦ Limit activities in the home that generate heat, such as cooking or ironing, during daylight hours.

- If you're taking medicine, ask your doctor or pharmacist if it will make you more susceptible to a heat-related illness.

- Excessive heat is particularly dangerous to young kids, the elderly, and people with disabilities or excessive weight, because these individuals don't have the physical ability to handle, or easily seek refuge from, the heat. Watch them closely. (Here's a noteworthy fact: Men are more susceptible, because they sweat more than women do and become dehydrated more quickly.)

- Never leave a person or pet locked in a car, even if the windows are left slightly open. Even on mild, sunny days, temperatures in an enclosed car can rise rapidly.

- It usually takes seven to fourteen days for the body to adjust to hot environments. Start slowly and build up the hours you spend in the heat.

- Bathe or shower several times a day in cool water.

- For ventilation, open windows on the shaded side.

- Take periodic rest breaks in a shaded or cool area to allow your body to cool off.

Watch What You Eat and Drink

- To keep cool, drink plenty of room-temperature or cool (not cold) water, juices, or sports drinks, even if you don't feel thirsty. Also, drink them before, during, and after vigorous activity. Electrolytes (sodium and potassium) are particularly needed after heavy exertion.

  Caution: If you have epilepsy, or heart, kidney, or liver disease, are on fluid-restrictive diets, or have a problem with fluid retention, you should consult a physician before increasing consumption of liquids.

- Eat lightly. The more calories you take in, the more body heat is produced. Avoid hot, heavy meals; eat smaller, more frequent meals.

- Choose foods high in water content, such as fruits, salads, and soups. Stay away from a diet heavy in proteins. They increase metabolic heat production and also increase water loss.

- Consult your doctor regarding the use of salt.

Workout Wisdom

- If you plan to exercise in the heat, start with brief workouts and increase them gradually over two weeks or more.

- Exercise in the early morning or evenings.

- Drink eight glasses of water throughout the day, whether you are thirsty or not. If you exercise intensely, drink even more water until your urine is regularly clear.

- Drink a glass of water fifteen to thirty minutes before going out. On a hot day, drink four to eight ounces every ten or fifteen minutes during your activity. A gulp is an ounce.

- Drinks with caffeine or alcohol can increase water loss. Avoid them.

- Put cold water on the back of your neck, under the arms, and on the wrists to cool your body faster.

- If you feel dizzy or weak, get out of the sun and drink cool fluids.

- After exercise, replace electrolytes with food or drinks.

- People at increased risk for heat ailments due to certain medications or chronic illness should exercise only in air-conditioned places.

Over Hill, Over Dale

Communing with nature is no walk in the park. Consider Laura, who set out with a friend for an afternoon excursion around the local reservoir: estimated time, four hours' hiking. In those four hours, Laura developed three blisters, scraped her knee, caught a bad case of poison ivy, twisted her ankle, got drenched in a rainstorm, and had a lovely hairdo ruined. Laura's new idea for a jaunty hike is a brisk walk through the shopping mall.

Whether you plan to hike for a few hours or a few days, you need to take precautions.

Have a Plan

♦ Get information on the weather, trail conditions, and animal hazards.

♦ Ask the police about known criminal activity in the area.

♦ If thunderstorms are predicted, avoid trips to high-risk areas, such as exposed ridges or open country.

♦ Be ready for emergencies. Pack a cell phone, flashlight, pocketknife, waterproof matches, whistle, compass, map, insect repellent, allergy medications, and first-aid instructions and supplies, including bandages, gauze, tape, antibacterial ointment, and a needle. Consider using a global positioning satellite (GPS) receiver, and the need for warm clothing and a Mylar blanket.

♦ Carry high-protein snacks.

♦ Pack at least one quart of water for every two or three hours of light-to-moderate hiking, and more if you expect to sweat a lot.

♦ For your hiking comfort, wear:

• a broad-brimmed hat, dress in layers, and bring raingear;

• long sleeves and full-length pants to protect you from sun, briars, and insects;

• clothing designed to wick moisture away from your skin (avoid cotton clothing);

• broken-in hiking boots, or good, sturdy walking shoes;

• two pairs of socks, one lightweight inner sock and a heavy outer sock. At the first sign of a blister, put a small patch of moleskin or "second skin" over the affected area to limit further irritation.

♦ Provide a whistle for children.

Don't Worry, Be Cautious

- Take the time to get in shape before you hike. During the hike, pause periodically to stretch, (especially in the morning, after you've gone a mile or two).

- Listen to your body. Your muscles, joints, and lungs will tell you when it's time to slow down.

- Use a sunscreen with a sun-protection factor (SPF) of 15–30, even on cloudy days. Reapply it often if you're sweating heavily

- Avoid using scented products.

- Don't hike alone. Travel in small groups. Make sure everyone knows the destination.

- Let someone know where you'll be going, and when to expect you back.

- Stay on well-marked trails.

- To prevent hypothermia, stay dry, beware of wind, put on your raingear or wool clothes before you start to shiver, and stop to rest.

- Next to hypothermia, stream crossings take more lives of backpackers than any other cause. To cross a stream safely:
  - unbuckle the hip belt on your pack;
  - never face downstream;
  - walk with your legs and body sideways to the current, always with only one foot or other means of support (a stick or another person) moving at any one time.

- Consider all backcountry water to be contaminated. Don't drink it, or treat it first.

- If you find yourself trapped in a thunderstorm, find a place to hide. Avoid metal structures and equipment, elevated areas, and natural electrical conductors, such as water. Seek out a low spot and sit or crouch. Do not lie down.

- To prevent altitude sickness, climb to higher altitudes slowly, to allow your body to get used to them. Drink lots of fluids. If you experience nausea, loss of appetite, or vomiting, go back down to lower elevations.

- Allow enough time to return before dark.

- Head back at the first sign of bad weather.

- If you get lost, stay put.

They Were There First

- Never approach or feed animals.

- Don't step where you can't see.

- Don't put your hand inside holes in logs, trees, or rocks.

- Assume snakes are poisonous.

- Carry a compact field guide to help you identify poisonous plants.

- Lyme disease precautions:
  - Apply tick repellent to your clothes, and wear light colors, which make ticks easier to see.
  - Check your hair and skin for ticks frequently.
  - Tuck your pants into your socks.
  - Avoid bushes and underbrush by sticking to the middle of the trail.
  - To remove ticks: place blunt-tipped, fine-pointed tweezers flat to the skin and slide under the tick. Gently pull the tick straight up without twisting. Put it in a plastic bag or jar, and have it tested for bacteria.

Color Me Careful

We turn to our hobbies to relax and to escape life's many stresses. Ironically, our source of comfort can also be a source of danger. Like many activities that are relaxing and therapeutic on the surface, arts and crafts carry their own dangers. Too often, toxic materials are included in art supplies. For instance, a Canadian art student fell down a stairway after he accidentally inhaled vapors from a freshly opened bottle of turpentine.

Before You Start

♦ Read the label. Be sure it states conformity to ASTM D-4236, the labeling standard of the American Society for Testing and Materials.

♦ If the label doesn't satisfy you, or if you intend to use a product in ways other than normal uses, contact the manufacturer for a Material Safety Data Sheet (MSDS).

♦ For information on specific products, contact Arts, Crafts and Theater Safety (ACTS) at (212) 777-0062, or www.caseweb.com/acts.

♦ Do not use products past their expiration date.

♦ Use all protective equipment specified on the label. Use a mask or gloves that are impermeable to whatever product you're using. Protect cuts and open wounds from exposure.

♦ Install a ventilation system that removes old air and brings in new air. To test, blow soap bubbles; if they fall to the ground, the system isn't working.

♦ Be sure you have good lighting and comfortable seating. Keep a fire extinguisher handy.

The Creative Process

◆ Do not eat, drink, smoke, or apply cosmetics in your work area.

◆ Take breaks and stretch often.

◆ Never use products for skin painting or food preparation unless they are labeled for that use.

◆ Do not transfer art materials to other containers. You'll lose valuable safety information listed on the product package.

◆ Wear a facemask and goggles when spraying paint or fixative. Do the spraying outdoors.

◆ When possible, use water-based paints and inks, and products that don't create dust or mist.

◆ Hobbyists with allergies or who are pregnant should consult a doctor before engaging in projects.

◆ Do not keep art materials on your skin — even nontoxic materials.

◆ Never use toxic solvents such as turpentine and paint thinner to cleanse the skin. Use baby oil (mineral oil), followed by soap and water.

◆ When you clean, use a wet mop or sponge rather than a duster. Dusts can damage lungs.

◆ Find substitute art materials for those which might be hazardous. For example, water-based adhesives can be used instead of flammable rubber cement.

◆ Take extreme care when using materials not sold as art materials, since they may not have been reviewed for safety. Get MSDSs.

◆ When they are not in use, keep all materials covered, stored in a safe place, and out of children's reach. Use unbreakable containers.

◆ Follow suggested disposal methods carefully.

◆ Do not store a flammable product near heat, sparks, or flame. Also, do not heat above the temperature specified on the label.

◆ After finishing the project, wash yourself and the work surface, and clean your supplies. Leave your work clothes in the work area.

Junior Picassos

Kids love the arts, too. Unfortunately, the fun can be dampened if they come in contact with toxic and dangerous materials. Don't be reluctant to ask their teacher if he or she is aware of these concerns.

◆ Make certain the product is clearly marked as appropriate for use by children.

◆ For children in sixth grade and under, use products that have *no hazard statements* and *no precautionary statements*. The word "nontoxic" should be on the label, but follow the same hygiene practices you would if the product were toxic.

◆ Older children must be supervised when using products labeled with warnings.

◆ Get an MSDS if you intend to use a product in creative ways, e.g., melting crayons.

◆ Young children should use only water-based marking pens, and not permanent markers.

◆ Children should not use any product containing lead.

◆ Teach children to use cutting tools safely, and to not place anything in their mouths.

Just Horsing Around

Watching the cowboy movies, you'd think falling off a horse was painless. Wrong, Red Rider!

The U.S. Consumer Product Safety Commission estimates that 150 deaths and 70,000 injuries are associated with horses and riding each year, including 6,000 head or spinal injuries. Probably no horse-riding accident caught the public's attention more than the tragedy that befell Christopher Reeve.

Horses helped us settle the West, but sometimes it's not so easy to settle *them*. Whether you're a novice or an experienced rider, here are some tips for staying safe in the saddle.

Some Preliminaries

◆ Falls are the most common riding injuries. Always wear a properly secured, hard-shell riding helmet that's been certified by the Safety Equipment Institute. Wear the helmet at all times when working around horses.

Studies show that the number of head injuries could be reduced by a third, and the number of severe head injuries cut in half, if riders would wear equestrian helmets.

◆ Batting and bike helmets are not acceptable for horseback riding.

◆ Wear smooth-soled riding shoes that cover the ankle. The shoes should have at least a half-inch raised heel to prevent getting a foot caught in the stirrup and being dragged.

◆ Wear long pants to prevent chafing and possible infections.

◆ Clothing must be snug to avoid becoming tangled with the saddle.

◆ Wear well-fitting gloves to protect hands from blisters, rope burns, and cuts.

◆ Don't wear jewelry, bracelets, or flapping clothing that might startle a horse, or get caught.

◆ Inform the stable of your experience level. If you're a beginner, get instructions from a certified trainer, and ask for a small, placid horse.

◆ When approaching a horse, speak softly, so the animal hears you coming. Walk where it can see you; approach at an angle from the shoulder; and stroke it on the neck or shoulder first.

- Do not run, yell, or play behind a horse.

- Avoid a horse's blind spot. Do not walk or stand directly in front of or behind a horse. If you must walk behind a horse, stay at least fifteen feet away.

- Do not feed a horse from your hand.

- Do not touch a strange horse unless its owner says the horse would welcome the attention.

- Walk around a horse, not under its body, neck, or tie rope.

- Carry a cell phone for emergencies, but keep it turned off.

- Watch for unusual objects in the horse's path.

- If you need to adjust your equipment or clothing, dismount.

- Never tie or wrap yourself to a horse. The American Association for Horsemanship Safety says you should always be able to escape your horse in three seconds or less.

- Never ride double.

- In a lightning storm, dismount and go to a low area, but not under a tree.

- Make sure an up-to-date first-aid kit is available at all times.

Saddle Up

- Check all leather gear for wear or cracking.

- Check stitching for loose or broken threads.

- Inspect the cinch strap that secures the saddle to the horse's back. It should be solid and tight.

- Be sure the saddle and stirrups are properly adjusted. With your foot in the stirrup, there should be a quarter-inch clearance between each side of your shoe and the stirrup.

- Always mount in an open area, away from objects you could fall on or the horse could get caught up in. Use a mounting block if necessary.

Most injuries occur when a rider is unintentionally separated from the horse. To stay with your horse:

- Avoid riding on heavily traveled roads. Always watch for traffic. Wear light-colored clothing.

- Ride single file on trails and roads. Keep at least one horse-length between horses.

- Don't ride alone. The lead rider should warn of upcoming hazards.

- Ride on the soil. Make sure the footing is good.

Kids and Horses

Kids love horses. What child hasn't asked for a pony at some point? According to the American Medical Equestrian Association, before you grant your child's wish, he or she should have:

- the desire to ride;

- the muscle strength to hold the proper position in the saddle;

- the balance to remain on the horse;

- the ability to understand instructions and follow directions;

- neck muscles strong enough to support fitted, approved headgear;

- a saddle that fits the child and the horse.

Only then should you find the proper, calm horse and the certified instructor with the experience and patience to teach your child.

Surgical Procedures

Kathy was scheduled for surgery at 9 A.M. As she was being wheeled into the operating room, the nurse smiled and assured her the surgeon would do a wonderful job with her hysterectomy. Kathy shrieked and sat bolt upright. Hysterectomy?! She was scheduled for gall bladder surgery! The nurse showed her the paperwork that specified a hysterectomy. Kathy dressed and fled immediately. She found a new physician and a new hospital, and had her gall bladder successfully removed a week later. Two years later, she gave birth to her third child.

| **While estimates vary, preventable incidents harm or kill tens of thousands of people in hospitals every year.**

Incorrect surgeries make the headlines, but infections and drug interactions cause most problems. Here are some tips for protecting yourself.

Prepare Yourself

◆ Look for a board-certified doctor. The American Board of Medical Specialists' "Directory of Board Certified Medical Specialists" is available at many libraries, or call (866) ASK-ABMS, or visit www.abms.org.

◆ Be sure that hospitalization is necessary, and you understand the diagnosis, options, and potential problems.

- Be direct when talking to a doctor. Don't minimize or trivialize your problems. Bring someone along on an important visit with a doctor.

- Read up on your disorder to become more knowledgeable. Write your questions in advance, and take along a notepad or tape recorder.

- Get a second opinion from a doctor with no connection to the first one.

- Learn as much as you can about your doctor, either informally or through professional groups. Ask tough questions, such as how many of these surgeries he has performed, and his success rate. Will he perform the operation, or will an assistant? Call the hospital to verify the numbers.

- Get the hospital's success rate for the procedure you will undergo, particularly for major surgery.

- Ask your surgeon about the optimal timing for surgeries and preventive antibiotics, and options for transfusions and pain control.

- Plan your recovery, including home care you will need.

- For more help, get the booklet, *Be Informed: Questions To Ask Your Doctor Before You Have Surgery* from the Agency for Healthcare Research and Quality. Write AHRQ Publications Clearinghouse, P.O. Box 8547, Dept. P, Silver Spring, MD 20907, or call (800) 358-9295; or visit www.ahrq.gov.

Monitor Your Medications

- Ask your doctor to help you compile a list of additional drugs you'll probably need, including nonprescription drugs. Include the name, dosage instructions, color, number, and shape of pills.

- Discuss well in advance any allergic reactions you have had.

- Bring the pill containers for all the medications you are taking, including over-the-counter drugs.

- Give your medications to your anesthesiologist, along with your complete medical history.

- Be sure your medications are recorded on your medical chart.

- Make sure your name and any allergies are correct on your wristband. Nurses should check it each time before administering a drug.

- If a drug appears different, get an explanation from the doctor or pharmacist before taking it.

During Your Stay

- Be certain you understand forms you're asked to sign. Get copies before going to the hospital.

- Ask the surgeon to mark the surgery site while you are awake.

- Have someone stay with you the first twenty-four hours following surgery, and as much as possible afterward.

- You should expect reasonable pain control. If you're not comfortable, notify your doctor.

- Request that doctors and medical personnel wash their hands before touching you.

- Allow only a registered nurse (RN) to perform the following procedures: inserting IVs, catheters, or gastric tubes; changing sterile dressings or treating damaged skin; giving shots; caring for a tracheotomy; or giving tube feedings.

- Discuss your treatment plan in advance, and question your doctor about unexpected treatments.

- Appeal your discharge if you don't feel ready to go home.

- Have a thorough review with your surgeon before you leave the hospital, so you'll know about possible side effects from medications, and what warning signs to look for during your recovery.

Gunning for Trouble

At age seventy-five, Jack was the picture of health. He loved life, and all his outdoor pursuits, especially squirrel hunting. It wasn't taxing, and he didn't have to travel far from home to do it. He arrived at his favorite oak tree at dawn and sat down. He knew the barrel of his shotgun had bumped the ground entering the timber, but there was no time for that now — he saw a squirrel! Jack fired, and his jammed barrel exploded, breaking his jaw and seriously cutting his right hand. He lost a good morning's hunt and a trusty shotgun. Luckily, he didn't lose more.

According to the International Hunter Education Association, in a recent year, more than eighty fatalities and 900 nonfatal injuries occurred to U.S. hunters.

If you're one of the millions of Americans who take to the fields with a loaded firearm, keep these things in mind.

Aim for Safety

Begin your hunting experience by taking a hunter-education course available in your area. These courses can be valuable whether you are a novice or an experienced hunter, and are required in most states.

- A gun requires periodic inspection, adjustment, and service. Check with the manufacturer or dealer for recommended servicing.

- Keep firearms unloaded, and keep the action open until you are hunting. Carry guns in their cases to the shooting area.

◆ Always assume that every firearm is loaded and dangerous. Treat it as if it could shoot at any time. A safety mechanism is not foolproof.

◆ Never take someone else's word that a firearm is not loaded. Always check for yourself.

◆ Never engage in horseplay with a firearm. Guns are deadly, and should be treated in a serious, cautious manner.

◆ Always point the muzzle in a safe direction, that is, one in which a firearm, if fired accidentally, will not cause injury or damage.

◆ Never point a gun at anything you do not intend to shoot.

◆ Before loading (or shooting), be sure the barrel and mechanisms are clear of obstructions, which is best done by looking down from the breech end of the firearm. Even a small bit of mud, snow, or excess lubricating oil can cause increased pressures, and the barrel could bulge or burst on firing.

◆ If the noise or recoil on firing seems weak or different, stop firing the gun at once and check to be sure the barrel is not obstructed.

◆ Be sure you have the proper ammunition for the firearm you're using — and know the maximum range of your ammunition.

◆ Do not hunt if you are using alcohol, drugs, or medication, any of which may impair your judgment and dull your senses.

On the Hunt

◆ Wear hunter orange or fluorescent clothing.

◆ Wear protective shooting glasses and some form of hearing protector while shooting.

◆ When carrying a gun, follow these simple rules:
  • Keep the muzzle under control and pointed away from yourself and others.
  • Be certain the safety is ON. Don't play with the

safety by putting it on and off. Leave it on until you're ready to fire.
  • Keep your fingers outside the trigger guard and off the trigger until you are ready to shoot.
  • Unload the gun as soon as you are through hunting or shooting.

◆ Clearly identify your target before you shoot. If you are not absolutely sure of your target, do not shoot.

◆ Know what's beyond your target. For example, if you can't see what's in the distance, do not shoot at an animal standing on the horizon of a hill. Some bullets can travel several miles.

◆ Never shoot at a sound or a patch of color.

◆ When a shell does not fire, keep the muzzle pointed in a safe direction for at least forty-five seconds and then remove the cartridge.

◆ Do not climb fences or trees, cross slippery areas, or jump ditches or creeks while carrying a loaded gun. Unload the firearm first. It takes only a few seconds, and it could save someone's life. If you are hunting with a partner, hand your gun to him before crossing the obstacle.

◆ Never pull a firearm toward you by the muzzle.

◆ Carry handguns in a holster.

◆ Do not shoot at flat, hard surfaces, or at water. Bullets will ricochet off these surfaces uncontrolled. Remember, a bullet or shotgun shell is your responsibility from the instant it leaves your gun.

◆ Always shout to alert other hunters of your presence as they approach you. Never assume you are the only hunter in an area.

◆ Be especially careful at the end of the day, as you become tired and the firearm you are carrying becomes heavier. Fatigue can make you careless; if you feel tired, stop, unload your firearm, and rest.

Hunting Lessons

A trained and experienced hunting guide, Dean spends his life around lethal weapons, wild animals, and amateur hunters who have no business leaving their living rooms. But he'll tell you those forces never frightened him as much as the blizzard that nearly drowned and froze him the morning he insisted on crossing a lake to reach his duck blind. In the end, Dean recalls, it wasn't natural forces beyond his control that nearly did him in, but his own ignorance and bravado.

Hunting should be a sport, not a life-and-death mission. It can be a dangerous pastime, however, and it requires special attention. Here are some reminders:

Getting Prepared

◆ Heart attacks are a real threat. Well before the season starts, have a physical exam, and establish a workout regimen that includes stretching and endurance exercises.

◆ Wear clothing that provides a layer of insulation for warmth, is thick enough to absorb perspiration, and is designed to shed rain and cut the wind.

◆ Dress in layers. As you feel your body beginning to heat up or cool down, remove or add an outer garment. Strive for maximum comfort.

◆ Always wear a hat. It blocks the sun to help you see, and prevents heat from leaving your body.

◆ Tell someone where you plan to go, and stick with your plan. This could help in an emergency.

◆ Carry a cell phone, if available.

Master the Ups and Downs

◆ Always wear fluorescent or "hunter orange" coloring when you are moving through the timber.

◆ Never assume you're the only hunter in the area. Better to assume that every sound or movement is another hunter until you can safely identify it.

◆ Never wave, whistle, or make animal calls to alert another hunter to your presence. Always stand still and shout to reveal your presence.

◆ When hunting in a new area, use a topographical map and carry a compass or global positioning system (GPS) device. They could help you avoid getting lost or getting into dangerous circumstances.

◆ To reduce the chance of being injured by another hunter, sit at the base of a tree trunk that's wider than your body. This way, you can see an approaching hunter and you are protected from the rear.

◆ Have a plan for carrying heavy game to your vehicle. Get help if necessary. If you down an animal, you can use the GPS device to pinpoint its location.

◆ Use a flashlight when walking in the dark. This lowers the risk of a fall or being mistaken for an animal.

National figures show that falls from trees outnumber all other kinds of deer-hunting mishaps. One study found that 4 percent of these falls are fatal.

◆ If you use a tree platform, be sure it is secured. Wear a shoulder harness with a safety belt attached to the tree.

◆ Don't hunt after drinking, and don't drink in the stand.

◆ Don't trust homemade stands built by someone else, and don't trust an old one. A commercial stand manufacturer says that failures of nailed-up stands cause more than half of tree-stand injuries.

◆ Don't trust nailed-on climbing steps. Use the metal screw-in kind.

◆ Be especially careful when climbing up and down. Unload your gun, take off your backpack and other encumbrances, and raise and lower them with a cord.

◆ Take care of your gun while in the tree. Don't hang it from a twig or lean it insecurely.

◆ Dress right for stand hunting. Wind chill is worse in a tree; you can get so cold that climbing down will be risky.

Water Hazards

Many hunts require getting from one place to another by water or, in the case of duck hunting, being on the water to hunt.

◆ Do not overload a boat.

◆ Walk and move cautiously in a boat. Keep your center of gravity low. Walk one step at a time, holding on to something stationary. Do not stand up or lean over the side.

◆ Wear a life jacket on the water. It's a must.

◆ If you fall into cold water, dry off immediately. Do not let the cold seep into your system. You risk hypothermia, a dangerous cooling of the body.

◆ Carry a change of clothing in a waterproof container.

Dangerously Cold

Old Man Winter can be a brutal companion if you're not adequately prepared to keep his company.

In the U.S., about 600 people die from excessive cold each year. Hypothermia can occur when the body temperature drops below ninety-five degrees as a result of prolonged exposure to cold temperatures. In extreme cases, it can cause death.

Because the body loses heat faster than it produces it, hypothermia can take a person by surprise, making it especially dangerous.

Know the Symptoms

Cold weather, extreme dampness, and rapid loss of body heat because of clothing made wet by perspiration can all lead to hypothermia. Even prolonged exposure to relatively mild temperatures can cause some individuals to lose too much body heat. In fact, some experts say that most hypothermia cases occur in air temperatures between thirty and fifty degrees.

When you feel uncomfortably cold, you're having the first warning of hypothermia. Muscle tension, fatigue, and uncontrollable shivering may follow.

Other danger signs include poor coordination, slurred speech, and blue or pale lips or fingertips. Eventually, these symptoms lead to drowsiness and apparent exhaustion. A person who reaches this stage may be confused or irrational and insist there is nothing wrong. Don't believe it — even a healthy person can be killed by exposure in only four hours.

If you see someone with the symptoms of hypothermia, don't take no for an answer. Get the person to a shelter and seek medical attention immediately.

To Protect Yourself

A well-designed apparel system has at least three layers: underwear, insulation, and an outer shell. Each component must work with the others to prevent you from becoming wet from sweat and the elements.

◆ Begin with thermal underwear of synthetic fibers such as polypropylene. This allows perspiration to escape. Don't wear cotton next to your skin.

◆ Wool and synthetic-fiber garments are preferred for the middle layer(s) because they stay warm when wet.

◆ A waterproof windbreaker should be the outer layer. Shed the layers as you begin to perspire.

◆ Woolen socks over a polypropylene inner sock are a good combination.

◆ Up to 50 percent of body heat is lost through the head, so a hat is a must.

◆ Mittens are more effective than gloves, because they allow heat to pass among the fingers.

◆ Avoid tight-fitting clothes and boots, which can restrict circulation.

◆ Avoid overdressing. Movement generates body heat. If that heat is retained by external layers of clothing, it can cause premature fatigue and discomfort.

Note: You're probably overdressed if you don't feel slightly chilled during the first five minutes of being in the cold.

◆ Eat a good meal to have the calories necessary to keep your body warm. Take along a thermos full of coffee or hot soup.

◆ Keep dry by not working up a sweat. If you're shoveling snow, or otherwise exerting yourself, shed a layer or two of clothing to keep from perspiring.

◆ Try to keep the wind at your back, and take periodic breaks.

◆ Use the "buddy system," or let someone know where you are and when to expect you.

◆ Avoid nicotine and alcohol. They dilate the blood vessels, which increases your heat loss. Certain drugs may have the same effect — check with your doctor.

So, You Just Have to Get Out

Regardless of the weather, some hardy souls insist on frolicking in the cold. That's cool, so long as they use good judgment. Joggers and runners are at special risk of hypothermia because their movement can increase the force of cold winds against their bodies, especially when there's a lot of moisture on their skin. If you are exercising outdoors:

◆ Wear modern, synthetic long johns, which keep moisture away from your body.

◆ Walk or run against the wind at the start, so you can return home with the wind at your back.

◆ Drink enough fluids.

◆ Know the route you're planning to run.

◆ Get back before extreme fatigue sets in.

◆ Carry concentrated snack foods, such as raisins, nuts, peanut butter, chocolate, or dried fruit.

◆ Wear mittens and a polypropylene hat. Spread a thin layer of petroleum jelly on exposed skin areas.

Wheels of Misfortune

It was a typical case of "Anything you can do, I can do better." Mona had been a very good ice skater as a girl, and had even played on a few ice hockey teams. She was athletic, tough, and competitive, so, when the teenage boy next door jokingly challenged her to a roller-blade race, she quickly accepted the dare. Mona, Super Mom and editor of the local newspaper, laced on a pair of borrowed skates, took a quick practice run, and rolled to the starting line. Ten yards into the contest, she hit a rough piece of pavement and skidded to a stop on bare hands and knees, breaking her wrist in the process. Her accident didn't make the front page of her paper, and Mona felt lucky it didn't make the obituary page, either.

More than 20 million people participate in roller-blading, or in-line skating, including many adults.

In a recent year, the Consumer Product and Safety Commission (CPSC) reported that twelve in-line skaters died and over 90,000 were treated in hospital emergency rooms.

Dress for Failure

Fractures of the wrist and lower arm account for nearly half of all injuries to skaters. Lacerations, abrasions, head injuries, and concussions are also a danger. The proper equipment can reduce the danger when the inevitable spill occurs. Equipment includes:

- a helmet with a hard plastic shell and padding underneath. It should have a chinstrap, and should not block your vision or hearing. An approved bicycle helmet will do.

- elbow and knee pads designed for skating. They should have a hard-shell cover and fit snugly so they don't slide out of place.

- wrist guards. They should have a hard plastic splint on the top and bottom. Wrist guards and elbow pads help reduce the risk to these areas of the body by more than 80 percent.

- a good pair of gloves.

◆ Purchase the proper skates (or boot), based on your skating experience and exercise goals. For best results, an in-line skate boot should fit snugly, but allow for a little extra toe room in the front. Go to a store with knowledgeable salespeople.

◆ Wear a thin liner of silk or polypropylene under a medium-weight athletic sock. Thick, all-cotton socks do not keep the feet dry, and contribute to blisters and other foot problems.

Don't Skate Around the Basics

◆ Before you start, take a lesson, including how to fall safely, from a qualified instructor. Contact a local retailer for recommendations.

◆ Achieve a basic skating level before taking to the road.

◆ Skate on smooth, paved surfaces away from heavy traffic and crowds of people.

◆ Do not skate on surfaces that have water, dirt, sand, or gravel on them. You'll lose traction and control of your skates.

◆ Avoid intersections at the bottoms of hills.

◆ Do not skate at night. It's difficult to see obstacles in your path, and to be seen by others.

◆ Skate on the right side of paths, trails, and sidewalks.

◆ Warn pedestrians when you're approaching from the rear.

◆ Observe all traffic regulations.

◆ Inspect your boots each time you skate.

◆ Rotate the wheels when they begin to wear unevenly.

◆ Skate defensively, especially on streets. Skaters are more invisible and vulnerable than bicyclists.

◆ Check out a new route by bicycle or car before skating it.

Skateboard Warnings

According to the CPSC, more than 50,000 skateboarders require emergency room treatment each year. Skateboarders with less than a week of experience have the most injuries, usually due to falls.

The American Academy of Pediatrics recommends that children under ten should not use skateboards unless supervised by an adult, and children under five should never use skateboards.

◆ Learn how to fall safely.

◆ Do not ride a skateboard in the street, and *never* hitch a ride on the bumper of a moving vehicle.

◆ Check out the area for holes, bumps, rocks, and debris before you ride. Seek out parks and areas designated for skateboards.

◆ Never skate in the rain.

◆ Always skate with friends: if you are injured, you'll need help.

◆ Wear closed, slip-resistant shoes, a helmet, wrist braces, gloves, and special padding for your elbows, hips, and knees.

◆ Before using a board, check it for hazards. Have any serious defects repaired by a professional.

Putting the Nix to Spiders and Ticks

Little Miss Muffet sat on a tuffet,
Eating her curds and whey.
Along came a spider and sat down beside her,
And she landed in the hospital with a severe brown recluse bite.

Spiders, ticks, and other tiny crawly creatures can be more than a nuisance; they can be downright bad for our health. While their bites rarely cause death, they can cause incredible pain and suffering.

Dealing with Spiders

Unless you are allergic to spider venom, bites cause little harm, but the bites of the black widow and brown recluse are exceptions. These spiders prefer out-of-the-way places, under rocks, debris, and woodpiles. They also like attics, cellars, and other damp storage areas. To avoid bites:

◆ Wear work gloves when handling boxes, firewood, lumber, and other items that have been stored for a long time.

◆ Shake clothing vigorously to dislodge any spiders, and inspect clothing carefully before wearing it.

◆ Dispose of unneeded clothing, papers, and stored boxes, unless they are airtight.

◆ Clean away webbing, spiders, and eggs with a vacuum cleaner.

◆ Keep undisturbed areas of a structure as free as possible of clutter. Periodically moving stored materials and vacuuming these areas during the "disturbing" is suggested.

◆ Vacuum the floor-joist areas of the basement if possible.

◆ Use a flashlight to scan dark, musty areas before you reach into attics or crawl spaces.

◆ Many spiders may be kept out by caulking cracks and crevices on the outside of the house.

◆ The safest method for removing a spider from your skin is to *brush* it away from your body. Do not mash it against you, as it could bite.

◆ If a spider or scorpion bites you, seek medical attention immediately. You might not feel the bite, so seek emergency medical help if you notice pain, redness, and swelling on your body, along with flu-like symptoms.

Warding Off Ticks

Tick-borne infections occur in virtually every state. Lyme disease, the most common tick-borne infection, affects more than 15,000 people annually.

To avoid tick-borne illnesses:

◆ Avoid tall grass. Stay on paved or marked trails.

◆ Cover your skin whenever you're in any area that can harbor ticks. Wear long-sleeved shirts, long pants, a hat, and enclosed shoes (no sandals) with socks. Tuck shirts into pants, and pants into socks or boots.

◆ Wear light-colored clothing, so you can spot a tick on it.

◆ Spray insect repellent containing DEET on exposed skin and clothing. Follow directions carefully, particularly for children.

◆ Always check for ticks after being in wooded, swampy, or grassy areas (including golf courses). Have someone examine hard-to-see areas, like the back of your neck and scalp. For added protection, wash with a washcloth.

◆ Spray your yard with an insecticide. Follow manufacturer's instructions, or have a professional do it.

◆ Use a blanket to cover any outdoor area where you want to sit.

◆ Check your pets regularly and remove any ticks immediately.

◆ To get rid of ticks in hiding, promptly wash any clothing you've worn in the woods. Spin clothes in the dryer for at least twenty minutes.

If the Tick Bites

◆ If you find a tick on your body, remove it promptly. Here's how:

  • Using sharp, pointed tweezers, grasp the tick as close to your skin as possible;

  • Pull it away with steady pressure. Don't use alcohol, jelly, a hot match, a lighted cigarette, or anything else to remove it;

  • Apply alcohol or some other disinfectant to the area.

◆ Every day for a month, check the site where you found the tick for any unusual rashes (usually in the shape of a bull's-eye). If a rash occurs, or you have flu-like symptoms, see your doctor immediately. Also, call your doctor if you have any of these symptoms after being in tall grass. Many people are not aware of having been bitten.

Medical Alert

> **According to an article in the journal of the American Association of Retired Persons, more than 7,000 people die every year because of medication errors. Additional thousands may die due to adverse side effects from drugs.**

Patients must be very vigilant regarding their health treatment! To protect yourself and your family:

Ask the Doctor

◆ When you get a new prescription, ask your doctor to spell the name of the drug, and tell you what it looks like and what the dosage is. Have him or her briefly note the drug's purpose on the prescription form. Be sure you (and the pharmacist) can read it.

◆ Make certain you understand:
  • when to take the medication;
  • what the drug should do;
  • its generic and brand names;
  • whether it should be taken with or without food;
  • how much you should take, how often, the maximum daily dose, and what to do if you miss a dose;
  • how to administer the drug, and whether you take a pill halved or chewed, or whether it must be swallowed whole;
  • what drugs could interact;
  • what side effects may occur, and when to contact the doctor;
  • how to store the drug, and when it expires;
  • what food, beverages, drugs, or other products to avoid while taking the drug, including alcohol, caffeine, non-prescription medications, dairy products, tobacco, vitamins, and herbal products.

◆ Some people cannot tolerate standard doses of medications, but can take lower doses. Talk to your doctor if you are an older adult, have a low body weight, have a chronic medical condition, or if you are particularly sensitive to drugs.

◆ Once a year, take all your medications (including non-prescription), vitamins, and herbs to your primary doctor for an evaluation.

◆ Maintain a list of your medications, the doctors who prescribed them, the pharmacy and prescription numbers, the amount you take, the time of day you take them, and any reactions you have. Take the list with you when you see any new doctor, and when you go into the hospital. Refer to it during interviews with various health professionals, especially the anesthesiologist if you're having surgery.

Ask the Pharmacist

◆ Keep a written record of prescription information to verify that you receive the correct prescription.

◆ Choose a pharmacy that:
  • keeps comprehensive records of all your medications and allergies. This will reduce the risk of a drug conflict or adverse reaction;
  • provides printed information regarding what medical condition the drug is designed to treat, dosage instructions, side effects, as well as any food, beverage, drug, or other product interactions;
  • willingly answers questions.

◆ Check refills. If they are a different color, size, or shape, contact your pharmacist immediately.

◆ If you use a different pharmacy or provider, inform the pharmacist of other medications and products you're taking, and any allergic reactions to drugs.

Ask Yourself

◆ Educate yourself and increase your awareness of the drugs that you and your family use. Ask yourself why you're using them.

◆ Read all labels and other information, and follow all directions.

◆ For non-prescription medications, never exceed recommended doses. Choose medications by their active ingredients and dosage, not by brand name. A brand may have several products or types.

◆ Avoid taking drugs prescribed for someone else, even if you share the same symptoms.

◆ Discard drugs that are past their expiration dates. Flush them down the toilet, then rinse the container.

◆ Keep drugs in their original containers.

◆ For liquid medications, use a measuring spoon or the plastic dosing cap. Tableware spoons are not an accurate measure.

◆ Make sure you have plenty of light when you take medications.

◆ Children aren't just small adults, so never estimate the dose based on their size.

◆ Never let children take medications unsupervised.

◆ If you are pregnant or intend to become pregnant, tell your physician before taking any medicine.

◆ Be sure the hospital staff carefully checks your identification bracelet before you take any medication. Verify that all medications are correct. A companion is helpful when you're not fully alert.

Decoding Your Prescription

By convention, Latin abbreviations, other notations, and metric units are used in prescriptions. The following are some common terms:

Term	Abbr.	Meaning
ante cibum	ac	before meals
gutta	gt	drop
hora somni	hs	at bedtime
oculus dexter	od	right eye
oculus sinister	os	left eye
per os	po	by mouth
post cibum	pc	after meals
pro re nata	prn	as needed
quaque 3 hora	q3h	every three hours
quaque die	qd	every day
bis in die	bid	twice a day
ter in die	tid	three times a day
quarter in die	qid	four times a day
c̄	with	
s̄	without	
†, ††, †††		one, two, three capsules, tablets, pills
milligrams	mg	
milliliters	ml	
disp	dispense	
signa	sig	you write (doctor's labeling instructions to the pharmacist)

Waterside Safety

Dolores and Bill had planned their trip to Hawaii for five years. It was to be a second honeymoon. As promised, everything about the islands was lush and exotic, and they were having the time of their lives. On the third night, they were invited to a luau half a mile down the beach. Dressed in eveningwear, they set off along the sand, stopping now and then to wade into the shallows. In the dusk, they didn't see the waves striking the shore. A powerful rip current hit them at the knee, and pulled them out to sea. Passersby were able to save Dolores, but Bill drowned—Paradise had turned vicious.

The ocean and the Great Lakes are beautiful, but they're also dangerous. **According to the U.S. Lifesaving Association, more than seventy-five drownings and 60,000 rescues occur annually at America's beaches.**

In and Around the Water

◆ Always check with the lifeguard on water and beach conditions, and equipment restrictions, before entering the water. Swim only in areas with lifeguards on duty.

◆ Look for and obey all beach safety signals and symbols.

◆ If you're not a strong swimmer, go no more than knee deep. Poor swimmers should not swim, and should use a life jacket when wading.

◆ Never swim alone.

◆ If you get caught in a strong current, don't panic. Wave one or both hands in the air, and scream or call for help.

◆ A rip current can pull you offshore. To escape, swim parallel to shore until you're out of the current.

◆ Always wear a swimsuit if you plan to get into the water. Shorts and long pants should never be worn in the water because they retain water and restrict your movement.

◆ Don't dive into unknown water, or into shallow, breaking waves.

◆ Use swim fins and a leash when body-boarding.

◆ Keep a safe distance from piers and rocks.

◆ Learn about organisms and critters in the water: how to avoid them and what to do if you're bitten.

◆ Some beaches have sharp coral reefs close to the shoreline. Use caution when swimming in shallow reef areas.

◆ Check for glass fragments and coral. Wear foot protection to guard against sharp objects and to avoid getting burned by the sand.

◆ Don't venture too far out on rocks, where you can be surrounded by a rising tide.

◆ Check local tide tables to know when the tide will be the highest.

◆ Keep children under constant supervision.

◆ Logs are unsafe if water is near, or if they can be reached by surges. Waves can cause a log to roll, and trap or crush you.

Keep the Sun Fun

◆ Limit the time you expose your skin go the sun. Exposure to ultraviolet rays is cumulative; eventually it can lead to skin cancer.

◆ Remember, ultraviolet rays penetrate clouds, so it's possible to get burned even on overcast days.

◆ Wear a wide-brimmed hat and sunscreen with a 15-SPF or higher. Apply it at the beginning of your time in the sun. Re-apply the lotion at least every two hours, more frequently when sweating.

◆ The sun's rays are most intense between 10 A.M. and 4 P.M., so limit your exposure then. When possible, wear long sleeves and pants.

◆ Use special sunscreens for babies. Always cover the baby's head. Infants less than six months of age should stay out of the sun.

◆ Use an umbrella shade to reduce exposure and keep you cool.

◆ Drink water throughout the day. Avoid drinks containing alcohol or caffeine.

◆ Use sunglasses that block 99–100 percent of UVA and UVB light.

◆ Large, wraparound frames can protect your eyes from all angles, compared to ordinary glasses that may allow light to enter.

Drinking Problems

Suzy's parents were delighted that she had graduated from high school: next would come college, then a job, followed by marriage and children — the opportunities were endless. If there was ever a night worthy of a toast, this was it. Of course, one toast led to another as the adults celebrated. Behind the scenes, Suzy and her friends sneaked in a few toasts of their own. Later, while driving her friends home, Suzy, carried away by excitement and alcohol, took a turn too fast. The car flew off the road, killing two of her friends. Suzy's bright future was clouded forever.

All too often, alcohol plays a prominent role in our celebrations, and the results can be tragic. Here are some suggestions to keep a healthy perspective on your party attitude.

For Parents of the Teen Party Host

Mothers Against Drunk Driving (MADD) offers these suggestions for an enjoyable teen party:

◆ Set ground rules with your teen before the party. Stress shared responsibility for hosting the party. Plan the party together.

◆ Notify police when planning a large party. This will help them protect you, your guests, and your neighbors.

◆ Plan to be home, and conspicuous, during the entire party.

◆ Select a location that allows comfort and adequate supervision.

◆ Replenish the food trays and the drinks yourself. Your occasional presence will help keep a lid on unwanted activities, such as drinking or drug abuse.

◆ Discuss the legal drinking age for alcohol with your child, and be sure you both enforce the law.

◆ Alert yourself to signs of alcohol or other drug abuse by teens.

◆ Notify the parents of teens who arrive at the party drunk, or under the influence of any other drug, to ensure the teens' safe passage home.

◆ Limit the party attendance (no crashers!) and set start and ending times. Call the police at the first sign of trouble.

For Parents of Teens Attending

◆ Know where your teenager will be. Get the address and phone number of the party host.

◆ Tell your child you expect a phone call if the location is changed.

◆ Contact the parents of the party-giver to:
  • verify the occasion;
  • offer assistance;
  • explain your rules for your child, including curfew and your stand against drinking;
  • make sure a parent will be present and will actively supervise;
  • be sure alcohol and drugs will not be permitted.

◆ If you don't like the answers you're getting from the host, don't let your child go.

◆ Tell your child never to ride home with anyone who has been drinking or taking drugs. About 40 percent of all traffic fatalities are alcohol-related. During holiday periods the percentages increase to nearly 50 percent!

◆ Know how your teen will get to and from the party. If necessary, provide the transportation yourself.

◆ Establish a time your teenager should be home and enforce it.

Adult Parties

If you are the host:

◆ Establish designated drivers in advance of the party.

◆ If underage people are coming, involve them in planning alternative activities. Supervise those activities.

◆ Avoid making consumption of alcohol beverages the focus of your party.

◆ Serve foods that are rich in proteins. Eating slows the rate at which the body absorbs alcohol.

◆ Don't serve salty foods — they make people want to drink more.

◆ Measure mixed drinks with a shot glass to avoid over-pouring. Pour sensible, one-ounce drinks. Do not let guests pour their own drinks.

◆ Stop serving alcohol to any obviously intoxicated person.

◆ At least ninety minutes before the end of the party, stop alcohol service and provide alcohol-free beverages with food and desserts.

◆ Arrange a ride for people who drank too much, or invite them to spend the night.

If you are attending a party:

◆ Eat before and while you're drinking alcohol.

◆ Make your first drink a large glass of water, juice, or soda to quench your thirst. Never drink alcohol because you're thirsty — you'll drink too much, too fast.

◆ Stand away from the bar. Dance, mingle, and talk to the guests.

◆ Space your drinks to a maximum of one an hour. Alternate between alcoholic and non-alcoholic beverages.

◆ Stop drinking alcohol ninety minutes before the party is over. There's no other way to sober up. Black coffee won't do it, and neither will a cold shower or any other so-called "remedy." Only time can make you sober enough to drive safely.

◆ Be able and ready to say no if you've had enough or simply choose not to drink alcohol.

Just a Walk in the Park

What could be safer than a casual walk in the fresh, open air? When automobiles are moving in the vicinity, a lot of things are safer. If you need proof, consider this: **More than 80,000 pedestrians are injured each year by automobiles, and more than 5,000 of them die from their injuries. That's about one fatality every ninety minutes to people who probably thought they would "be right back."** And in most cases, the incident was the fault of the walker, not of the driver.

If you're walking for your health, or just to get from here to there, there are precautions to take.

Beginning Steps

◆ Before crossing a road, always stop at the curb, look left, then right, then left again before crossing.

◆ Never assume a driver will stop; make eye contact with the driver before proceeding.

◆ Walk fast, but don't run. Keep looking until you're safely across.

◆ When your view is blocked by a parked car, or when crossing between parked cars (and this is not recommended), move out slowly to where you can see traffic clearly.

◆ Leave the Walkman at home. It may put some extra bounce in your step, but it could also get you bounced into a hospital bed. You're better off tuning in to your surroundings and the dangers that exist there.

◆ If there is a sidewalk, use it.

◆ Where there are no sidewalks, always walk or run facing traffic and stay as far to the left as possible.

◆ Don't try to save a few seconds by crossing against the light.

◆ Remember, a flashing DON'T WALK light means do not begin to cross the street (especially with the growing penchant for drivers to run red lights). Pedestrians already in the street should continue walking and complete their crossing.

◆ Be alert for cars backing out of parking spaces.

◆ Certain locations require added caution:

• along high-speed highways and strip shopping areas where motorists don't expect pedestrians;

• near construction work zones. Often sidewalks are closed, and drivers are distracted. Select an alternative route;

• on rural roads where there are no sidewalks;

• train tracks, because it's difficult to judge a train's speed.

◆ If you use a motorized scooter or wheelchair, display a brightly-colored flag about five feet high.

◆ More than half of all adult pedestrians killed at night have blood alcohol levels of 0.10 percent or higher. If you drank too much, call a cab or have a friend take you home. Friends shouldn't let friends *walk* drunk, either.

Bright Ideas for Walkers

Pedestrians are more likely to be killed when visibility is poor. Fatal pedestrian crashes occur most often between 6 P.M. and 9 P.M.

◆ Wear light-colored clothing or clothes with reflective material.

◆ Carry a flashlight or light-stick at night.

◆ Cross where the lights are bright and visibility is good.

◆ Be especially alert in winter, which brings reduced visibility for pedestrians and drivers.

◆ The sun can blind drivers at dawn and sunset. Be extra careful then.

Kids, Young and Old

◆ If there's concern about being able to cross the street, wait until the light has just turned green. The first few steps into the street are the most dangerous. Drivers will have noticed you by the time you approach the other side.

◆ Stay away from traffic after taking medication that causes dizziness, blurs vision, or impairs your judgment.

◆ Keep children away from streets, driveways, and parking lots. Often children don't see motor vehicles, and drivers don't see children.

◆ When an adult is walking with a child, the adult should walk between the child and the roadway, acting as a buffer more visible to vehicles.

◆ When crossing the street with a child under ten years of age, always hold the child's hand.

Special People, Special Needs

People with impaired vision, hearing, balance, or mobility face special safety challenges that we might not have considered. Here are some things we can do to be more helpful to disabled people, whether their disability is temporary or permanent.

Vision Impairment

Whether caused by refusal to wear corrective lenses or a serious medical problem, impaired vision can lead to severe injury. However, denial is powerful, and many people refuse to acknowledge their vision is failing. But there are special precautions we can take on their behalf.

◆ Brighter lighting is generally helpful, but avoid glare, which can blind a person to a hazard.

◆ Push chairs in, close doors, keep stairs clear, and pick up toys.

◆ Show and tell the person about furniture rearrangement, and remove obstacles from pathways.

◆ Place luminous tape or directional signs on the walls, near the floor, and pointing to exits.

◆ Practice fire escape plans regularly.

◆ Store everyday items in easy-to-reach locations.

◆ Use a daily pill organizer to take medicines.

◆ Put bells on the dog and cat so their whereabouts are evident.

◆ Talk to rehabilitation professionals for more safety suggestions.

Hearing Impairment

Any hearing loss interferes with communications and can lead to safety problems. People who can't hear high-pitched warnings need alarms that they can *see*.

Honesty is the most important safety essential. Help the person realize they have a problem.

Ask an audiologist for more facts on these additional safety steps:

◆ Assign at least two people to notify a hearing-impaired person of emergency warnings. Make sure he or she understood what you said. Ask him to repeat the message.

◆ Get smoke detectors equipped with strobe lights.

◆ Arrange for lamps to flash when the doorbell or phone ring, and for other significant sounds. Get visual or vibration alarm clocks.

◆ Vibrating pagers can inform users of alarm signals and messages.

◆ Get cars outfitted with visual signals of emergency sirens.

◆ If using a phone is difficult or impossible, install a text-phone.

Mobility and Balance Impairment

Mobility impairments range from an awkward gait to quadriplegia, which can severely hinder a person's ability to escape in an emergency. To reduce the dangers:

◆ People with crutches and canes are most vulnerable to slipping or tripping. Keep floors dry and clear of obstacles, and be sure rugs or carpets are secure.

◆ Install and use handrails or grab bars everywhere necessary; e.g., bathrooms, and where one or more

steps or slopes change elevation.

◆ Learn how to fall safely. Martial-arts instructors and physical therapists are possible resources. Get a helmet if needed.

◆ Look for and eliminate hazards that could lead to serious injury in case of a fall.

◆ Wear shoes that fit well, fasten securely, and have thin, nonskid soles. Thick soles can cause falls.

◆ Use carpeting or relatively soft flooring. Ceramic tile or stone increase the consequences of a fall.

◆ Stronger muscles may reduce fall frequency and injuries. See a fitness professional for a program.

Security

Disabled people are more vulnerable to crime, and should learn and follow prevention strategies.

◆ Contact local firefighters and police to familiarize them with the situation and to request advice.

◆ Be realistic about limitations. Avoid places or situations that might be excessively risky.

◆ Install a home alarm system with a panic button.

◆ If possible, go out with a friend.

◆ Large assist dogs can be a security advantage.

◆ Take a self-defense course from an instructor who's knowledgeable about disabilities. Ask a physical therapist for recommendations.

◆ The "handicapped" symbol on license plates advertises vulnerability; use a removable placard, instead.

◆ Contact the police department to see if they have a special indication to show the driver is deaf.

◆ Look for organizations that will do a home safety inspection.

◆ In case of an emergency, always carry medical information.

This Is No Toy Story

Roxanne and her teenage friends spent the afternoon taking turns on the two-seater personal watercraft (PWC). Riding the waves and splashing around was a great way to enjoy the bay. In a moment of inattention, Roxanne and her partner fell off. Before she could get out of the water, Roxanne was struck by another PWC; she died at the scene.

PWCs are not toys, but too many people treat them as if they were. Each year, about eighty people across the country die in accidents involving personal watercraft.

Before You Go

◆ Know your craft. Read the owner's manual to learn operating techniques and to develop riding skills. Share this information with others who might ride on it.

◆ Check over the craft. Be sure:
  • the throttle and all switches are working properly;
  • the fuel and battery lines are properly connected;
  • you have enough fuel;
  • the cables and steering are functioning properly.

◆ Never exceed proper passenger weight or capacity.

◆ Have a Coast Guard-approved fire extinguisher onboard.

◆ Wear life jackets and a wetsuit.

◆ PWC riders have an increased risk of abrasions due to contact with their PWC, other vessels, docks, rocks, coral, or the water's surface, particularly as speeds increase. A wetsuit also protects you from hypothermia. Consider wearing a helmet, water-shoes, gloves, and other protective apparel. Normal swimming attire is not good enough.

◆ Know and obey navigational rules of the road and posted instructions.

◆ Practice re-boarding before going out for the first time.

◆ Know local water conditions and where the obstacles are.

The Operator

◆ Insist on training when you rent a craft. Ask questions until you're confident you know how to operate the controls. Be sure the instructor is competent to teach.

◆ Never drink and ride — at least 25 percent of all recreational boating fatalities involve alcohol.

◆ It is recommended that PWC operators be sixteen years old and have valid driver's licenses, which indicates that the operator has demonstrated some degree of maturity, responsibility, and good judgment.

◆ Parents should guide and supervise a teenager's use.

◆ Know your limits. Don't stay on the water too long; you'll become tired and more prone to accidents.

◆ Take time to master the basic techniques before attempting more difficult maneuvers.

◆ Many craft have a lanyard connected to the start/ stop switch. Never start your engine without attaching the lanyard to your life jacket or wrist.

On the Water

◆ Ride with someone nearby in case you run into trouble.

◆ Allow plenty of room to turn safely when you're near swimmers, scuba divers, surf-boarders, boats, and docks. Remember — you don't have brakes.

◆ Sailboats, and commercial and fishing vessels always have the right of way.

◆ Watch out for sail craft; they cannot maneuver as quickly as you can.

◆ Stay to the right of *oncoming* boats. They must pass on your left side. When *overtaking* a boat, pass on the right or left, but stay clear.

◆ Always stay within sight of land.

◆ Be especially alert around water skiers, since you may distract the driver or skier.

◆ Wake jumping is dangerous. You are a distraction to that boat, and a potential hazard to oncoming craft. Also, you might injure yourself or damage your boat when landing. Crossing a wake should always be done cautiously and courteously.

◆ If you lend your craft to friends, make sure they're of legal operating age for your area and know how to operate your craft and follow safe boating rules.

◆ Never operate a personal watercraft after dark.

◆ Be especially alert at dawn and dusk, when the sun's glare makes it harder to see you.

◆ Take a boating-safety course and regular refresher courses. For information, call the U.S. Coast Guard Information Line, (800) 368-5647, or visit www.uscgboating.org.

Some Serious Pet Peeves

Ryan's family had a cat, two dogs, a rabbit, and a parakeet. Then, his teenaged sister brought home a pet iguana. During a brief time, young Ryan was scratched by the cat, pounced on by the male dog and had a rib cracked, bitten by the female dog protecting her puppies, and messed on by the parakeet. He then contracted a mild case of infectious diarrhea from the new reptile. Bruised and battered, but undaunted, the ten-year-old adventurer stands ready to offer more pets a home. His parents might want to nix that idea.

We love our pets, and we endure a certain amount of aggravation and inconvenience for the pleasure of their company. However, we should not have to sustain injury or disease. Here are a few suggestions for sharing a world with animals.

Dog Bites Man

Each year, nearly 5 million Americans are bitten by dogs: approximately 800,000 seek medical care, and twenty die. Knowing that:

- Stay away from a dog that looks frightened or angry.

- Do not pet a dog that is chained or alone.

- Never pet or run up to a strange dog.

- Avoid running past a dog.

- Do not yell at a dog, or sneak up behind it. Frightened dogs will bite out of fear.

- Don't disturb a dog that's sleeping, eating, or caring for puppies.

◆ Never grab anything away from a dog. It feels possessive about its toys, food, and bones, and is willing to fight to keep them.

◆ Dogs are protective of their owner, yard, and house. Respect their territorial instincts.

◆ Ask permission before handling someone else's dog. If you receive permission, let the dog come to you. Speak quietly. If the animal is friendly, let him sniff the back of your hand to get to know you. Then stroke him under the chin.

◆ Always stay calm and quiet around new animals.

◆ Teach children to play gently with a dog. Never leave children alone with a dog.

If you encounter an angry dog:

◆ Do not stare it in the eyes.

◆ Try to remain motionless until the dog moves away, then walk away slowly, sideways. Do not turn your back on the dog.

◆ Be firm. Say, "No!" to the dog, and act as if you are in control of the situation.

If that fails and you are attacked:

◆ "Feed" him your jacket, purse, or anything else.

◆ Curl up in a ball on the ground and protect your face.

◆ After the attack, report the bite and seek medical attention.

Little Tabby

◆ The risk of infection from cat bites is high. See a doctor for antibiotic treatment. Cat scratches require careful monitoring.

◆ Since cats can cause allergic reactions, keep them away from areas where you spend a lot of time. If symptoms persist, consult a veterinarian for preparations that can be applied to the cat.

Our Pets Have Pests

◆ Keep your cat indoors, and humanely confine your dog to reduce exposure to diseases and parasites carried by other animals.

◆ Wash your hands thoroughly after handling pets or cleaning up after them.

◆ Children can become very ill if they eat dirt or sand contaminated with infected dog or cat feces. Keep kids away from areas with possible feces. Cover sandboxes when not in use.

◆ To protect from infectious diseases, such as diarrhea or salmonellosis, use gloves when cleaning litter boxes and bird and reptile cages. Never wash them in the sink.

◆ Pregnant women and people with compromised immune systems should not change cat litter, and should avoid contact with soil or sand to avoid toxoplasmosis, which is transmitted through cat feces and can cause birth defects.

◆ Reptiles harbor salmonella, which can be very dangerous for children under five, the elderly, pregnant women, and people with compromised immune systems.

◆ When cleaning accumulated bird droppings, wear gloves and masks that prevent breathing dust. Wear gloves when cleaning a bird feeder or bath.

◆ Follow your veterinarian's advice about examinations and vaccinations.

While You're Joggin'... Use Your Noggin

Susan was a slave to her schedule: rain or shine, she laced on her running shoes, and set out on her daily jog. Like clockwork, she left at the same time, ran the same route, and arrived home at the same time. And the schedule that gave Susan comfort gave the mugger opportunity. Susan knew there was trouble the moment he pulled his car beside her at the curb and asked for directions. She kept running; he kept following. This day belonged to Susan, though: a mounted policeman crossed her path, and she yelled for help. The car sped off, but was caught two blocks later. The driver, wanted for armed robbery and rape, admitted that he had singled out Susan because he knew when and where to find her.

On Your Mark

◆ If you are a new runner, visit your physician for a complete medical examination if you have high blood pressure or lipids; a personal or family history of health problems; or if you are over thirty-five years of age, overweight, physically inactive and easily fatigued, or a smoker.

◆ Get fit before starting to run. Consult a medical professional for strengthening exercises and stretches for running.

◆ Warm up before you run. Afterward, cool down to allow your body a gradual return to normal.

Plan Carefully

◆ Choose a safe time and place to run. Walk the route first.

◆ If possible, run on grass or dirt. Knee injuries can occur if you run on hard surfaces.

◆ Avoid running on roadways. However, if you must run there:

  • Avoid peak traffic hours.

  • Run on the shoulder facing traffic at all times.

  • Obey all traffic signals.

  • Do not run on snow or ice-covered roads — automobile drivers have enough distractions.

◆ Wear light-colored clothing at dawn or dusk, and bright clothes in daytime.

◆ Alter your route. Don't be predictable, allowing someone to assume you'll pass by at a certain time. Think of Susan.

◆ If you must run at night or in inclement weather, choose well-lighted, populous areas. Wear highly visible white or reflective clothing. To improve your chances of being seen, carry a flashlight.

◆ Save the safest area of your route for the end of your run. You're most fatigued then and less able to deal with a crisis situation. Reserve some energy for emergencies.

◆ Make eye contact with drivers before crossing in front of a car, even when you have the right of way.

◆ Avoid running on narrow, twisting, or hilly roads with no shoulders. You are hard to see there, and, when two cars approach each other, a hazardous situation occurs.

◆ Carry personal identification, including the name and phone number of the person to contact in an emergency, and important medical information, such as blood type or allergies.

◆ Join a running association to get training tips.

Stay Alert at All Times

◆ Never run with headphones.

◆ Avoid running near doorways, alleys, or dense shrubs.

◆ Always tell someone where you'll be running and when you'll return. Better yet, run with a friend.

◆ If you use a jogging path, run during the popular hours.

◆ Do not wear bright or expensive jewelry. It can attract thieves.

◆ Ignore verbal harassment.

◆ Do not daydream. Run with your head up. Be aware of your surroundings.

◆ Know the places where you could get help if you needed it.

◆ Avoid areas with aggressive dogs. The best way to treat a barking dog is to act as if you are ignoring it, but stay alert for an attack.

◆ Do not run between a dog and its owner, especially a child.

◆ If you suspect that a car is following you, turn back and run the other way. If you suspect someone is following you, draw attention to yourself: don't hesitate to holler, "I'm being followed!"

Gifts That Keep On Giving

Having trouble selecting the perfect gift for the hard-to-please wife, husband, aunt, or son? Does your mom return every birthday gift you ever buy her? Never see your brother in the silk necktie you bought him for Christmas? Well, there's a solution. Instead of trying to figure out what they want, give them what they need. Following is a list of practical products that might not exactly tickle the cockles of your sister's heart, but will help keep her and her loved ones safe. Isn't that gift enough? (We don't recommend specific brands or prices — we'll leave those choices up to you.)

Detectors and Lighting

◆ *Smoke detectors.* Most fires occur at night while people are asleep. A smoke detector on each floor and outside each bedroom is a must.

◆ *Carbon monoxide detectors.* Like smoke, carbon monoxide is a lethal killer that sneaks up on its victims, often from faulty heaters, furnaces, and stoves. In fact, hundreds of people a year die of accidental poisoning, and thousands end up in the hospital from this odorless, colorless, and tasteless gas. Detectors are best placed outside the bedroom.

◆ *Flashlights.* They come in all sizes and powers. A powerful one that lights up a whole room is very useful during electrical outages. There should also be one in the glove compartment of each car or truck.

◆ *Nightlights.* Simple and inexpensive, they can prevent dangerous falls during the night. They're especially needed near stairs and places where children and elders are likely to roam.

◆ *Emergency light*s. They go on when the power goes off.

Upstairs, Down, and All Around

◆ *Fire extinguishers.* It's hard to go wrong with a multipurpose type A-B-C fire extinguisher with a UL listing. They're effective for kitchen, garage, and house fires.

◆ *One-step stool.* These are much safer than climbing on a table or chair to get to those hard-to-reach closets, cabinets, and light fixtures.

◆ *Safety goggles.* For the man or woman who works around flying debris in the basement, garage, or garden. They're a must around power machinery, like saws, leaf blowers, and edgers.

◆ *Hearing protection.* Great for woodworkers, snowmobilers, hunters, target shooters, attending loud concerts, and mowing the lawn.

◆ *First-aid kit.* Buy a good one that can be used for travel or in the home. You can even personalize, matching the contents to the lifestyle of the recipient: insect repellent for the hiker, for example, or an icepack for the weekend athlete.

◆ *Survival kit.* A good one can be used in the larger emergencies, such as storms, earthquakes, or prolonged power outages. A kit should include water, tools, a battery-operated radio and flashlight, plenty of fresh batteries, and bedding. You can also add containers, nonperishable food, and the aforementioned first-aid kit.

◆ *Rubber-suction bathmats.* These are very important in stalls and tubs to prevent falls. A nonskid rug outside the tub will prevent slips when the bather steps to the floor.

◆ *Grab bars.* Again for the bathroom, to help the bather get into and out of the tub or shower safely.

◆ *Fire escape ladders.* These chain ladders are stored under a bed or in a closet. Each upper-level room should have one.

◆ *Child-resistant locks.* They come in a variety of sizes and functions, from locks for cabinets, to latches for toilet seats.

◆ *Ground fault circuit interrupters.* These are essential for electrical outlets near water.

◆ *Electrical outlet covers.* These prevent children from poking any item into an open socket.

◆ *Safety gates.* They'll protect toddlers from dangers on the stairs.

◆ *Anti-scald devices.* They stop water flow when the temperature exceeds 115° F; particularly useful when children are around.

◆ *Disability aids.* There are many devices to help people with impaired sensory, speech, mobility, or mental ability, whether temporary or permanent.

◆ *Highway emergency kit.* A great help in those nerve-wracking breakdowns that can occur anytime.

Shopper Beware

As Anita approached the escalator during the holidays, she noticed a little girl standing by herself, apparently hesitant to get on. The girl's father was at the top of the escalator with another child in a stroller. Anita took the girl's hand and helped her onto the escalator. As they neared the top, the child suddenly bolted for her father. Anita hadn't been holding the rail tightly because she had a package in her hand. The girl's unexpected movement caused Anita to lose her balance and fall backward. Fortunately, its safety mechanism stopped the escalator, and the heavy coat Anita was wearing cushioned her fall. She survived to shop another day.

As with other routine activities, shopping has its hazards. To confine the damage to your wallet and not your person, here are a few things to consider.

In the Parking Lot

Just parking your car in a busy shopping mall parking lot can be a high-risk adventure. To protect yourself:

◆ Go slow. Drive defensively and be patient.

◆ Watch for illuminated taillights to spot cars pulling out.

◆ Improper backing ranks as the top cause of parking lot mishaps. To back safely:

• Allow sufficient space when you pull into the spot. When your vehicle is wedged between other vehicles, you have less room for your exit maneuver and your vision is obscured.

• Avoid parking beside high-silhouette vehicles.

• Turn your head to watch where you're going and what's coming. Don't rely on your side or rearview mirrors.

• Stop once after you begin backing, to double-check that no pedestrians or vehicles are approaching.

◆ Follow the arrows that direct flow down the parking aisles. It will be easier to steer into parking spaces, and you won't surprise others who are backing up.

◆ Do not cut between unoccupied spaces.

◆ Be prepared to yield the right of way.

◆ Always assume the pedestrian does not see you. Without direct eye contact, you can't be sure. Be extra-careful at night.

◆ Drive no faster than five to ten miles an hour in parking areas, even relatively empty ones.

◆ Use your turn signals.

Walking To and From

◆ Try to park in well-lighted areas, as close to the front door of the store as possible.

◆ Avoid shopping alone.

◆ If you're worried about walking to your car alone, ask a security guard or a store employee to accompany you.

◆ Have your keys in your hand before you exit the store.

◆ Body language is important: look confident and aware of your surroundings, as opposed to preoccupied, with your head down and overloaded with packages.

◆ Glance under the car as you approach it. Check the backseat before you enter.

◆ Lock the doors immediately once you're inside.

◆ Be particularly aware of your surroundings while using an ATM.

◆ If accosted by a robber, scream.

◆ On icy surfaces, wear shoes with good traction, and look where you're going.

Inside the Store

Escalators

◆ Do not place packages on the steps or balance them on the handrails.

◆ Don't take carts, strollers, or wheelchairs on an escalator.

◆ Never allow children to ride an escalator unattended. Do not let them sit or drag their feet along an escalator's side; a shoe can get caught between the step and the side panel.

◆ Hold on to the handrail.

◆ If your hands are full, take the elevator.

Shopping Carts

Each year, there are about 25,000 trips to emergency rooms due to falls from shopping carts, most of them involving young children. These are serious injuries: concussions, fractures, and occasional fatalities.

To avoid these injuries:

• Use a backpack to carry your child.

• Shop where they have supervised play areas.

• Have your child wear a safety belt in the cart. Strapped-in children can still be subject to injuries from tip-over.

• Don't let kids hang on the carts.

Carts with infant carriers are more likely to tip over due to their high center of gravity.

Made in the Shade

When it came to working in the sun, Ray had a lot going for him: he was Mediterranean, with a dark complexion, brown eyes, and coal-black hair, and his skin was thick and rugged. Ray was so tough, in fact, that he refused to apply a sunscreen, choosing instead to let his skin "breathe out" the heat. Despite his many physical advantages, Ray's mental "toughness" worked against him, and by middle age he had lost both his ears to skin cancer. Now, he tells anyone who'll listen to avoid the sun and use the maximum-strength sunscreen.

According to the Skin Cancer Foundation, over a million new cases of skin cancer are reported in the U.S. each year, and more than 8,000 Americans will die. Studies show that 20 percent of Americans will develop some form of skin cancer during their lifetime.

No one can be outdoors without risk, but the people most at risk have fair skin; red, light brown or blond hair; blue, gray, or green eyes; freckles; and large, numerous, unusual, or changing moles. They don't tan easily, often burn badly, and may have a family history of melanoma. As children or youths, they had a record of painful or blistering sunburns.

Basic Protection

To protect yourself, the Skin Cancer Foundation recommends that you:

◆ Avoid direct exposure to the sun from 10 a.m. to 4 p.m.

◆ Limit your time in the sun, regardless of the hour or season.

◆ Apply sunscreen liberally a half-hour before going out. For an average-sized person, that's enough to fill a shot-glass.

◆ Use a sunscreen with an SPF (sun protection factor) of 15 or higher. Be sure it protects against UVA and UVB rays.

◆ Reapply sunscreen every sixty to ninety minutes, when you come out of the water, and after you perspire.

◆ Cover up with tightly woven clothing, a hat with a brim at least four inches wide, and sunglasses.

◆ Seek the shade.

◆ Stay away from tanning parlors and artificial tanning devices.

◆ Be careful around highly reflective surfaces, such as water, sand, snow, and concrete. Their glare can nearly double your exposure to the sun's rays.

◆ Plan sun-smart activities.

◆ Use sunglasses that protect against both UVA and UVB rays.

◆ Some prescription and non-prescription medications, herbs, and vitamins increase sensitivity to UV light. Check with a doctor or pharmacist.

Kid Alert

◆ Regular use of a 15-SPF sunscreen throughout childhood and adolescence may reduce the risk of the most common skin cancers by almost 80 percent.

◆ Use special sunscreens for babies. All babies should wear hats.

◆ Never expose children under the age of six months to the sun, nor use sunscreen on them.

Heightened Self-awareness

◆ Get familiar with your skin and your pattern of moles, freckles, and "beauty marks." Be alert to changes in the number, size, shape, and color of pigmented areas. If you see any changes, call your dermatologist.

◆ About 80 percent of skin cancers develop on the head and neck. However, check your entire body often for any changes or suspicious spots. Warning signs include:

Asymmetry: One half of a mole doesn't match the other half.

Border irregularity: Ragged, notched, or blurred edges.

Color: Changes in color from black to brown to red, often with a combination of other colors; or, a spot or sore that continues to itch, hurt, crust, scab, erode, or bleed.

Diameter: Any mole or spot that grows larger than one-fourth of an inch (size of a pencil eraser).

◆ Perform monthly self-exams. Use a hand-held mirror to check hard-to-see areas, e.g., your toes, and the soles of your feet.

◆ Have a total-body skin exam by a qualified skin specialist regularly.

◆ For more information, contact the Skin Cancer Foundation at (800) SKIN490, or visit www.skincancer.org.

Sleepless in America

It was Jake's first real job. The pay was good, his co-workers were fun, but the shift-work schedule was grueling. He'd been warned of the toll it could take on his system, but he was young and energetic. He plunged into that first midnight shift with no preparation, and by 4 A.M. was barely awake. Jake struggled through the next three hours and stumbled to his car in a haze. He got halfway home before he ran off the road into a pasture. The shock woke him briefly, and he pulled into a filling station and slept until he was alert enough to make his way home. Being unprepared was a mistake he only made once.

Sleeplessness can be dangerous to our physical and mental health. When our bodies need sleep, we are less alert, attentive, and productive, and at higher risk for mistakes and injuries. If you have trouble staying alert during a dull or routine situation, you're probably not getting enough sleep.

It's estimated that at least 1,500 people die in fatigue-related crashes each year. A recent National Sleep Foundation poll found that more than 60 percent of American adults have sleeping problems; one-third are so sleepy during the day that it interferes with their daily activities.

Pillow Talk

Sleep needs per night vary, but most adults need about eight hours; teens nine hours or more; and children eight to nine hours.

These tips from the National Sleep Foundation can help you get the shut-eye you need:

◆ Avoid stimulants, such as caffeine and nicotine, in the late afternoon and evening.

◆ Although alcohol is a depressant, it interferes with sleep during the night and can wake you early.

◆ Check your medications to see if they could be keeping you awake.

◆ Avoid heavy foods and spicy foods, such as pizza, tacos, hamburgers, etc. at night. Carbohydrates, such as pasta, breads, cereals, and soups, are easier to digest.

◆ Exercise regularly, but not within three hours of bedtime.

◆ Establish a regular bedtime routine, such as taking a warm bath.

◆ Associate your bed with sleep — no work or TV.

◆ Keep a regular schedule. Go to bed and get up at the same time every day, during both weekdays and weekends, even if you had trouble sleeping the night before. This will help you develop a sleep-wake rhythm.

◆ If you can't get to sleep after about twenty minutes, get up and find a relaxing activity, such as listening to soothing music or reading, until you feel sleepy. Clear your mind. Don't use the time to work out your daily problems. Milk, which contains tryptophan, really does help you go to sleep.

◆ A fifteen-to-twenty-minute nap can improve alertness, sharpen memory, and briefly reduce the symptoms of fatigue.

◆ If you have trouble sleeping for several weeks, or if you're sleepy during the day, consult your doctor or a sleep-disorder specialist.

Problems with Shift Work

About 25 million Americans are rotating-shift workers. Tips for shift workers include:

◆ The drive home is particularly dangerous. Carpool to help stay awake. At the first sign of drowsiness, stop and walk around.

◆ Eat a light meal when you get home, and get to sleep as soon as possible. Perform chores when you're refreshed.

◆ Schedule your sleep, and inform others of your schedule. Keep sleep a priority.

◆ Make the room where you are sleeping pitch-black. Use dark shades, or hang heavy, lined curtains to cut the room light. Use earplugs and a sleep mask.

◆ Block out background noises by turning on a fan, air conditioner, or other source of "white noise."

◆ Keep the room temperature between sixty-five and seventy degrees.

◆ Turn off the phone and doorbell ringers. Use an answering machine.

◆ A short nap before starting a night shift can be beneficial.

◆ Avoid using caffeine to keep you awake, especially when you plan to sleep after your shift.

◆ For more information, contact the National Sleep Foundation at (888) NSF-SLEEP, or visit www.sleepfoundation.org.

Shoosh! Shoosh! Ouch!

The tragic deaths of Sonny Bono and Michael Kennedy remind us that sliding down the side of a mountain, like any recreational activity, must be approached with safety in mind. **Each year, approximately thirty people die while skiing, and 135,000 are injured.** The good news is, serious injuries are rare among America's millions of skiers and snowboarders. The better news is, almost all of these injuries can be avoided.

Getting Ready

◆ Get in shape and learn how to warm up. If you don't have a regular workout routine, exercise four to six weeks before you ski. Don't expect to ski yourself into shape.

◆ Use the proper equipment. Buy or rent from experts who can instruct in its proper usage. If you own equipment, have a professional check it at the beginning of each season.

◆ Before starting, take lessons from a qualified instructor. Learn how to fall safely.

◆ If you're at the intermediate level, take more lessons before you move to advanced terrain.

◆ Ask an expert to adjust the setting of the bindings according to your height, weight, and skill level. Too tight and the skis won't fall off when you fall; too loose and a ski might come off underneath you.

◆ Dress in layers. Wear a waterproof, wind-resistant shell. Invest in waterproof mittens or gloves and a warm hat.

◆ Wear eye protection designed for skiing.

◆ Boots should fit snugly in the heel and around the ankle, but allow for some toe movement.

◆ **According to the American Medical Association, nearly 3,500 potentially serious head injuries each year are related to snow skiing.** Wear a helmet. Helmets protect the wearer from some injuries, but they provide limited protection to skiers moving at higher speeds. That's why experts stress that the first line of defense is skiing responsibly.

◆ Ski sober. Liquor dulls your abilities and dims your judgment.

◆ Wear sun protection. The sun reflects off the snow and is stronger than you think, even on cloudy days.

Downhill Etiquette

The National Ski Areas Association publishes *Your Responsibility Code* for skiers. For more education materials, call (303) 987-1111, or visit www.nsaa.org.

1. Always stay in control, and be able to stop or avoid other people or objects.

2. People ahead of you have the right of way. It's your responsibility to avoid them.

3. You must not stop where you obstruct a trail, or are not visible from above.

4. Whenever starting downhill or merging into a trail, look uphill and yield to others.

5. Always use devices to help prevent runaway equipment.

6. Observe all posted signs and warnings. Keep off closed trails and out of closed areas.

7. Prior to using any lift, you must have the knowledge and ability to load, ride, and unload safely.

Additional tips:

◆ Know your limits. One study found novices are ten times more likely to be injured than experts.

◆ Don't overdo it. You're most vulnerable at the end of the day, when fatigue begins to set in.

◆ Most ski injuries occur when skiers reach high speeds and lose control. Make round, continuous turns to stay in control. Don't ski on a slope that scares you.

◆ When possible, keep ten feet or more between you and other skiers.

◆ If you pass another skier, shout, "On your right!" or "On your left!"

◆ Give skiers with disabilities a lot of space.

◆ At the bottom of the slope, move out of the way as quickly as possible.

◆ Trail and slope conditions vary constantly. Ski the reality of the situation, not your memory of it.

◆ Be careful not to become dehydrated. Drink water frequently.

◆ To avoid hypothermia, go into the lodge to warm up periodically.

◆ Avoid skiing alone. If you do go out alone, tell someone your plans.

Snowboarding

About 30,000 snowboarding injuries are treated in emergency rooms each year. Almost half of these injuries occur during the first three attempts at the sport.

◆ Take lessons before you begin.

◆ Practice skier's etiquette tips.

◆ Wear a helmet.

Ice And Snow?
Away We Go!

The elements were ripe for disaster. Following a snowstorm, Rick and Josh decided to take a late-night ride on their snowmobiles. Both were drunk, and the snowmobiles didn't have adequate lights. Intoxicated by weather, alcohol, and high speed, it wasn't long before Josh struck a rut in the road and collided with Rick. Both suffered broken bones and cuts. The snow stayed around for weeks, but Rick and Josh couldn't enjoy it.

Each year, snowmobiling results in more than 100 deaths, and over 10,000 injuries requiring emergency room treatment. The American Academy of Pediatrics has said that operating snowmobiles is inappropriate for children under sixteen. To stay safe on your ride:

The Human Element

◆ Learn safe snowmobiling procedures by taking a course, or attending a clinic sponsored by your local snowmobiling association.

◆ Inexperienced drivers should be especially careful, as should those driving new or unfamiliar machines.

◆ Never ride alone.

◆ Ride to the right, and use hand signals.

◆ Drinking and snowmobiling don't mix. Alcohol slows reaction time and impairs perception.

◆ Stay alert at all times, and drive defensively. The combination of wind, sun, glare, vibration, motion, and cold can cause fatigue.

Most snowmobile injuries involve collisions, especially when driving on or beside public roads. The loud noise of most snowmobiles makes it hard to hear other vehicles.

◆ Wear an approved safety helmet, ear protection, eye protection, and possibly a face shield. This also applies to your passenger.

◆ To combat glare on bright, sunny days, wear goggles with dark-colored lenses.

◆ Wear warm, windproof clothing, and dress in layers. Check for frostbite frequently.

◆ Do not wear long scarves or loose-fitting apparel that could get caught in the vehicle's moving parts.

◆ Check the weather forecast.

◆ Carry a cell phone for emergencies. Consider using a GPS (Global Positioning Satellite) receiver.

Proper Operation

◆ Know your snowmobile and become familiar with its operation.

◆ Keep the snowmobile in good working condition at all times. Follow maintenance schedules, and have a safety inspection regularly.

◆ Be sure all lights are clean and working. Keep them on at all times.

◆ Always carry a flashlight, spare bulbs and parts, and a toolkit.

◆ Never have the engine running while the hood is open.

◆ Be extra-cautious when riding at night. Don't over-drive your lights.

◆ Never tailgate, or carry more than one passenger.

◆ Passengers must keep their feet on the running boards and maintain a firm grasp on the passenger strap or grips, or the driver.

◆ Do not jump your snowmobile.

◆ Snowmobiles are more likely to turn over at high speeds. Drive cautiously.

◆ Support your weight on your feet, as if posting a horse by standing on the stirrups. This will help you keep control and absorb jolts.

Know Where You're Going

◆ Know the rules of the local trails and community. Many states prohibit snowmobiles on public roads, and have minimum age requirements.

◆ Let friends and/or local authorities know your intended journey and when you plan to return.

◆ Make a careful study for hazards in the terrain you'll be riding.

◆ Know what trail signs mean, and follow the directions they give.

◆ Stay on established trails to reduce your exposure to hazards.

◆ Avoid road traveling. The snowmobile is not designed to operate or turn on pavement. When crossing a road, make a full stop before proceeding.

◆ Give a wide berth to fence posts and telephone poles.

◆ Be alert for hidden wires, especially in areas that may have been farmed at one time or another.

◆ Do not ride on railroad tracks.

◆ Traveling frozen lakes and rivers can be fatal. Avoid waterways.

◆ If you must cross ice, be absolutely sure of its thickness. Never cross in a single file. Allow plenty of room for stopping and turning, especially at night.

Planning for a Rainy Day

It started out as a simple trip to the grocery store, but ended up in terror. Heading out in the dark on a rain-swept night, the three young people in rural Missouri never saw the rushing water that had risen treacherously from the creek bed to swamp the narrow road ahead. Their car was immediately caught in the current and swept downstream. Two of the passengers managed to escape the sinking vehicle, but the driver could not get free and drowned. "We never saw the water," one of the survivors marveled. "It just blended in with the color of the road."

While storms are necessary to our existence, they also present a threat to it. Still, there are steps we can take to outwit the forces of nature.

Thunderstorms and Lightning

Lightning kills more than seventy-five Americans a year, and can strike ten miles from the rain area. If you can hear thunder or see lightning, you are already at risk. During an electrical storm:

- Get inside a home, large building, or automobile (with the windows rolled up).

- Stay away from open doors and windows, plumbing, fireplaces, and all metal objects.

- Don't use plug-in electrical equipment, such as hair dryers, toothbrushes, or electric razors.

- Don't take a bath or shower.

◆ Do not use the telephone, except in an emergency.

◆ If you are caught outside:

• In a group of people, spread out to minimize potential injuries.

• Avoid being in or near picnic shelters, baseball dugouts, bleachers, or metal fences.

• Avoid hilltops and tall objects, such as isolated trees or poles.

• In the open, seek a low area, squat with your hands on your knees, and keep twice as far from nearby trees as the trees are tall.

• Get off golf courses, athletic fields, tennis courts, bicycles, and mowers. Remove shoes with metal cleats.

• Get out of the water and off small boats.

• In a forest, find a low area under a thick growth of small trees.

Tornado Warning

Over 1,000 tornadoes strike the U.S. each year, killing about seventy people and injuring hundreds more. In a house or apartment:

◆ Go to a basement if one is available. Seek shelter under sturdy furniture, a workbench, or a stairwell. Cover your head (keep a helmet handy in your home or basement).

◆ In homes without basements, take cover in the center of the house. Go to a small room on the lowest floor, preferably one without windows, or a closet or hallway, or hide under heavy furniture against a strong inside wall. Put as many walls as possible between you and the storm.

◆ The National Weather Service (NWS) recommends keeping all windows closed.

◆ Draw blinds and shades over windows to reduce glass damage.

While only 5 percent of Americans live in mobile homes, about 45 percent of people killed in tornadoes were in mobile homes when the twisters hit. The best advice:

◆ Evacuate your mobile home and seek shelter in a building.

◆ If necessary, find a low spot, such as a ditch or ravine.

Flash Floods

Flash floods and river floods have become the biggest weather-related killers across the U.S., causing about 100 deaths annually.

◆ Do not camp near small streams. Rain upstream can cause a flash flood. Camp on higher ground.

◆ Pay attention to signs warning of areas prone to flash floods.

◆ Do not try to cross a flowing stream on foot if the water is above your knees.

◆ It only takes two feet of water to make a car float. If your car stalls, abandon it immediately and move to higher ground.

◆ Be very cautious at night, when it's harder to see flood dangers.

◆ Never try to cross rushing water. If you must cross standing water, be sure the water is below your floorboards. Drive slowly so you don't create waves.

More Survival Tips

◆ Buy and use a NOAA Weather Radio for continuous broadcasts of weather information from the NWS.

◆ For more suggestions, visit www.fema.gov/impact/tipsheets.

The American Meteorological Society provided some information.

Street Smarts

Kevin was in a great mood. He'd had a few drinks, danced for hours, and exchanged phone numbers with a pretty woman. Things couldn't be better. His head swimming with excitement, he left the nightclub alone just past midnight and walked slowly to his car. It was a perfect summer night. The moon and stars were out — and so was the armed robber who popped from the shadows to rob Kevin of his wallet, hitting the former football player in the face with a gun and knocking him to the ground. Kevin admits he let his guard down that night, and vows he'll be more attentive to his surroundings and his personal safety in the future. He's lucky to have a second chance.

Walking Tips

◆ Look aggressive. Walk confidently and briskly. Act like you know what you're doing. Your body language should say, "Don't mess with me." Attackers select people who look vulnerable.

◆ Know your route, where to go for help, and areas where someone could lurk.

◆ Stay alert. Be aware of your surroundings. If your intuition tells you something is wrong, it probably is. Leave immediately.

◆ Make eye contact with people as you walk.

◆ If a stranger approaches, don't be polite. If the person persists or asks for money, the time, or directions, tell him to call the police for help. Briskly walk away.

◆ Do not walk alone, especially at night or in poorly lighted areas. Wear tennis shoes or flats.

◆ If you think someone is following you, cross to the other side of the street and change directions several times, or step into an open business or other safe haven. Do not go home, which lets the person know where you live.

◆ Avoid people loitering on the street or near buildings.

- Don't flash cash or expensive jewelry. Keep your money and credit cards in your front pockets, or carry a "fanny pack."

- Cooperate with an armed robber. Don't make any quick movements, and limit eye contact. In gun and knife robberies, 95 percent of the people who give up their property without resisting are not injured, and very few suffer serious injuries.

- Carry your purse close to your body. If someone tries to grab your purse, let it go.

- Some experts suggest throwing the money in one direction and running in the opposite direction.

- Try not to carry a lot of packages at one time. It makes you an easy target, and vulnerable.

- Carry a whistle around your wrist or on your key chain, and blow it loudly if you feel threatened.

- A set of keys, one protruding from between each finger, can be an effective weapon.

- If you suspect someone is threatening you, make a scene immediately. Most women who fight off assailants do so in the first moments of attack.

- Don't expect bystanders to help you; they often won't. If you are accosted, don't just yell, "Help!" Instead, shout "Fire," or "Call 9-1-1." That gives people something positive and specific to do.

- Where there is apparent danger, running and yelling are two of the most common and successful self-defense tactics.

In Your Car

- Keep your vehicle running well, and the gas tank above a quarter full to avoid running out of gas in a dangerous location.

- Park in well-lighted areas that are easily accessible. Check the backseat and under your car before entering.

- Don't be a "pattern parker." Vary your routine so you don't become an easy target.

- Have your keys ready in your hand as you approach your car. Immediately lock the doors and windows.

- Consider installing a car alarm that can be set off remotely.

- Car phones are another important security measure.

- Keep your purse out of sight.

- At stoplights, leave space between you and the car in front of you for a quick escape.

- Don't travel unfamiliar routes at night.

- Don't leave your car if you are bumped from behind or someone says one of your tires is flat. Once you leave your car you are open for attack. Instead, drive to a well-lighted service station or local police department.

- If in doubt, tell a police officer who has stopped you that you wish to drive to a safe, lighted location where other people are before talking.

- *Never* get into a car with an assailant. It's the worst possible situation. Do anything to avoid it: run, fight, scream.

H-2-oh-oh!

Jeb was going to take his daughter, Denise, trout fishing with him for the first time. Jeb wanted her first fishing experience to be a memorable one, which meant wading to his favorite spot on the far side of a fast, shallow river. Halfway across, Jeb stepped into a hole, and Denise slipped from his grasp. She was immediately swept downstream, but Jeb was a loving and careful parent, so Denise was wearing a life jacket. She washed safely ashore, a little bruised but intact. Before she had caught one trout, her first fishing trip turned out to be a most memorable day, indeed.

> **According to the American Red Cross, every year, nearly 4,000 people die by drowning. Most drowning deaths are the result of sudden, unintentional entry into the water. If you're going to pursue any activity in or around water, there are some things you want to do and others you want to avoid doing.**

Let's Start with some Classic DO's

◆ Take swimming lessons from a qualified water safety instructor.

◆ Make safety a top priority when choosing a place for recreation.

◆ Know and obey the posted safety rules. Learn where the lifeguards are, and where to find rescue equipment. Keep a cell phone handy.

◆ Always wear a life jacket when boating, playing in a river, or fishing near deep water.

◆ Be cautious in murky water. It may conceal dangerous objects on river or lake bottoms, as well as sharp drop-offs.

◆ Wade or slowly enter feet first into unfamiliar waters (or familiar waters the first time each trip).

◆ Stay out of water that feels too cold. The shock of cold water to the system can cause hypothermia and render a swimmer unconscious in minutes.

◆ Stay close to shore. River currents are deceptively strong. Try to swim in river bends or backwaters, where currents are weaker.

◆ Check the weather before swimming. Do not swim in severe weather, and if you hear thunder or see lightning, get out of the water immediately.

◆ Follow boating traffic rules.

◆ Have a plan for responding to emergencies before entering the water. Know your limitations. Unless you are trained as a lifeguard, you are putting yourself and the swimmer in trouble at risk by attempting to swim to his or her rescue. If you see someone in trouble, take these steps in order:

• Reach out with a stick or paddle. Keep your balance.

• Throw him something that floats, such as a cooler or large piece of wood.

• Paddle or motor to him.

• Swim to him.

Some Important DON'Ts

◆ Use alcohol and drugs while participating in water recreation.

◆ Dive into unfamiliar waters, which are often too shallow or have hidden obstructions.

◆ Swim *too* long, *too* far away, stay *too* long in cold water, or play *too* hard.

◆ Swim alone. Try to confine your activity to areas supervised by lifeguards or qualified adults.

◆ Engage in horseplay.

◆ Leave children alone near water. Swimming lessons don't make your child "drown-proof."

◆ Rely on inflatable objects like rafts or toys to keep you afloat if you are a poor swimmer. The only reliable flotation device is a properly fitting life jacket. Here's a tip for the kids: Check for snug fit by picking the child up by the shoulders of the life jacket. If it fits correctly, the child's chin and ears will not slip through.

◆ Swim or wade in swift water. If you get caught in swift water, swim with it and angle toward the shore. Or, relax and take deep breaths, and keep your feet up and pointed downstream. You will float, almost always into a bank downstream.

◆ Swim near boat docks. A boater might not see you.

◆ Remember: As you grow older or more out-of-shape, you may lose the stamina needed to swim long distances or in fast-moving rivers.

Dangerous Water Falls

Kathy was sure she was ready; true, she hadn't been on water skis in fifteen years, but she had skied a lot as a girl. Water skiing, she reasoned, was no different from riding a bicycle — it all comes back to you once you climb on. So, even though Josh didn't want to drive the boat faster, Kathy insisted he crank it up. Faster! Faster! Ah, the exhilaration of the wind in her face and the water at her feet. Ouch! The pain of losing control and flying head over heels, landing on her back, and having to be pulled from the water with a seriously sprained shoulder.

According to the National Safety Council, more than 6 million Americans water ski each year, and over 10,000 require emergency room treatment. Most of these injuries result from carelessness and poor preparation.

Driver Prepare

- Learn and obey the "rules of the road" on water.
- It takes three to water ski:
  - the skier;
  - the towboat operator;
  - an observer in the boat. The driver cannot watch and know if the skier has fallen while also seeing where the boat is going.
- Operate in a corridor at least 200 feet wide, giving a safety area of 100 feet on both sides of the boat. The ski path should be at least 2,000–3,000 feet in length.

◆ The boat driver is responsible for keeping the skier away from dangerous areas. Take time to get familiar with the shoreline, shallow areas, and obstructions. Keep the boat a safe distance from the shore, docks, and objects in the water.

◆ Be alert for boats entering the ski area; if one does, shut down the engine and wait for the area to clear.

◆ Always pull novice skiers slowly. High speeds are not essential to pleasurable water skiing.

◆ Always approach a skier in the water on the driver's side of the boat.

◆ Picking a skier from the water is a dangerous proposition. Your boat engine must be turned off and the propeller fully stopped.

◆ The boat should run parallel to the shore and come in slowly when landing.

◆ When your skier is down, raise a ski flag to alert other boaters.

◆ Equip your boat with a wide-angle rearview mirror.

◆ A towing pylon, boarding ladder, and speedometer are also advisable.

Skier Beware

◆ Know how to swim!

◆ Do not ski in unfamiliar waters, where there could be unseen dangers. When skiing in new waters, take along someone familiar with the area.

◆ Never ski in shallow water, at night, or in front of another boat. Rough water is particularly dangerous, since waves and a running sea will prevent the towboat from keeping a smooth speed and course.

◆ Always wear a snug-fitting Coast Guard-approved life jacket. Life jackets are required in most states. The life jacket should be Type III, and designed as a ski vest. The life jacket must keep the skier face up in the water if he or she falls.

◆ The skier and the boat driver should agree in advance on the general boat path and signals to use.

◆ If a skier falls, he or she should clasp both hands overhead to be seen and to signal he is OK. In a congested boating area, a downed skier should hold up a ski to show that everything is OK.

◆ Buy age-appropriate skis. Make sure the bindings are snug, but will release in case of a fall.

◆ Wear a helmet to protect against head injury.

Other Water Hazards

◆ Don't stay on the water too long. The sun, wind, waves, and vibration can make you tired.

◆ Whether you are pulling or being pulled, do not drink alcohol, take prescription drugs or over-the-counter medications, or use illegal drugs, all of which can impair your judgment.

◆ Use and renew sunscreen.

◆ Some special advice for those who like to water-tube:

  • Stay well away from shore. Most injuries occur when water-tubers come too close to shore.

  • Before water-tubing, inspect the rope for fraying and the tube for defects.

  • Wear a Type III life jacket.

  • Two people should be in the boat.

Some information came from U.S.A. Water Ski, (800) 533-2972, or www.usawaterski.org.

Critter Cautions

Peggy has a lifetime membership to the Audubon Society, and nobody loves nature and wildlife more than she does. Maybe you know a Peggy. She's the delightful neighborhood woman who sets out dog food on her back porch each night for the raccoons and foxes. Nice gal, Peggy, luring untamed critters into your backyard, where they can overturn your flowerpots and try to get into your house. Wasn't it fun when you had to call out the sheriff to trap the rabid fox? And no, Peggy doesn't think she was wrong—she was just helping out Mother Nature.

Urban sprawl is drawing blurred lines between the places that people and animals now call home. It's time we learned that most dangerous and potentially harmful encounters occur because people fail to leave the animals alone. To ensure harmony with our wild friends:

Don't Feed the Animals

◆ Do not feed wildlife. Intentional and inadvertent feeding is the major cause of most wildlife problems. Knowing that, bring in your dog and cat's food bowls, or they'll become a welcome place to eat for your wildlife neighbors. Wild animals can find plenty of food on their own; don't give them an invitation to come knocking.

◆ Feeding songbirds is fine, but be aware in bear country that bears find certain bird foods attractive.

◆ Use tight-fitting lids on your trashcans, or tape or tie them shut. Also, don't take your garbage out too early. Left overnight, it's a perfect attraction to nocturnal foragers like raccoons and coyotes.

◆ Pets left unattended, even in a fenced yard, are potential food for coyotes, and, in some parts of the country, even alligators or mountain lions. Keep your pets close by, and do not let them roam outside at night. Remember: fences are not always an effective deterrent against the growing threat of coyotes. These predators can climb fences up to five feet high and can also crawl under them.

◆ Screen or cap chimneys, and furnace, attic, and dryer vents, and keep dampers closed. Animals can use these spaces as nests, and they provide access to your home. To prevent fire and safety hazards, consult a professional before performing this work.

◆ Seal all cracks and holes larger than one-quarter inch in diameter to keep out rats, mice, bats, and snakes.

◆ Close holes around and under the foundation of your house, so animals will not be tempted to build a home there. Bury wire mesh one to two feet deep in places where animals might gain access.

◆ Be careful what you plant around your home and in your garden. You'll have to do some homework to learn what the local creatures are eating. And fence your garden.

◆ Keep your yard free of brush and low branches, which create good hiding spots.

Oh, Dear! More Deer

To avoid serious injury from the growing number of deer encountered on our roadways:

◆ Scan the road while driving, especially at dusk and dawn. That's when deer do most of their moving.

◆ Watch carefully for deer where roads cross creeks or go through wooded areas.

◆ If you see one deer, expect to see others. Deer tend to travel in family groups.

◆ Slow down if you can safely do so. Try to scare away the deer by sounding your horn or flashing your lights.

◆ Consider installing a deer whistle on your car.

◆ Most fatal incidents involving a deer occurred because a driver swerved or got hit by another car. If you cannot avoid a collision, hit the deer rather than swerving into a ditch or the oncoming lane of traffic.

Confronting Wildlife

◆ If you encounter a young animal, leave it alone. Don't assume it has been abandoned; its parent is probably nearby, and will likely return to it. Let Nature take its course.

◆ If you are going into an area where wildlife will be present, call the local wildlife office to review possible dangers and what to do if you encounter a wild animal.

Freeze Warning

It seemed so simple and routine: all Thad had to do was walk down his short driveway incline and get the morning paper. However, during the night, a winter storm had blanketed the area in a sheet of ice. Thad slipped and slid down the hill; try as he might, he couldn't climb, or even crawl, back up the small incline. He called for help, and eventually his teenaged son came to his rescue, wearing golf cleats and lugging a garden hose. Thad suffered only a bruised ego that morning. Mrs. Burns, next door, was not so lucky: she fell and broke her arm.

There's nothing prettier than a frozen world sparkling in the sun, but there are also few things more treacherous.

Staying on Your Feet

◆ Plan ahead. If you can, shop before the winter storm hits. Afterward, don't buy more than you can easily carry.

◆ Stay inside when there's ice on the ground. Most people fall while getting the mail, picking up the paper, or taking out the trash.

◆ Be very cautious with your first step onto slick surfaces. Sometimes it's hard to detect slippery surfaces, particularly at night. Use a flashlight.

◆ Walking on snow or ice, take it slow. Keep your body position slightly forward and put your feet down flat, not on the heels. Bend your knees and take short, slow steps, or move your feet forward without lifting them from the ground.

◆ Always wear shoes with good traction. (Thad had on his house slippers.) Snow boots, hiking boots, and tennis shoes are the best choices. Some people like to wear strap-on ice cleats, or cleated golf shoes.

◆ If possible, walk on the grass.

◆ If you must walk in the streets, be careful around intersections; cars might slide through them.

◆ Keep looking ahead to avoid slick spots.

Sliding and Gliding

The U.S. Consumer Product Safety Commission estimates more than 50,000 sled injuries and 30,000 ice-skating injuries each year, including many serious head injuries and some fatalities.

Sledding

◆ Sled on spacious, gently sloping hills. Avoid sledding on overcrowded hills.

◆ Check slopes for bare spots, holes, and other obstructions that could cause injury, especially hazards that might be hidden by snow.

◆ Avoid slopes near streets and roads, where your momentum could carry you into traffic.

◆ Be sure there is a level run-off at the end of the slide path, so the sled can glide safely to a halt.

◆ Do not sled at night unless the run is well lighted.

◆ Ride a sled lying down with your head to the rear. Snow disks and plastic sliders are designed for upright use.

◆ Always wear a helmet.

◆ If a spill is unavoidable, roll off the sled. Remember: don't collide headfirst!

◆ After the ride down, get off the slope and use a safe path to go back up.

Ice Skating

When playing on the ice, follow these general guidelines:

• Generally, two or three inches will support a skater of average height and weight.

• Large groups require four to six inches.

• Stay off the ice during thawing periods.

◆ When in doubt, check with local authorities. If you can't get a ruling, stay off the ice. Have a bonfire, instead.

◆ Skate in specially designated areas, such as indoor and outdoor rinks, or frozen, shallow ponds.

◆ Make sure children's skates fit *now*. Kids lose control in skates that are too big.

◆ Keep blades properly sharpened.

◆ Children should wear bicycle helmets to protect their heads, and kneepads and wrist guards.

◆ Try not to break a fall with your hands, which could shatter a bone. Instead, try to land on your backside.

Kids' Safety

Introduction

Children and youths are the most vulnerable members of society. A combination of inquisitiveness, lack of knowledge, and feelings of invincibility contribute to this vulnerability. It's up to adults to protect children in their early years, and then to guide them in forming good safety habits as they acquire the knowledge to make decisions on their own. Unfortunately, much work needs to be done, as accidents are the leading cause of death from ages one through nineteen.

The principal causes of death among children and youths, based on recent National Safety Council statistics, are:

Motor Vehicle	8,100
Drowning	1,300
Fires	800
Suffocation	500
Firearms	300
Poison	300
Falls	200
All Other	1,300
Total	**12,800**

Restrain Your Children

Karen was confident her husband had properly installed their daughter's safety seat in their small car. Still, she was conscientious about family safety, and when she learned she could receive a free child safety seat inspection at the local SAFE KIDS coalition, she jumped at the chance. A certified inspector found Karen's safety seat straps were threaded through the wrong slots, the harness clip was missing, and the seat was not strapped into the vehicle tightly enough. The benefits of the free inspection were realized a week later when a reckless driver crashed head-on into Karen's car, totaling it. Properly restrained in the back seat, her daughter suffered only a small cut on her mouth, and Karen wonders what might have been if she hadn't found time in a hectic schedule to put safety first.

A Crash Course on Safety Seats

1. **According to the National Safety Council, child safety seats reduce fatal injury in cars by 71 percent for infants under age one, and 54 percent for those from one through four.** But to work effectively, they must be used consistently and properly.

2. No single child safety seat is considered best for babies, and not all safety seats fit all vehicles. Try the seat in your car before you buy it, and place your child in it to see that he or she sits and is restrained comfortably and properly.

3. Send in the registration card to stay informed of problems or recalls.

4. Keep your vehicle owner's manual and safety seat instructions handy for details about how to secure children. These instructions are the best source of information on correct use of the seat.

5. Set a good example by always wearing your seatbelt. Praise your child often for sitting in the safety seat or wearing a seatbelt.

6. Make it a rule that your child cannot ride until safely restrained.

Proper Seating Arrangements

♦ Children under thirteen should be properly restrained in the backseat.

♦ Infants should ride in a rear-facing safety seat as long as possible — until they are at least one year old and weigh at least twenty pounds. Consult the manufacturer's instructions about positioning your baby in the safety seat and determining the proper recline angle.

Note: If your vehicle has a passenger-side air bag, do not use a rear-facing restraint in the front seat. The only exception is if there's no backseat and there is a switch to deactivate the passenger bag.

If there's no switch, the child should never ride in that vehicle.

♦ Children who are at least one year old, weigh twenty to forty pounds, and can no longer ride facing rearward should ride in forward-facing safety seats.

♦ Kids over forty pounds should be correctly secured in belt-positioning booster seats until adult lap and shoulder belts fit correctly (around age 8). The lap belt should be snug over the upper thighs rather than the soft abdomen, and the shoulder belt should be snug across the chest and collarbone.

♦ To fit correctly in only a safety belt, kids must be tall enough to sit with knees bent at the edge of the seat without slouching. Shoulder and lap belts must be used correctly.

♦ If a child must ride in the front seat, make sure the seat is all the way back, the child stays belted, and sits back in the seat.

Departing Thoughts

♦ Get a tight fit. A child safety seat should not move more than one inch from side to side or toward the front of the vehicle. You might need to kneel in the child safety seat while tightening the straps to achieve a tight fit.

♦ Each time you use a child safety seat, be sure:
  • the harnesses are snug and flat against the child's body, and the harness clip is at armpit level — an adult should not be able to fit more than one finger comfortably between the child's collarbone and the harness;
  • the lap harness rests low across the hips.

♦ Contact your local or state SAFE KIDS coalition for information about child passenger safety events and services in your area. More information is available at www.safekids.org, along with a listing of coalitions. If necessary, call the National SAFE KIDS Campaign at (202) 662-0600 for information.

Driver's Education

Teens and automobiles are a dangerous combination. **In fact, car crashes are the leading cause of death for people between the ages of thirteen and nineteen. More than 5,500 teens die each year in collisions, and hundreds of thousands are seriously injured. According to the Insurance Institute for Highway Safety, the risk of crash involvement among drivers sixteen to nineteen years old is four times the risk among older drivers. Risk is highest at ages sixteen and seventeen.**

For these reasons and more, you need to be sure your teen is adequately prepared to get behind the wheel of an automobile.

Before Turning the First Key

Some states have a graduated licensing program. Even if your state doesn't, you might wish to adopt a similar practice. Graduated licensing programs include six to twelve months in a learning phase, during which adult supervision is required. That's followed by another six to twelve months in an intermediate licensing phase, during which unsupervised driving isn't allowed in high-risk situations, e.g., at night or with other teens in the car.

The National Safety Council sells a video kit, *Coaching the Beginning Driver*, which contains valuable coaching and defensive driving examples. For information, call (800) 621-7619. Also, AAA has a video kit, *Teaching Your Teen to Drive*, with similar safety tips. Call your local AAA office for information.

◆ Although most teens prefer smaller cars, the death and injury rates are lower for occupants of larger cars. Bigger is generally better, and high-performance cars are not.

◆ Enroll your teen and yourself in a defensive driving course.

Practice, Practice, Practice

While driver's education classes and driving schools are worthwhile, they might not provide the comprehensive car-control skills a young driver needs to handle the challenges of today's driving. Parents can provide that extra time behind the wheel, however. When teaching your teen, start with the basics:

- Only one parent in the car.
- Keep the sessions short, usually no longer than an hour at first.
- Be patient! Keep a constructive, helpful tone. Avoid sarcasm.
- Teach by example. The way you drive while your teen is growing up is far more important than the advice you give.

◆ Have the teen operate the controls while the car is standing still.

◆ Confine early learning to quiet streets and large, open parking lots. Then move onto streets with slow speed limits, where there will be minimal contact with other vehicles.

◆ Practice at night and in inclement weather, too, but not until the teen has learned to handle dry pavement. Large, vacant parking lots are safe places to learn to handle a skid and to cope with the diminished braking capabilities caused by hydroplaning.

◆ Demonstrate the particulars of an emergency highway stop.

◆ Only after many hours of practice and demonstrated ability on the part of the young driver are you ready to move the classroom to more complex situations, e.g., highways, shopping malls, and rural roads.

Enforce Your Rules for the Road!

Teenage drivers also need to know *your* rules of the road. Make sure they understands that:

◆ He or she will always wear a seatbelt, *as a driver or passenger.* **According to a recent study, 70 percent of fifteen-to-twenty-year-olds who died in passenger-vehicle crashes weren't wearing seatbelts.**

◆ Driving should have a purpose.

◆ There are restrictions on nighttime driving, and no driving between midnight and 6 a.m. Weekend nights are the most hazardous. Give teens a driving curfew.

◆ Consider a vehicle-monitoring device.

◆ Teens cannot have more than one or two friends in the car. Peer pressure leads to risk taking and bad judgments. **In one study, 85 percent of teen drivers involved in crashes were carrying teen passengers, and risk increased with each additional teen passenger.**

◆ No alcohol or drugs! This will be difficult to enforce, but it must be stressed time and again. If nothing else, get your teen to buy into the concept of the "designated driver."

◆ Some experts recommend that teens not have their own cars during their first two years of driving.

◆ Set penalties for driving infractions when the teen learns to drive.

◆ To encourage responsible driving, have your teen pay for part or all of the auto insurance.

◆ Sign a contract, with rules on using seatbelts, and the number and ages of passengers. Include consequences for breaking the rules.

◆ Develop guidelines that minimize distractions: no loud music or talking on the phone.

◆ Children should never be allowed to ride with inexperienced drivers — regardless of how responsible the drivers are in other areas of their lives. Spell out in advance who the unacceptable drivers are.

The First Six Months

*A*nn *was only six weeks old when her mother placed her in the middle of a neighbor's bed. Her mother didn't think Ann could scoot very far, so she left her alone and went to another room to visit. A short time later there was a "thud" and a scream from the bedroom. Ann had scooted off the bed, onto the floor. Fortunately, the only damage was to her mother's state of mind.*

Sometimes, it seems a miracle that kids live to be adults. **According to the National Safety Council, each year, about 600 children under one year old die accidentally from other than motor-vehicle incidents. About 300 of those deaths are due to suffocation.** Despite doting parents and safe home environments, children find ways of imperiling themselves. Here are some things parents and grandparents should watch out for:

Cribs

- Don't use a crib manufactured before 1974, the year tougher standards took effect. Look for a crib with the seal that says it meets national safety standards.

- The slats on a crib should not be more than two and three-eighths inches apart.

- Do not use a crib with corner posts higher than one-sixteenth of an inch above the end panel. Children's clothing can tangle on them and strangle the child.

- The mattress should be the same size as the crib to prevent gaps in which arms or legs could be trapped. If you can fit two fingers between the mattress and crib, the gap is too wide.

- Do not use thin plastic material, which can cling to a child's face and cause suffocation, to cover mattresses or pillows.

- Never leave crib rails down when a child is in the crib.

- Be sure all hardware is securely in place. Check it regularly.

- Cribs should not contain large stuffed animals or pillows. Not only could these items serve as stepping stones to help a child climb out, but they can also suffocate.

- Put your baby to sleep on her back or side in a crib with a firm, flat mattress and no soft bedding underneath. **About 30 percent of the 6,000 babies who die each year from sudden infant death syndrome may have suffocated when placed on top of pillows, comforters, and other soft, fluffy coverings.**

- Do not leave toys in bed with a sleeping child.

- Inspect every crib a child uses for safety.

- Never put infants (up to twelve months) to sleep on adult or youth beds.

- Do not place a crib near draperies or blinds, where a child could become entangled.

- Do not hang objects with strings or elastics, such as laundry bags or toys, around the crib.

- Place crib bumpers around the bed. Cut off excess string length. Remove the bumpers when the child can stand.

- The National Academy of Pediatrics recommends babies not sleep with their parents. Deaths have occurred when a parent rolled over on top of a child.

Mobiles

- Hanging crib toys should be beyond the child's reach.

- Avoid mobiles with small, removable parts that can be easily grasped and swallowed.

- Remove the mobile from the crib as soon as the child can push her way up to her hands or knees.

Tables and Chairs

- Changing tables should have:
  - safety straps to prevent falls;
  - drawers or shelves that are easily accessible while you keep one hand on the baby.

- Highchairs should have waist and crotch straps that are not attached to the tray. The tray must lock securely.

- Caps on highchair tubing should be firmly attached so a child can't remove and choke on them.

Other Tips

- Never leave a child alone in a bathtub.

- Avoid clothing with ribbons or strings. Remove any drawstrings.

- Never leave the soft sides of portable cribs and playpens down.

Carriers

- Choose a carrier seat with a wide, sturdy base for stability.

- Stay within arm's reach of the baby when the seat is on tables, counters, couches, and chairs.

- Do not set it on soft, plush surfaces that will make it unstable.

- Always use the safety belt.

Pacifiers

- A pacifier's protective shield should be too large to fit into the baby's mouth.

- The shield should have ventilation holes in case the child does place it into his or her mouth.

- If the pacifier has holes or tears, dispose of it.

- Do not string a pacifier (or any other object) around your child's neck.

Getting the Right Sitter

Ann needed a babysitter for her two young children. Marisa and Kendall needed money for their summer vacation, and babysitting provided a viable income for the perky fifteen-year-old cousins. It looked like a good match for everyone involved. The girls seemed responsible, and the two young children were easy to handle. So easy, in fact, that when the girls' boyfriends stopped by one afternoon, it was easy to be distracted from their job. When a vigilant neighbor came to the door toting little Eric, who had wandered from the house instead of taking his nap, the girls were terribly embarrassed and quickly unemployed. And Ann resolved to be more careful in her next choice of a sitter.

Entrusting your children to others is a serious step. The following tips can help ensure that you trust the right people to watch after your most precious ones.

Finding a Suitable Sitter

◆ Is the sitter at least thirteen years of age, and responsible enough to care for your child?

◆ Look for a sitter who has received training from local agencies such as the "Y" or a hospital. Ideally, find a sitter who is certified in infant-and-child CPR.

◆ Meet the sitter ahead of time for a personal interview. Introduce him or her to your kids to see how they interact.

◆ Ask the sitter for references, and call them to check on qualifications and competency.

◆ Pose "What if...?" questions that will show you the sitter's degree of preparedness for the job. Admitting they don't know an answer is a more positive response than bluffing a wrong answer.

Before You Leave Home

◆ Have the sitter arrive early so you can show her around your house. Be sure to point out the locations of telephones, hard-to-find light switches, the first-aid kit or medicine chest, extra keys, flashlights, and blankets. Practice using the door locks and the burglar alarm system.

◆ Also, instruct the sitter on the safety precautions you have taken: point out baby gates, child-resistant locks, smoke alarms, carbon monoxide detectors, electrical outlet covers, toilet locks, etc.

◆ Show him all the entrances to your home.

◆ If preparing a meal is part of the job, train the sitter in how to use the stove or microwave.

◆ If your child is allowed to ride a bike or scooter, skateboard, or in-line skate while you're away, tell the sitter where the protective gear is stored, and that it must be worn.

◆ Leave written information and guidelines, including:

  • who and when to call for help;

  • feeding, bathing, bedtime, and special-needs instructions;

  • safety tips appropriate for your children (updated as necessary);

  • your name, home address, and home phone number;

  • how to reach your home from major intersections;

  • important phone numbers, including where you can be reached, the phone number and relationship of someone to call in case you can't be reached, the doctor, ambulance, fire department, police, poison control center, and veterinarian;

  • phrasing for the sitter to use to answer the phone or doorbell.

Set Clear and Rigid Rules

◆ Instruct the sitter to never leave your child alone — even for a second.

◆ Clearly establish areas that are "In Limits" and "Off Limits." For example, the sitter should know if it's permissible to play in the backyard or enter the basement.

◆ Allowing guests is not advisable (remember Marisa and Kendall?). Discuss whether it's okay to make phone calls to friends, watch TV, or use the computer.

◆ Ask the sitter to keep the drapes or blinds closed at night, and to keep both an outside light and inside light turned on.

◆ No smoking, drugs, or alcohol are allowed.

◆ Tell the sitter to get your child out of the house immediately if she sees flames or smells smoke or gas.

◆ Show her your family-gathering spot outside the house in case of an emergency evacuation.

Note: If you leave your child at your sitter's home, make sure you review the above information and check out the home beforehand to see that it is childproofed.

Some information courtesy of the National SAFE KIDS Campaign.

Serious Business

Remember the first time you supervised your baby brother or sister, or were asked to watch the kid next door for a few hours? A little scary, wasn't it? And it should have been; taking responsibility for another person is a huge commitment. Still, it's a common practice, and it can be a good way for young people to earn money. The goal is to keep it a positive experience for all involved.

Kids, before beginning your babysitting career, enroll in a class offered locally. Most teach basic childcare techniques, such as feeding and diapering, plus first aid, age-appropriate activities, fire safety, and home-emergency skills.

Before the Parents Leave

◆ Get the names and phone numbers for emergencies, including fire and police departments, poison control center, the nearest hospital, a relative, a reliable neighbor, and a veterinarian, if applicable.

◆ Get the phone number where your employers can be reached. Know when they expect to return.

◆ Always leave your employer's name, address, and phone number *at your own home* before going to baby-sit. And let your family know what time to expect you home.

◆ Get a schedule of activities (playtime, feeding, bedtime).

◆ Tour the house with the parents. Know the locations of phones, emergency exits, first-aid supplies, fire escape routes, and specific hazards that might attract children. Find out how to lock and unlock the doors.

◆ Find out where the items you will need are located, such as the children's clothing and playthings.

◆ Familiarize yourself with potential hazards in the house, such as electrical outlets, appliances, and exposed heating elements.

◆ Find out where the "danger" items are — medicines, bleaches, household cleaners, and inappropriate toys. Keep them out of reach if parents have not locked them away in a secure place.

◆ Know who should be admitted to the home and who may take the child, such as relatives or friends.

◆ Know where a flashlight is kept in case the lights go out.

On the Job

◆ Dress for the job. Wear low-heeled shoes and practical, washable clothing. Do not wear jewelry or decorative pins.

◆ Unless instructed by the parents, do not bathe an infant.

◆ If you're changing the baby's diapers, place everything you need within immediate reach, so you won't have to step away from the infant, even for a second.

◆ In case of accident or illness, don't try to be doctor or nurse except for minor cuts and bruises. Call the parents, or others on the emergency list, for instructions.

◆ Keep children within safe play areas, preferably in your sight. Keep toddlers away from stairs.

◆ Cook only with permission from the children's parents, and only if you can do so safely.

◆ Never play the stereo or television so loud that you can't hear a child cry or call out. If you must use the telephone, make your conservation brief.

◆ The safest place for a young child when you're unable to watch her is in the playpen.

◆ Stay with her when she is eating.

◆ Don't take the child outside unless the parents have given you permission. Then, make sure the child is dressed properly for the weather.

◆ If you're playing with or feeding a baby, and the phone or doorbell rings, take him with you, or put him in his crib, carriage, or playpen before answering.

◆ Keep all toys and objects small enough to be inhaled or swallowed away from babies and toddlers.

◆ Remember: infants should sleep on their backs.

◆ In case of fire, get the children out first, and then call the fire department from a neighbor's house.

◆ If someone calls, say the child's parents are unavailable, and take a number.

◆ If your employer has been drinking, arrange your own ride home.

Hot Tub Alert

D̶ebra had just completed her master's degree in psychology, and there was a jubilant mood in the house as she boiled a pot of hot water for tea. Her three-year-old son, Michael, was helping her make chocolate chip cookies. When she lifted the pot off the stove and set it on the table, Michael leaned over and eagerly sucked at the steam rising from the spout. He screamed in pain, and Debra rushed him to the hospital, where they prescribed lots of cold water and ice, and told her that Michael was fortunate to have avoided serious injury.

Why do kids do these things? Even a psychologist can't tell you.

What we know is that each year, according to the National SAFE KIDS Campaign, an average of sixteen children under age fifteen die of, and more than 30,000 children are treated in emergency rooms for, scald burn-related injuries. Here are some ways to reduce the risk in your home.

In the Kitchen

- When you're busy in the kitchen, your toddler should be in a playpen or highchair, away from hot liquids and splattering grease.

- Establish a stay-away safe zone in the kitchen.

- Never carry or hold a child and hot liquids at the same time.

- Use extra caution when cooking with oil.

- Keep pans and pots on rear burners, with their handles turned toward the back of the stove.

- Install a safety shield or guard on the stove.

- Keep hot foods twelve inches away from the table edge, and hot pans at the back of the counter.

- Don't put hot containers on tablecloths or place mats, which children can pull down on themselves. Use tablecloths and place mats only when children aren't around.

- Unplug appliances when not in use. Avoid dangling cords.

- Store snacks and other foods away from the stove, so no one is tempted to reach across a burner.

- Microwaves present special dangers:
  - Be careful when heating and removing liquids; they may be scalding even when the container is not.
  - Before serving food, check for even heating.
  - Supervise children, particularly under age seven. Never let them remove food from the microwave.
  - Review microwave operations with a babysitter.

In the Bathroom

Hot tap water accounts for nearly one-fourth of all scald burns among children, and is associated with more fatalities and hospitalizations than other hot liquid burns. These burns most often occur in the bathroom, and tend to be more severe and cover a larger portion of the body. To prevent tap water burns:

- Reduce the temperature of your hot water to 120° F.

- When filling a tub, add the cold water first, then follow with hot until the tub is ready.

- After the bathtub is filled, put your forearm in the water and move it quickly back and forth for several seconds. If it feels even a little bit hot, it is *too* hot for your child. Add more cold water and retest until it feels comfortable.

- Install anti-scald devices that stop water flow when the temperature exceeds 115° F in your shower and bathtub fixtures.

- For extra safety, buy a bath thermometer. The water should not be higher than 100° F.

- Never leave a child unsupervised in a bath.

- Seat the child at the rear of the tub, preferably with his or her back to the faucet handles. Children will turn on the water if they can reach it.

- Don't use toys, as this implies the bathtub is a play area.

- Keep children away from hair curlers and curling irons. Each year, thousands of children require emergency room treatment from touching these products.

- Put a slide-bolt latch on the upper half of the outside of the bathroom door, above a young child's reach, so children can't get into the bathroom by themselves.

Garage Door Perils

Each year, automatic garage doors kill a number of children, and injure many others. The fault can lie in childhood naiveté or mechanical failure. To protect the children in your home:

◆ The button inside the garage should be installed at least five feet high, so young children can't reach and activate it.

◆ Make certain the area around the garage door is clear of children before using it.

◆ Keep door-opener controls away from children. They are not toys.

◆ Keep the door in full view when you're lowering it.

◆ Instruct children to never "race the door."

◆ Never allow a child to stand under the door or walk through the doorway when the door is moving.

Maintain the Hardware

◆ Inspect your garage door and openers monthly. Check the hardware for signs of wear. If it is properly balanced, the door should stay open when it is three to four feet off the ground, with the release mechanism disconnected.

◆ Lubricate moving parts as recommended in the owner's manual.

◆ Remove the pull down rope from electrically operated doors, and disable the locks.

◆ Install restraining cables, which can help contain an extension spring that breaks.

◆ Most automatic door openers have an automatic reverse mechanism that stops and reverses the door when it contacts an object. To test this critical safety feature, place a roll of paper towels in the path of your descending garage door periodically. The door should stop and reverse when it strikes the roll of towels. If it doesn't, call a qualified technician. Do not attempt to repair it yourself — the springs can be very dangerous.

Note: According to *Consumer Reports*, a garage door could pass the paper-towel test but still injure a child. For maximum safety, *Consumer Reports* recommends installing a "safety reversing sensor" that will cause the door to reverse if it senses anything in its path.

Accident Facts

Age	Annual Accidental Deaths	Annual Motor Vehicle Deaths
Under one year	754	162
one	614	205
two	511	178
three	435	181
four	375	195
five	354	181
six	300	159
seven	321	180
eight	279	150
nine	290	164
ten	278	153
eleven	276	165
twelve	310	178
thirteen	375	222
fourteen	471	316
fifteen	635	462
sixteen	1215	967
seventeen	1411	1111
eighteen	1744	1400
nineteen	1585	1221

Source: National Safety Council

A Few Grand Safety Tips

Grandchildren are truly a blessing. They rejuvenate their elders, and bring a great new sense of excitement and discovery. And there's always the wonderful feature of knowing that you can hand them back to your children when you're exhausted or can't handle them anymore. But there's also the serious downside of knowing that if anything happens on your watch, you've failed your own children. Grandparents face a lot of pressures, but there are ways to lighten the load. (These tips also apply to non-grandparents when kids visit.)

> **To underscore the importance of eternal vigilance, according to the National SAFE KIDS Campaign, each year, more than 2,000 children under fifteen die of, and 4.5 million are injured in, home mishaps.**

Put Yourself in Their Shoes

For younger kids, get down on your knees and crawl around the rooms and yard to look for things a small person could get into. Open doors and drawers; as you do, ask yourself these questions:

- Is it poisonous?
- Is it a choking hazard?
- Could it start a fire?
- Could it fall over, or fall down?
- Could a child fall from it, or through it?
- Could a child trip over it?
- Could it scald or burn?
- Could it strangle or suffocate?
- Could a child drown in it?
- Could it electrocute?
- Could it cut?
- Does it contain alcohol?

Other Things to Do

- Post emergency numbers near all phones.
- Learn CPR and the Heimlich maneuver for children.
- Purchase hearth guards for the fireplace, and corner guards for furniture with sharp corners.
- Place stickers on sliding glass doors at child and adult eye levels.
- Tie up dangling drapery and blind cords and appliance wires.
- Keep plants beyond a child's reach. Philodendron and dieffenbachia are poisonous. Learn the names of your plants, so you can help the poison control center if a child eats them.

- Cover electrical outlets with one-piece safety covers; children can choke on small, individual covers.

- Unload guns, and lock up the guns and ammunition separately.

- If you have a pool, install four-sided fencing and keep emergency equipment poolside.

When They Visit

- Lock cabinets with childproof latches.

- Store matches, lighters, plastic bags, and plastic wrap high out of children's reach.

- Keep potentially "poisonous" products locked up, including medications. Have a bottle of syrup of ipecac handy for use (only if directed by a poison specialist).

Note: Each year, more than a million poisonings among children under six are reported to U.S. poison control centers. According to the U.S. Consumer Product Safety Commission, grandparents' medicines account for almost 20 percent of all drugs swallowed by children.

- Don't feed kids under six hard candy, popcorn, nuts, hot dogs, raisins, or food with seeds or pits. Some foods, such as peanut butter or fruits, can be choking hazards in big portions. Provide small portions.

- In the kitchen, secure infants and toddlers in a playpen or a highchair with straps.

- Remove the tablecloth, because a child could pull it off and be burned by hot foods and liquids.

- Use the rear stove burners, keep pot handles out of reach, and never leave the stove unattended.

- Don't drink hot liquids while holding a child.

- Give formula and food a personal test for proper temperature before feeding a child. Don't heat formula in the microwave.

- Place things you *want* a child to have, like healthy snacks, within easy reach.

- Lock liquor cabinets, or move the bottles out of reach.

- Watch the recliner: fingers, arms, legs, and heads can get caught between the chair and the leg rest.

- Move furniture away from windows to prevent falls.

- Keep the bathroom door closed and the toilet lid down.

- Do not leave electrical appliances plugged in, especially near the sink or tub.

- Never leave a child alone in a tub, or near a pool or water-filled containers.

- Lower your water-heater thermostat to 120° F, and always test the water with your forearm or a bath thermometer before putting a child into it.

- Pick up any small items lying around that a child could swallow.

- Check toys for small parts, sharp edges, or broken pieces.

- Lock up all tools and garden chemicals.

- Crib slats should be no more than two and three-eighths inches apart. Look for a certification seal to confirm that the crib meets Juvenile Product Manufacturers Association standards. Use a firm mattress, and crib sheets that fit snugly. Position the crib away from wall hangings, windows, and cords. Dress infants in warm clothes. Don't use comforters, bulky blankets, or pillows. Once the baby can pull herself up, remove stuffed animals she could climb out on; remove any mobiles, too.

- Tie plastic dry-cleaning bags in a knot and dispose of them safely.

- Store your purse on a top shelf, and remove potentially dangerous items from your dresser.

- Install safety gates to block off the tops and bottoms of stairways.

The Gift of Safety

While winter holidays weren't created expressly for the benefit of children, youngsters take great delight in the festivities surrounding this magical time of year. However, the magic can quickly turn to disaster from simple oversight or poor planning. **One of the greatest gifts we can give our children is our concern for their safety.**

Well-planned Decorations

Decorate your house with children in mind.

◆ Avoid room decorations that are sharp, easily breakable, or very small.

◆ Avoid trimmings and decorations that resemble candy or food. Children could mistake them for the real thing.

◆ Keep small ornaments, tinsel, small figurines, and other decorations out of reach of young children.

◆ Place breakable ornaments, or those with small detachable parts, on upper tree branches.

◆ Keep lighting wires away from young children.

◆ Push the wires into the tree branches and clip them securely to the branches. Never allow children to play with light strings or other electrical decorations.

◆ Trim lower tree branches to prevent eye injuries.

◆ Keep candles, matches, and lighters out of reach.

◆ Make sure all electrical decorations are safety tested. Look for the UL Label.

◆ Keep toddlers away from electrical fixtures. Use large outlet covers on electrical sockets that are not in use.

◆ Secure electrical cords so children can't pull or trip over them.

Well-chosen Toys

◆ Be sure the toy matches the age, skills, abilities, and interests of the child.

◆ Avoid toys that have sharp or metal edges, glass, cords and strings, or sharp points.

◆ For infants and toddlers, buy toys that are too large to fit in their mouths. Here's a valuable rule of thumb: If a toy or part can slide through an empty toilet-paper roll, it's too small for small children.

◆ Be sure the eyes of dolls, and buttons on stuffed animals, are securely fastened.

◆ Do not allow children under age six to blow up a balloon or be alone with one. Balloons are the most dangerous "toy" for small children.

◆ When purchasing toys for older children, consider the possibility they might fall into the hands of younger children.

More Precautions

◆ Supervise youngsters carefully during holiday activities and parties.

◆ Keep toddlers away from the kitchen when cooking and baking are in progress. If they must be present, keep them in highchairs or playpens.

◆ If you build a fire, use a fireplace screen. Do not leave young children or the fire unattended.

◆ Keep "fire salts," which produce colored flames on wood fires, away from children. They can make a child sick if swallowed.

◆ Keep round, hard foods and candies, such as candy cane pieces, mints, nuts, and popcorn, out of reach of children under age six.

◆ Keep holiday plants away from children. Some are toxic. Call the poison control center if your child eats part of a plant.

◆ Keep alcoholic drinks and containers, baking ingredients with alcohol, and cigarette butts, out of reach.

◆ Post poison control center and emergency phone numbers near all phones. Keep syrup of ipecac handy, but use it only on the advice of a poison control center or physician.

◆ If you travel to the house of a relative or friend, perform an immediate safety check. Look for such things as visible prescription drugs or poisonous products, unguarded appliances and stairs, toxic products under sinks, and unprotected electrical outlets.

◆ Keep a close eye on your child. When visiting someplace you go frequently, take along necessary safety devices for temporary use.

◆ When shopping with small children, sew or pin their name, address, and phone number inside their clothing in case you become separated.

Some of this information is courtesy of the National SAFE KIDS Campaign.

Watch Out — Baby's Walking!

*B*etty is one of the best grandmothers ever, but the day she entered the bedroom and saw the window-blind cord tangled around her grandson's neck, she felt like the worst person alive. How could it have happened? She had cut the cords short, but still, the child had pulled them into his crib. When Betty found the baby alive and well, she wept with relief. Then she moved the bed away from the window.

Between the ages of six months and two years, children are beginning to walk, run, climb, jump, and explore everything. It's a wonderful time in their development, but a time when adults need to watch them like hawks. We can't allow for every danger a child will face here, but we can list some of the most common ones. **According to the National SAFE KIDS Campaign, the biggest threat to a child's life and health at this age is an accidental injury.**

Fire and Burns

- Cover unused electrical outlets with rotating-style safety plugs.
- Keep appliance cords out of reach by tying them up or taping them down.
- While working in the kitchen, keep children in playpens or highchairs.
- Turn pot handles toward the back of the stove, where they're out of reach of curious hands.
- Use place mats instead of tablecloths, because toddlers may try to pull themselves up by grabbing hold of the cloth.
- Never carry a child and hot liquids at the same time.
- Turn your water heater down to 120° F or lower to prevent scalding.

Falls

◆ Move chairs and other furniture away from windows to discourage young climbers.

◆ Don't let toddlers play on or near stairs. Use permanent safety gates at the tops and bottoms.

◆ Remove or cushion sharp-edged furniture wherever a child is likely to go.

◆ Avoid accordion gates with large openings; a child's neck could get trapped in the openings.

◆ **Highchairs cause almost 10,000 injuries to small children each year**. Use restraining straps that run around the child's waist and between the legs to keep him from escaping from the seat and falling to the floor or getting his head caught in the structure.

◆ The American Academy of Pediatrics recommends that baby walkers not be used.

Choking and Poisons

◆ Do not store household cleaning products under the sink. Keep them, and all poisons, locked up and out of reach.

◆ Small children use their mouths to explore the world. Keep them away from objects they can pick up and swallow, such as toys for older children, safety pins, coins, broken or deflated balloons, jewelry, and batteries. Remove refrigerator magnets.

◆ Remove wall hangings and mobiles over the crib.

◆ Avoid all foods that could lodge in a child's throat, such as hot dogs, nuts, raw carrots, grapes, candies, gum, popcorn, and foods with pits.

◆ Learn how to save the life of a choking child. Consult your doctor.

◆ Use a small-parts tester "choke tube" to see if small toys or parts present a choking hazard.

◆ If small children are present, keep potentially hazardous cleaning compounds capped while in use.

◆ Use safety caps on medicines and toxic household products.

◆ Keep all purses out of reach.

◆ Dispose of plastic cleaning bags safely and immediately.

◆ Post the number of your local poison control center at all household phones.

◆ Keep a one-ounce bottle of syrup of ipecac in the medicine cabinet for each child in the house in case of accidental poisoning. Use it only on the advice of the poison control center or a physician.

The Dangers Never Cease

◆ Keep window cords out of reach. Cut looped chains or cords of window blinds in half and attach large safety tassels to the ends.

◆ Never leave a child alone in or near a bathtub, pail of water, or any other water for even an instant.

◆ Lock all cabinets and drawers from the countertop down, and oven, dryer, and dishwasher doors.

◆ Buy clothes with snaps, buttons, or Velcro instead of long, loose drawstrings, which can snag and present a choking or falling hazard.

◆ Encourage grandparents and caregivers to child-proof their homes.

◆ There are numerous products designed to keep your child safe. You should consider: toilet-lid locks; bathtub products, such as cushioned covers for spouts and knobs; anti-scald devices; cabinet and drawer latches; corner and edge bumpers; door guards; electrical-cord products; electrical-outlet covers; medicine-cabinet latches; stove guards; window-blind products; and window locks.

Access Denied

Pokemon, Beanie Babies, Tickle Me Elmo, and Harry Potter are childhood fads that will come and go. The Internet, however, is a growing phenomenon that is here to stay. It can be a source of entertainment and information for your children, and will be a useful workplace tool as they grow older. Sadly, it also poses threats to their safety. Take a few minutes to review these suggestions on how to make your child's Internet experience wholesome and productive.

Tell Your Children

♦ Never give out identifying information — name, home address, school name, or telephone number — in a public message, such as a chat room or bulletin board.

♦ Always ask your parents' permission before using your full name, address, telephone number, or school name anywhere on the Internet.

♦ Never send a person a picture of you without first checking with your parent or guardian.

♦ Never respond to messages or bulletin board items that are obscene, suggestive, belligerent, threaten-ing, or make you feel uncomfortable. If you get such a message, don't respond. Instead, show it to your parents or a trusted adult. A response just encourages the sender.

♦ Never meet a new online "friend" without adult supervision. (Parents: If a meeting is arranged, make the first one in a public spot, and be sure to accompany your child.)

♦ Remember that not everything you read online is necessarily true. Be very careful about any offers that involve your coming to a meeting or having someone visit your house. The biggest danger to your safety lies in getting together with someone you "meet" online.

◆ Regardless of who asks, you don't have to provide any information that you don't want to share.

◆ Never give out your password to anyone, even if they say they're from your Internet service.

Suggestions for Parents

◆ Set reasonable rules and guidelines for your children's computer use. Discuss the rules and post them near the computer as a reminder. Remember to monitor the children's compliance, especially when it comes to the amount of time they spend on the computer.

◆ Be sure your child is using kid-friendly search engines. Check with your Internet service provider for suggestions.

◆ Keep the computer in view in the family room or kitchen — not in a child's room.

◆ Monitor your child's chat rooms and e-mail. Set and enforce time limits for chatting, e-mailing, and surfing.

◆ Consider software that can monitor where your children have been online, block sites with objectionable words or images, limit computer time, and prevent children from divulging too much information. Remember, however, that filters aren't perfect. Even if they were 100 percent effective, software is no substitute for your involvement and guidance.

◆ Find out which safeguards are in use at other locations your child visits.

◆ Young children should not be allowed to "surf the Net" alone.

◆ Get to know the service your child uses. If you don't know how to log on, have your child show you.

◆ If your child receives a message that is harassing or threatening, or of a sexual nature, forward a copy of the message to your service provider and ask for their assistance.

◆ Get to know your children's online friends just as you get to know all their other friends.

◆ Watch for these danger signs and take prompt action if your child:
  • spends large amounts of time online, especially at night;
  • has pornography on the computer;
  • receives phone calls from people you don't know;
  • makes calls to numbers you don't recognize;
  • turns the monitor off or changes the screen when you enter the room;
  • receives mail, gifts, or packages from a stranger;
  • becomes withdrawn from the family.

If you become aware of any incidents that could put your child at risk, or indecent material involving children, call the police or the FBI immediately. For additional information, visit the FBI Web site, www.fbi.gov, and search for "Internet safety."

A Kitchen Recipe

It was just an evening among friends, and the kitchen was a busy place. Six-month-old Greg had made it known that the aroma from the kitchen was making him hungry, so Kay offered to feed him while Greg's mother prepared food for the guests. While Kay was feeding him, she turned aside for a moment to talk. In that instant, Greg stood up and toppled to the floor, landing squarely on his head. Fortunately, there was no damage to Greg's head, but it did knock some sense into the heads of the adults present, concerning the need for constant vigilance when children are in the kitchen.

Kitchens are fascinating places for children — filled with warmth, good smells, wonderful tastes, and myriad shiny objects. Each of those attractions represents a potential hazard to the curious, unsupervised child. To keep young children safe in the kitchen:

Kitchen Basics

- Never leave a child unattended in the kitchen.

- Store dangerous or poisonous substances, and plastic bags, in a high cabinet with a childproof lock.

- Unplug appliance cords when not in use, and keep them tied up and out of children's reach.

- Store canned goods and dry foods in low cabinets, and put potentially harmful products in upper cupboards.

- Keep utensils in a safe place, preferably in a childproof drawer.

- Store knives in a secured drawer.

- Install stove shields, or remove control knobs from burners and ovens when not in use.

- Insert childproof plugs into unused electrical outlets.

- Keep your trashcan in a closed cabinet or pantry.

- Keep refrigerator magnets out of reach.

- Keep highchairs away from the table, counter, wall, or any surface from which a child could push off.

- Don't put dishwasher detergent or sharp objects in your dishwasher until just before you turn it on.

- Never heat your child's formula in the microwave. The bottle may feel cool, but the milk inside may be hot enough to cause burns.

Remove Temptation

- Don't store treats over the stove, or in a place a child can climb to reach. Store snacks in a low cabinet.

- Keep pets and small children out of the kitchen while you're cooking. If you feel you need to keep an eye on babies or toddlers, secure them in a highchair or playpen.

- Turn pot and skillet handles away from the edge of the stove and beyond a child's easy reach.

- Never hold a child while cooking, drinking, or carrying hot liquids.

- Place hot foods and liquids away from the edges of counters and tables.

- Pay extra attention to items sitting on tablecloths or place mats, so children can't pull hot food or liquids down and scald themselves.

- Store matches in a fireproof container, out of reach of children.

When to Start

Here are some tips and age-appropriate tasks from the National SAFE KIDS Campaign, to help keep the kitchen a fun, safe place:

- Keep a close eye on the kids, and set strict safety rules.

- Never let a young child (under age ten to twelve) remove heated items from the microwave.

Over age 5:
Stir ingredients together in a bowl; rinse foods under cold water; use a cookie cutter; use a butter knife or plastic knife to spread peanut butter or slice soft cheese.

Over age 10:
Use electrical appliances, such as a blender, food processor, electric mixer, microwave, or toaster oven.

Over age 12:
Chop or slice with a paring knife; peel vegetables; use the stovetop to turn burners on and off and select temperatures; flip pancakes on a griddle; place a cookie tray in the oven; use an electric can opener.

Over age 14:
Operate the stovetop without adult supervision; drain cooked spaghetti into a colander; remove a tray of cookies from the oven.

Lacking Supervision

Parents don't want to leave young children home without adult supervision, but for many families there is no choice. **According to the National SAFE KIDS Campaign, approximately 5 million children spend time at home alone every day, and 4.5 million children are injured at home each year.**

First Steps

Before you leave your child alone, check with your local child-protection service on the legal age a child can be unsupervised. Contact your school district or the "Y" for possible latchkey programs.

To minimize the trauma to child and parent:

◆ Enroll your child in a self-care or babysitting course.

◆ Engage in "role-playing" activities. Act out each situation and coach your child on proper behavior. Possible situations include a fire emergency, a stranger at the door, a scary telephone call, a sibling who does not return from school, and an injury.

◆ Begin by leaving the child alone for a short time.

◆ Consider buying an easygoing dog for security and companionship.

◆ Develop and post clear house rules, from cooking, to play, to having guests. Buy snacks that don't have to be heated. Teach kids which appliances are off-limits.

◆ Make the house look occupied. Turn on the lights and radio or TV.

◆ Decide whether you want your child to simply not answer the door, or say through a closed door, "My mom is busy. Can I take a message?" The same applies to phone calls.

◆ Be sure children can operate window and door locks and the alarm system, and that they use them when they are home alone.

◆ Sit down as a family to discuss fire escape routes from each room.

◆ Keep guns, ammunition, prescriptions, liquor, matches, lighters, and cigarettes locked up.

◆ Point out potential hazards in the home, and teach children how to avoid injuries from them.

◆ Make sure kids know where the smoke alarms and carbon monoxide alarms are located and what to do if one sounds. Also, review procedures for power failures and overflowing toilets.

◆ Create a survival kit for a weather emergency or blackout. Include a flashlight, portable radio, extra batteries, bandages, jug of water, and games to pass time.

◆ Show kids where the first-aid kit is and how to use its contents.

◆ Tell the child where you will be, how you can be reached, and when you'll return home.

The Telephone Connection

Help children memorize important information, such as:

- their full name, complete address, and telephone number;
- their parents' full names;
- the nearest intersection to their home, to help direct police and fire officials;
- how to report an emergency to 9-1-1 or the Operator.

◆ Post a list of important telephone numbers next to each phone, including parents' workplace; police and fire departments; poison control center; and neighbors or relatives.

◆ Purchase Internet filter and blocker programs. Tell children never to divulge personal data.

◆ When in doubt about whether to call 9-1-1, always place the call.

◆ Consider carrying a cell phone or a beeper for emergencies.

◆ Occasionally, go home early and unannounced to be sure your rules are being followed.

Comings and Goings

◆ Take a "safety walk" through the neighborhood. Point out the safest route to and from school and other activities. Caution children against taking shortcuts. Tell them:

◆ Do not go into an empty home if they think they are being followed.

◆ Do not enter the home if there is anything unusual. Go to a trusted neighbor's home.

◆ Make a scene when threatened. Yell, "fire," instead of "help."

◆ Do not wear their house key where others can see it. Place the key on a chain around their neck and inside their clothing, or pin it inside a pocket.

◆ Never talk to a stranger, particularly one who tries to start a conversation. Define "stranger," so children are not confused.

◆ Never accept rides or gifts from anyone unless they have a parent's permission.

◆ Check in with a parent as soon as they get home.

Pool Perils

Swimming is great exercise and wonderful entertainment for children. **Nonetheless, drowning is the second leading cause of injury-related death in children. Each year, about 1,000 children drown, and another 4,000 are hospitalized for nearly drowning, usually in a pool owned by their family. More than 60 percent of children who drown in pools are under age four.** These tragedies do not have to happen.

Poolside Fortifications

◆ Install a fence at least four to five feet high, with vertical slats no more than four inches apart to keep children from squeezing through. It should have no foot- or hand-holds that could help a young child climb it.

◆ The fence should completely surround the pool, and prevent direct access from the house and yard.

◆ The gate of the fence should be self-closing and self-latching. Never prop a pool gate open.

◆ The gate latch should be higher than your children can reach, and should open away from the water, so small children can't use their weight to push it open.

◆ If the house forms one side of the barrier, then doors should be protected with alarms that produce an audible sound when a door is unexpectedly opened.

◆ Steps and ladders leading from the ground to an aboveground pool should be secured and locked, or removed when the pool is not in use.

◆ Remove shrubs or trees that obstruct your view of the pool from inside the house.

◆ The Consumer Product Safety Commission (CPSC) recommends layers of protection, including fence, pool cover, and an alarm system. To obtain detailed barrier recommendations, write the CPSC, Pool Barriers, Office of Information and Public Affairs, Washington, D.C. 20207.

Poolside Precautions

◆ Keep a telephone near the pool area. It's vital for emergencies, and you won't be tempted to desert a swimming child to answer the phone in the house.

◆ At poolside, keep a strong, lightweight pole that's at least twelve feet long and has a blunt end.

◆ Invest in a ring buoy firmly attached to a long throwing rope.

◆ Install ladders at both ends of the pool.

◆ Do not leave objects such as tables or chairs near the fence, where children can use them to climb into the pool area.

◆ The water depth should be clearly marked on the pool deck and, if possible, above the waterline of the pool wall.

◆ Indicate the break between the deep and shallow areas with a semi-permanent float line.

◆ Before using the pool or spa, always remove the cover completely. Beware: lightweight, floating solar-type pool/spa covers are *not* safety covers. A child can become trapped under this type of cover.

◆ A motorized pool cover operated by a switch that meets the standards of the American Society for Testing and Materials (ASTM) adds to the protection of your children, but should not replace the fence between your house and the pool.

You Can't Be too Vigilant

Constant, attentive supervision is the key to poolside safety when children are nearby.

◆ Never leave a child alone near any body of water... even for an instant.

◆ Do not assume that a child can swim just because he or she has had swimming lessons.

◆ Do not rely on inflatable toys or water wings to keep a child afloat. They are not life jackets.

◆ Do not bring tricycles or wheel-toys into the pool area. Children could accidentally ride them into the water.

◆ Forbid horseplay. Pools are for swimming, not wrestling.

◆ During social gatherings, designate an adult to supervise children. Rotate the assignment so the watchers stay alert.

◆ If a child is missing, check the pool first. Seconds count in preventing death or disability.

◆ Remove toys from the pool area when not in use. Toys can attract young children into a pool.

◆ Learn cardiopulmonary resuscitation (CPR). Babysitters and other caretakers should also know CPR.

Tykes 'n Bikes

Kids love their bicycles. **However, that affinity does not change the fact that about 250 children are killed and more than 350,000 children go to emergency rooms each year due to bicycle injuries, more than any other sport. Bikes are associated with more childhood injuries than any other consumer product other than automobiles.** To keep the joy in biking:

No Helmet, No Bicycle

Bike helmets reduce the risk of serious head injury by 85 percent. According to the Children's National Medical Center, universal use of bicycle helmets by children ages four to fifteen would prevent between 135 and 155 deaths, and between 39,000 and 45,000 head injuries, every year.

◆ Your child should participate in helmet selection to assure a proper fit. Do not buy one that a child can "grow into."

◆ A helmet should fit snugly, but comfortably. It should have a chinstrap and buckles that will stay securely fastened. A properly adjusted helmet covers both the front and back of the head.

◆ All helmets manufactured or imported for sale must meet a uniform Consumer Product Safety Commission standard. Look for the certification. However, helmets that meet ASTM, ANSI, or SNELL standards provide adequate protection.

◆ Never buy a used helmet. Do not use a helmet that has been dropped, or involved in a collision.

◆ Don't use markers on helmets.

And keep this is mind: If parents wear helmets when they bicycle, about 98 percent of their kids wear them, too. If parents don't wear helmets, the number drops significantly.

Rules to Ride By

◆ Take a bicycle-safety course.

◆ The American Academy of Pediatrics recommends that children under age eight should ride with adult supervision and off the street. The decision to allow older children to ride on the street depends on traffic patterns and individual maturity.

◆ Check your brakes before you get on the bike.

◆ Ride on the far right and travel with the flow of traffic. It is never safe to ride against traffic.

◆ Stop at stop signs and red lights, and obey all traffic laws.

◆ Do not ride two abreast unless you're on a bike path.

◆ Stop at the end of the driveway to look for cars.

◆ Be predictable; don't do anything that could surprise the driver of a car, like swerving or acting foolish.

◆ Signal when making a turn. Let motorists know what you intend by using proper hand signals.

◆ Don't ride too close to parked cars. The driver might open his door in your path. Leave at least three feet between you and parked cars.

◆ Avoid broken pavement, loose gravel, and fallen leaves.

◆ Don't ride at night or in wet weather.

◆ Don't clown around. Never hitch a ride on a moving vehicle, or do stunts or "wheelies" on roads with cars and trucks.

◆ Be seen. Wear light-colored clothing when you ride, including a brightly colored helmet.

◆ Put reflectors on the front and rear of the bicycle, on the pedals, and on the wheels.

◆ Wear close-fitting clothing to avoid getting caught in moving parts.

◆ Never wear headphones — they hinder your ability to hear the traffic around you.

Finding the Right Bicycle

Parents, choose a bicycle that fits your child's present size, not one she'll grow into later. The bike should fit the rider's ability and type of riding. To be sure your child's bike is the right size:

• Sitting on the seat with hands on the handlebar, your child must be able to place the balls of both feet on the ground.

• Straddling the center bar, he should be able to keep both feet flat on the ground, with about one inch of clearance between his crotch and the bar.

• When buying a bike with handbrakes, be sure the child can comfortably grasp the brakes and apply sufficient pressure to stop the bike. Under ages six to seven, buy a bike with foot brakes.

◆ Look for rubber-treated pedals or metal pedals with serrated rattrap edges. Avoid plastic pedals.

◆ Don't get a small child a bike with gears.

Heads-up Advice

Tommy now had the coolest bike on the block. It was sleek, shiny black, and made for speed. The bike came with a new helmet, but how cool was that? Girls weren't impressed by helmets. He was a dashing figure until he hit the manhole cover and flew face-first into the street, knocking out two front teeth and causing a concussion that sent him to the hospital for two days. Today, Tommy's smile is a little crooked, but he keeps his safety helmet on perfectly straight.

According to the Brain Injury Association, every year, one million people in the United States are treated for traumatic brain injury (TBI) in hospital emergency rooms. More than 50,000 die each year from TBI, and 80,000 experience the onset of long-term disability.

Major causes of TBI are: transportation incidents (44 percent); falls (26 percent); assaults and firearms (17 percent); and sports, recreation, and other (13 percent). Alert parents need to know how to protect their children from brain injuries, and how to identify a serious injury.

Some of the Facts

Nearly 300,000 traumatic brain injuries occur on U.S. sports fields each year. Repeated concussions not only impair memory and mental function over the long term, but may also trigger "second impact syndrome" — a sudden, fatal brain swelling.

There is no such thing as a "modest" concussion, and you don't have to be knocked out to suffer one. More than 90 percent of concussions don't involve loss of consciousness.

Experts agree that *nobody* who still exhibits symptoms of a brain injury should be allowed to play again until all symptoms have cleared.

After a brain injury, the risk for a second injury is three times greater; after the second injury, the risk for a third injury is eight times greater.

Helmets First

A properly fitted helmet is the most important piece of safety equipment for many activities. **For example, medical research shows that helmets could prevent 85 percent of brain injuries to cyclists.**

◆ Different activities require different helmets:
  • Bicycle helmets are OK for bicycling, in-line skating, skateboarding, and roller-skating;
  • When around or riding horses, wear an equestrian helmet;
  • Use motorcycle helmets on motorcycles, ATVs, snowmobiles, and mini-bikes;
  • Snow skiing and snowboarding require special helmets.

◆ Buy only helmets that meet the certification requirements for a particular activity. For details on helmet selection and fitting, talk to an expert, contact a national association for the activity, or contact the Consumer Product Safety Commission.

◆ The child should participate in selecting the helmet. Do not buy one that a child can "grow into."

◆ Never buy a used helmet! Do not use a helmet that has been dropped or involved in a collision.

◆ If parents wear helmets, almost all kids wear them, too. If parents don't wear helmets, the number of kids who do drops considerably.

In the Event of a Brain Injury

◆ After any fall or activity involving contact to the head, see a physician if any of the following symptoms are present: thinking problems; memory loss; dizziness; headache; nausea; sensory changes; balance, sleep or pain problems; changes in personality, mood or behavior; or trouble communicating.

◆ Ask your child's teacher(s) to call you if they see any symptoms.

◆ When your child leaves the emergency room or office following a brain injury, the doctor or nurse should give you instructions on caring for your child over the next twenty-four hours, and describe any important changes to watch for. If you do not get these "Head Sheet" instructions, ask for them.

◆ The effects of a "mild" brain injury may not be seen immediately. **See a doctor who specializes in such injuries right away if you notice any of these changes in your child:**
  • severe headache that does not go away or get better;
  • seizures, eyes fluttering, body going stiff, staring into space;
  • child forgets everything, amnesia;
  • hands shake, tremors, muscles get weak, loss of muscle tone;
  • recurring nausea or vomiting.

Choosing Childcare

Jay was a whiz at research. He had a Ph.D. in chemistry, prided himself in the thoroughness of his technical reports, and had no tolerance for sloppy documentation. All of which heightened his shock when he turned on the evening news and saw that his daughter's daycare center had been closed down for a long list of safety violations. How could that be? Why hadn't he seen those problems himself? After all, he was the master of research — at least he would be the next time he checked out a daycare center for little Sarah.

Current studies show that more than half of American children under the age of five are enrolled in daycare programs. To find a good program for your child:

Basic Research

◆ Begin by visiting the best center in your community, even if your child can't get in. It will give you a model of high-quality childcare.

◆ The staff should be certified, and the center should be licensed.

◆ Child/staff ratios are an important factor in quality daycare. The American Public Health Association (APHA) and the American Academy of Pediatrics (AAP) recommend the following child/staff ratios: thirteen to twenty-four months (3:1); 25–30 months (4:1); 31–35 months (5:1); three-year-olds (7:1); four-year-olds and kindergartners (8:1); and first-graders (10:1).

◆ Look for a childcare facility where you see a great deal of positive interaction between caregivers and children, and among children.

◆ Don't rely on first impressions. Visit at stressful times, such as when kids are dropped off or picked up.

◆ Read the caregiver's parent handbook carefully.

◆ Review the procedures used to check the backgrounds of employees. A well-run center makes careful checks of references, background, and previous employment.

◆ Talk with other parents who use the facility.

◆ Trust your intuition and observations.

Ask the Right Questions

Don't be afraid to ask questions. Some important ones are:

◆ What type of training and education do the caregivers have?

◆ How many staff members have left in the past three years? High turnover is disruptive to children.

◆ How long has the caregiver or center been operating?

◆ Is the facility accredited? Accredited homes and centers voluntarily follow much stricter standards.

◆ How often does the state inspect? Ask for documentation.

◆ Do the caregivers know how to maintain control?

◆ Are the staff members trained in first aid and CPR? Do they receive periodic retraining?

◆ Is there a basic exit plan? Have it explained to you. Are evacuation drills conducted regularly?

◆ Do they sanitize and disinfect changing tables after a child is changed?

◆ Do caregivers and children wash their hands frequently?

◆ Is bedding assigned for use by only one child and washed weekly?

◆ How do they clean the toys that go in a baby's mouth?

◆ Do they use a no-choke device to test baby toys?

◆ Are appropriate first-aid supplies easily available, inside and outside?

◆ Is there a plan to get a badly injured child to an emergency room equipped to handle children?

Look For the Right Things

◆ Are toys, games, play equipment, furniture, books, etc., in good shape, with no sharp edges? This indicates the facility has the children's best interest in mind.

◆ Do stairs have safety gates?

◆ Are fire exits clearly marked and accessible?

◆ Are smoke detectors and fire extinguishers located in appropriate areas? Are they tested regularly?

◆ Are hot water heaters and heat sources guarded to prevent burns?

◆ Is the kitchen clean? How about the eating area?

◆ Are windows screened and protected to prevent falls?

◆ Are sliding glass doors marked at both child and adult eye levels?

◆ Are matches, cleaning supplies, and poisonous or hazardous materials stored in child-resistant, locked containers, out of reach of children?

◆ Is there enough room for movement and play without danger or injury to the children?

◆ Are the electrical outlets covered when not in use?

◆ Are outdoor toys, such as swing sets, in good working order?

◆ Are indoor and outdoor surfaces appropriately carpeted or cushioned? Rubber mats, sand, or wood chips absorb the impact of children's frequent falls.

◆ Is there a fenced-in outdoor play area with a variety of safe equipment?

◆ Is the area free of hazards, such as culverts, drainage ditches, and open sewers? Is it clean, with no broken glass or trash?

◆ Is the play area visible and accessible to supervising adults?

Fearless Years of 2-5

Just after his second birthday, Tristan uttered his first sentence: "I need help."

Dangers inside the House

With active young children, you need to be alert to these dangers (to name just a few) in your house, or any house you visit.

While he might not have understood the full wisdom of that statement, the truth is that young children need our constant help when it comes to safety. **More than 1,500 children, aged two through five, die of accidental injuries each year.** Children in this age group will run, jump, and climb. They love to take "risks" and test their physical strength and skill, but they don't understand what dangers exist.

- Crawl through your house to look for hazards from a child's level.

- Keep lighters and matches out of sight and reach of children, preferably locked up. Teach children to tell an adult if they find them.

- Keep children away from space heaters and fireplaces.

- Never leave a child alone near water. If you must leave, take the child with you. Learn CPR (cardiopulmonary resuscitation).

◆ Keep young children out of the bathroom unless they are closely watched. Install a hook-and-eye latch on the door, above a child's reach.

◆ Never leave water in a bathtub, bucket, or pail.

◆ Set the water temperature at 120° F. A third-degree burn can occur in only three seconds when water is 140° F or hotter.

◆ Place plastic safety caps or covers on electrical outlets.

◆ Use unbreakable dishes.

◆ Make sure pot and skillet handles are pointed toward the back of the stove. Use the back burners.

◆ Don't store snacks above the range.

◆ Don't feed children foods that may block their airway, such as hot dogs, nuts, popcorn, raisins, large chunks of meat, chunks of bread or peanut butter, hard fruit or vegetables, grapes, or chewing gum. Also, keep toys with small parts and tempting small objects, such as coins, jewelry, crayon pieces, and marbles, safely away from young children.

◆ An adult must be present every time a child plays with a balloon.

◆ Discard plastic bags and balloon pieces safely and immediately.

◆ Use safety latches and locks to keep children from getting into cabinets and drawers.

◆ Keep medicines and hazardous products out of children's sight and reach, preferably locked up. This includes your purse.

◆ If a child places something poisonous in his mouth, call the poison control center or your doctor immediately. Have syrup of ipecac on hand to make your child vomit, but only use it if instructed.

◆ Move chairs and other furniture away from windows.

◆ Install safety gates securely at the tops and bottoms of stairways. Buy gates with openings too small to entrap a child's head.

◆ Block the entrance to pet doors. Children may follow a pet outdoors.

◆ Install edge guards on sharp furniture and fireplaces.

◆ Stop using a crib when the rail is about two-thirds of your child's standing height, and when there is evidence he or she can climb out.

◆ Cribs should not contain large stuffed animals or pillows. They can serve as stepping stones.

Dangers Outside, Too

◆ Use a car seat every time you drive with your child. Learn how to properly install the seat and fasten the belts. Have it checked by an expert. Children twelve and under should ride in the backseat.

◆ The National SAFE KIDS Campaign recommends children under ten never cross the street alone. However, teach young children to:

  • STOP at the curb, and never run into the street.
  • LISTEN and LOOK for traffic to the left, to the right, and to the left again.

◆ Wear life jackets when boating.

◆ When biking, avoid busy streets. Use bike helmets.

◆ Fence in your pool or hot tub on all four sides.

◆ Do not allow young kids to play in driveways or near busy streets.

◆ When shopping, use seatbelts to keep your child safely in her seat; or use backpacks; or shop where they have supervised play areas.

◆ Put twelve inches of sand, sawdust, or wood chips underneath play equipment.

The 6-12 Years

How good is your memory? What do you remember between your sixth birthday and your thirteenth? Maybe the time you climbed the tree and jumped into the sandbox? Or the time you took the dare and rode your bicycle with "no hands" down Maple hill? How about that time you and Johnny found some cigarettes and decided to light one up?

Do any of these shenanigans sound familiar? Probably. Which is exactly why you worry about your own kids at a similar age. And you *should* worry. **Each year about 2,000 children in this age group die from unintentional injuries**.

It's impossible to warn of every danger facing inquisitive children, but we can alert you to some of the hazards. The rest is up to you.

Basic Rules for You and Your Child

◆ Set the example, to encourage your children to do as you do.

◆ Teach personal safety habits in a calm and confident manner, without terrifying them.

◆ Tell children to:
  • never go with strangers;
  • run away when trouble arises;
  • say *no* to inappropriate requests;
  • tell you if anyone touches them, or tries to touch them, in their "bathing-suit" areas.

◆ Get to know the families of any friends your child might visit. Discuss safety issues with the parents, such as guns, swimming pools, older siblings, TV policy, dangerous animals, smoking, etc.

◆ Know where your kids play. Do not allow them to play near railroad tracks, quarries, ponds, abandoned buildings, roadways, new construction sites, or other local hazards.

◆ Keep safety in mind when deciding on activities. Talk to the leaders to review safety procedures.

◆ Teach children when and how to use emergency phone numbers. If they have doubts about whether to call, they should call.

◆ Post emergency numbers near the phone: police, fire, where parents can be reached, a neighbor who can help in an emergency.

◆ If you decide to have a gun, keep it unloaded, and lock up the gun and ammunition separately. Teach your kids gun safety rules.

◆ Children of this age group should not use power lawn mowers.

◆ Don't let children play with matches, lighters, or fireworks.

◆ Fire is always a concern. Teach this one early: if their clothing catches fire, *Stop, Drop, and Roll*. Also teach and practice what to do when the smoke alarm sounds.

Transportation Issues

◆ **Motor-vehicle incidents cause about 60 percent of the deaths in this age group**. Insist that children always wear safety belts.

◆ All kids in this age bracket should ride in the back if possible.

◆ Kids over forty pounds should be correctly secured in belt-positioning booster seats until adult lap and shoulder belts fit correctly (around age eight). The lap belt should be snug over the upper thighs rather than the soft abdomen, and the shoulder belt snug across the chest and collarbone.

◆ To fit correctly in only a safety belt, kids must be tall enough to sit with their knees bent at the edge of the seat without slouching. Shoulder and lap belts must be correctly used.

◆ If a child must ride in the front seat, make sure the seat is all the way back, and the child stays belted and sits back in the seat.

◆ Never let a child ride in a carpool without wearing a safety belt.

◆ When crossing a street with a child under ten, always hold the child's hand. Supervise children until they've proven that they're safe pedestrians.

◆ Plan and enforce the safest routes to school, friends' houses, play areas, and stores.

Each year, about 350,000 children under fifteen are treated in emergency rooms for bike-related injuries. To avoid injuries:

◆ Buy a bike they can control.

◆ Make them wear a helmet. Choose a new helmet with a federal label from the U.S. Consumer Product Safety Commission (CPSC). A used helmet could have flaws. To test the helmet's fit, tighten the straps and wiggle it around. If you can slip it off without unbuckling it, try another helmet. Never reuse helmets after a fall.

◆ Teach them to ride on bike paths, sidewalks, or in protected areas, but not in the street, and never ride after dark.

◆ Never carry passengers.

◆ Avoid loose clothing, which can catch in chains and spokes.

Don't Toy with Safety

◆ Keep safety in mind when selecting toys.

◆ Buy the right size of playground equipment for your child's age and height, and make sure there are approximately twelve inches of safe surfacing beneath it.

◆ If you do not have the proper playing area, don't buy items that shoot, propel, or need to be thrown. The CPSC recommends that children under fourteen should not use high-velocity pellet or BB guns.

◆ To keep children from playing with the garage door, mount the wall switch out of their reach.

◆ Review safety precautions and gear associated with in-line skates, skateboards, scooters, and any new toys. Bike helmets are okay for roller-skating, in-line skating, skateboarding, and scooters.

Some information is courtesy of the National SAFE KIDS Campaign.

Explosive Consequences

Danny and his pals had made a really neat discovery: if they held a soda bottle in their hands and lit a bottle rocket inside it, they could fire it like a weapon. They weren't totally dumb, either; they put on their sunglasses so no one would get hit in the eye. They should have worn suits of armor, too, because it wasn't long before two of the gang were hit in the face and burned. The pain was bad enough, but it went away. The scars will be there forever.

According to the U. S. Consumer Product Safety Commission, there are more than 7,000 emergency room cases related to fireworks each year. Sadder still, there are deaths. Injuries from the intense heat of fireworks, typically harming the eyes, head, hands, arms, or legs, can cause burns, lacerations, blindness, and amputations. Many of the injuries involve children under the age of fifteen.

When the Fourth of July or other holidays featuring fireworks are approaching, keep these things in mind:

Do Your Homework

◆ Check with your local police department to learn what fireworks, if any, may be legally discharged in your area.

◆ Class-B fireworks are the ones most often used for public display. The federal government has outlawed them for consumer use.

- Consumer (Class-C) fireworks are legal for public sale in many states. Class-C fireworks include fountains, bottle rockets, cylindrical fountains, Roman candles, rockets with sticks, mines and shells, helicopter-type rockets, certain sparklers, party poppers, missile-type rockets, illuminating torches, toy smoke devices, revolving wheels, and firecrackers with no more than fifty milligrams of powder.

- Remember: Even fireworks that are legal cause hundreds of blinding injuries each year! **For example, bottle rockets can move as fast as 200 miles per hour, explode in midair, and fly in any direction.** What's safe about that?

- Find a safe and legal fireworks display conducted by licensed professionals. Even then:

  - Stay in the designated watching area.

  - Do not allow children to retrieve a souvenir shell, even one that has exploded. Shell fragments could contain dangerous explosives.

Family Backyard Pyrotechnics

If community ordinances allow fireworks, take these precautions when using them:

- Always read and follow the manufacturer's directions.

- Store fireworks in a cool, dry area, hidden from children.

- Fireworks should only be lit outdoors on a smooth, flat surface, and away from structures and flammable materials. Thousands of fireworks incidents cause millions of dollars in damage each year.

- Do not light fireworks inside a can or bottle.

- Don't assume that Class-C fireworks are harmless. **The heat from a sparkler (1,800° F) can melt gold.** Imagine the harm it can do to a child's flesh or eye.

- Make sure spectators are at least thirty to forty feet away before lighting fireworks. **It's estimated that nearly 40 percent of fireworks injuries happen to bystanders.**

- Keep a water bucket or hose nearby for emergencies.

- Do not try to light fireworks that have misfired. Soak duds with water, pick them up with a long-handled shovel, and put them in a nonflammable container.

- Wear hearing protection.

If the Kids Use Fireworks

Only adults should handle fireworks. However, if you decide to let older children use fireworks under your supervision:

- Discuss safety procedures. Teach children to *Stop, Drop, and Roll* if their clothes catch fire.

- Show children how to put out fireworks by using water or a fire extinguisher.

- Never place your face or any other body part over fireworks.

- Never carry fireworks in your pockets.

- Leave the area immediately if friends are using fireworks without parental supervision.

- Do not dismantle fireworks or try to make your own.

- Do not hold any fireworks in your hand once you have lit them.

- Do not throw fireworks.

Things that Go Bump on the Turf

The soccer game should never have been played that day. It was dangerously cold, and ice puddles in parts of the field had been shredded into sharp slivers. Still, the adults in charge wanted to get the final game into the record books. The game ended abruptly for Timmy when he slid to steal a ball, and a piece of the jagged ice put a gash in his thigh that took nine stitches to close.

Like it or not, contact sports, like soccer and football, are an integral part of childhood for millions of American boys and girls. **Unfortunately, as the Consumer Product Safety Commission reports, each year, football and soccer result in about 360,000 and 170,000 emergency room visits, respectively.**

Because adults are sometimes more childish in their thinking than the children they supervise, parents need to remain vigilant.

Youth Football

If your child is playing youth football, check on the rules and policies for equipment and supervision. Ask these tough questions:

◆ Are there any weight and age requirements for players? Are birth certificates required?

◆ Is protective equipment required for both practice sessions and games? Is it in good condition?

◆ What are the rules and penalties for practicing without protective equipment?

◆ Who has training in first aid? Some organizations require that a trainer be present at all games and practices. It is also advisable that coaches be certified in CPR (cardiopulmonary resuscitation).

◆ What is the emergency plan in case of injury?

◆ What is the program's policy about cancellation due to weather or hazardous playing conditions?

◆ Are the coaches teaching proper techniques? If a coach is teaching kids to block or tackle with their heads (called "spearing"), he shouldn't be coaching — remove your child. The same goes if Coach thinks water during practice is for sissies.

◆ Set the rules for informal games in your backyard or up in the park, and enforce them.

  • Encourage passing and running scrimmages without body contact from blocking or tackling.

  • Encourage children to play touch football.

For the Soccer Players

◆ Make your child wear shin guards. Remind them that the professionals wear them. Shin guards reduce the force of kicks to the leg by up to 70 percent.

◆ Be sure your child is doing the proper stretching exercises before she starts a game or practice. All leg muscles should be stretched.

◆ Players under the age of nine or ten should not wear cleats. Instead, buy shoes with nubs on the bottom for traction.

◆ The playing field should be free of holes, rocks, and debris.

◆ In the rain, use a non-absorbent, synthetic ball.

◆ Padded goal posts reduce injuries. Encourage their use.

◆ Do not allow children to jump up or swing on the soccer goal posts. Falls from goal posts, and goal posts falling onto players, have resulted in serious injuries and deaths. Many of these "moveable" goal posts are unsafe, because they are unstable and not properly anchored or counter-balanced.

◆ For information on installing and moving goal posts, write the Consumer Product Safety Commission, Washington, D.C. 20207 for the booklet, *Guidelines for Movable Soccer Goal Safety.*

General Rules of the Games

◆ Look for leagues with formal certification procedures for coaches.

◆ Compensate for the weather. When it's hot, get plenty of liquids and avoid soft drinks. Sit in the shade when you're not on the field. In winter, wear layered clothing and — especially for younger kids — a hat.

◆ Don't let injured children continue to play.

◆ To avoid blisters, wear shoes that fit properly. Also, wear thin inner socks and thick outer socks.

◆ If a blister is forming, put a glob of petroleum jelly on the affected area, and another glob between the sock and the shoe.

Frightful Possibilities

Fall is the time of year for ghosties, and ghoulies, and things that go bump in the night. Sometimes, those bumps are intended to be scary; other times, they're unintentional and terribly serious. Whenever your children are getting ready for trick-or-treating, be alert to the dangers lurking.

According to Prevent Blindness America, emergency room statistics indicate that a child is more likely to be injured on Halloween than at any other time of the year.

A Word to the Parents

- No child should trick-or-treat alone.

- Plan and discuss the intended route. Stay in familiar areas.

- Accompany children under twelve on their rounds.

- Cars pose the biggest threat to children after dark. To make them highly visible, dress children in light colors, and sew or tape retro-reflectors or reflective tape onto their costumes.

- Costumes should be loose and comfortable, but not baggy or long enough to cause falls or to catch fire. No high heels.

- Purchase only costumes and props labeled as fire-retardant. Note, however, that these items may still burn.

- Capes and other costume accessories that might pose a strangulation hazard should be fastened with Velcro rather than with fabric ties.

- Avoid costumes with wigs, floppy hats, or eye patches, which block vision. Beards should be fastened so they don't hamper the child's vision or breathing.

- Wear FDA-approved, nontoxic makeup instead of masks, which can block vision.

- Avoid pointed props, such as spears, swords, or wands, which could endanger children's eyes.

- For young children, pin a slip of paper with the child's name, address, and phone number inside a pocket, in case the child gets separated from the group.

- Around your home, remove any items children could trip over. Turn your outside lights on.

- Inspect all candy before allowing your child to eat the treats.

Some Reminders Before They Go

- Establish a return time.

- Never dart out between parked cars, or from hidden corners such as alleys.

- Obey all traffic signals.

- Walk, don't run, from house to house.

- Stay off the lawns. Unseen objects or uneven terrain could trip them.

- Carry a flashlight or light-stick so they can be seen.

- For better visibility, wear masks on top of their heads between trick-or-treat locations.

- Refuse to enter strange homes or apartments.

Play It Safe

Most kids are going to play organized sports, but they aren't always aware of the potential for injury. Accept the fact. However, that doesn't mean adults can't be involved in making play as safe as possible for our enthusiastic young athletes. Here are some tips to help make games fun and painless.

A Set of Helpful Standards

The National Alliance for Youth Sports, (800) 729-2057 or www.nays.org, has developed standards for parents in developing and administering youth sports for children. Involved parents should:

◆ Consider and carefully choose the proper environment for their child, including the appropriate age and development for participation, the type of sport, the rules in the sport, the age range of the participants, and the proper level of physical and emotional stress.

◆ Select youth programs that are developed and organized to enhance the emotional, physical, social, and educational well-being of children.

◆ Encourage a drug-, tobacco-, and alcohol-free environment.

◆ Recognize that youth sports are only a small part of a child's life.

◆ Insist that coaches be trained and certified.

◆ Make a serious effort to play an active role in the youth sports experience of their child.

◆ Be a positive role model, exhibiting sportsmanlike behavior at games, practices, and home, while giving positive reinforcement to their child and support to the coaches.

◆ Demonstrate a commitment to their child's youth sports experience by annually signing a parental code of ethics.

Keeping Sports Fun

◆ If you decide to let your child play on a "Select" team, recognize that he or she might face additional pressures, and you might need to take steps to keep sports at that level in perspective.

◆ While virtually all coaches want to make sports an enjoyable activity for kids, a few coaches will use their positions to exploit children. Following are questions for parents suggested by the Florida branch of the National Center for Missing & Exploited Children:

1. Does the organization do a background check on coaches?

2. What is the coach's philosophy about winning and sportsmanship?

3. Are there other adults who supervise off-site travel?

4. Do children use a locker room to dress, and are there multiple adults present in the locker room when children are using it?

5. Do you, as a parent, have input into the sporting activity?

6. Does the coach promise to make your child a champion player, or want to spend time alone with your child outside of scheduled activities?

7. Do you talk to your child about how he or she likes the coach or the sport?

Where Does It Hurt?

There is a risk of injury in every sport. To reduce the risk:

◆ Take your child for a complete physical exam before taking part in any sport. Some children have serious physical conditions that can be aggravated by exertion.

◆ Become educated about the possible injuries that can occur in the sport. Talk with a sports medicine doctor or trainer to develop a fitness plan, and to get guidelines on preventing overuse injuries.

◆ Begin conditioning exercises before the season begins.

◆ Make sure your child has good equipment that fits properly.

◆ Use eye guards and mouth guards for high-risk sports.

◆ Don't ignore pain. If a child says something hurts, see a sports-medicine doctor.

◆ Buy a book on sports medicine and keep it handy. It will help you treat minor injuries at home. It will also help you oversee your child's general physical condition.

◆ Insist on safe playing facilities, healthful playing situations, and proper first aid applications. Know the answer to these questions: Where is the nearest hospital? How would I get there in an emergency? Who can I call for immediate attention if my child is injured?

◆ A trainer, parent, or coach trained in CPR, and access to a telephone, should be available near the playing field.

◆ Children are especially vulnerable to overuse injuries, because of the softness of their growing bones and the relative tightness of their ligaments and tendons during growth spurts. One way to avoid overuse injuries is to never increase intensity, duration, frequency, or distance by more than 10 percent a week.

◆ Watch the weather. Heat illness can occur when it's hotter than eighty-five degrees with humidity of 70 percent or higher.

◆ Make sure your child drinks enough water during a sporting contest. If children ask for water, give it to them; their bodies are sending an important signal.

Go Fly a Kite

Children and grown men and women have been flying kites for more than 2,000 years. Ben Franklin did it; Charlie Brown tries to do it. Whether you're a seasoned kite flyer or a novice, you'll want to follow these important safety practices.

- Do not fly a kite in wet or inclement weather. The wet cord can conduct electricity, and if you're standing in wet shoes on wet ground, you increase your chances of electrocution.

- Learn how to launch and land a kite properly. Running is the worst way to launch a kite.

- Fly your kite in a safe area. The best ones are level, open spaces, such as city recreational areas or beaches. Avoid rocky or bumpy terrain — it can cause you to trip and fall.

- Do not fly a kite in a street or highway.

- Never fly a kite near electric power lines, antennas, or utility poles. Also avoid buildings, electric signs, and railroad tracks.

- Do not use wire or tinsel to fly the kite. Metal lines can carry an electrical charge from a power line or atmospheric electricity. Use cord.

- When flying a large kite, use a reel and wear gloves. The pressure of controlling a strong kite can burn bare hands.

- If your kite lands in a tree, leave it there. Kites are inexpensive and replaceable. Your body parts are not. (You might be able to free the kite by loosening the line and letting the wind blow it out.)

- Do not fly a kite in air traffic patterns, such as near a local, rural airport.

- Be aware of bystanders who can trip you or be injured by your kite's antics.

Sports Accident Facts
Under Age 15

Sport	Annual Injuries*
Archery	900
Baseball & softball	138,600
Basketball	195,900
Bicycle riding	374,700
Billiards, pool	2,200
Bowling	5,900
Boxing	800
Exercise	36,000
Fishing	19,300
Football (touch and tackle)	173,200
Golf	14,300
Gymnastics	23,700
Hockey (ice, street, roller, and field)	25,800
Horseback riding	14,800
Horseshoe pitching	800
Ice skating	16,700
In-line and roller skating	87,300
Martial arts	7,600
Scooters	34,400
Skateboarding	33,300
Snow skiing	17,800
Snowboarding	8,100
Snowmobiling	1,500
Soccer	81,700
Swimming	55,400
Tennis	3,500
Track & field	6,600
Trampolines	78,800
Volleyball	15,200
Water skiing	600
Weight lifting	11,300
Wrestling	18,800

* Injuries treated in hospital emergency departments — under age fifteen. Source: National Safety Council

Monkeying Around

Urging children to "Run along and play" should not amount to sending them off to harm themselves. Unfortunately, that's all too often the result. According to the U.S. Consumer Product Safety Commission (CPSC), more than 200,000 children are treated in hospital emergency rooms each year as a result of injuries related to playground equipment, and approximately 15 children die. Here are some suggestions to help your children "Run along and play safely."

The Backyard Playground

◆ Buy well-made equipment and assemble it correctly. Place it on a level surface and anchor it firmly.

◆ About 70 percent of all playground injuries are caused by falls. The surface under any playground should be made of wood chips, shredded wood mulch or rubber, sand, or pea gravel, and should be at least twelve inches deep. This use-zone surface should extend six feet from the play area's perimeter. Lawns are not soft enough for children to fall on safely.

◆ Swing seats should be made of soft materials, like lightweight canvas, soft rubber, or plastic.

◆ Do not use swings in the shape of animals. They have been associated with several deaths a year. Also, the CPSC recommends full-bucket seats for younger children.

◆ Do not buy equipment with open "S" hooks, sharp edges, or openings between three and a half and nine inches. A child's head may get caught in openings that size, and he might strangle. This hazard has been especially common on rings and guardrails.

◆ Install playground equipment at least six feet from fences or walls.

◆ Put equipment in shady areas or facing north.

◆ Place protective caps on all exposed screws or bolts. Check for loose nuts and bolts periodically.

Community and School Playgrounds

Check out your public playground carefully before letting your children play in it.

- Be sure there are fences, hedges, or open spaces to prevent children from running into the street or parking lots.

- Make sure the use zones have the recommended surfaces. For swings, the use zone in front and back of the swing should extend out a minimum distance of twice the height of the swing, as measured from the ground to the crossbar. For example, if the crossbar is ten feet high, the use zone must be twenty feet in front and twenty feet in back of the swing seat.

- Surfaces elevated thirty inches or more above the ground need guardrails.

- The highest climbing platform for preschool children should not exceed six feet. For school-age children, eight feet is the limit.

- To avoid painful collisions, swings should be spaced at least twenty-four inches apart, and at least thirty inches from the supportive structure.

- Moving equipment should be separated from other equipment by twelve feet. This gives children a safe area in which to fall and walk. Also, these rides should have no accessible parts that can crush or pinch fingers.

- Ideally, preschoolers should have separate areas.

- There should be no sharp points or edges that can cause cuts.

- All "S" hooks should be closed.

- Be sure all sliding equipment has a platform, so children can climb down if they become scared. There should be a bar across the top of the slide, to force children to sit down before they slide.

- There should be no V-shaped openings, or open areas close to the tops of slides, where clothing could get caught.

- There should be no exposed concrete footings, tree roots, or rocks that could be tripped over.

Stay Involved

- **Approximately 40 percent of playground injuries are due to inadequate supervision.** Be sure an adult actively supervises your child at the playground.

- Do not allow pushing or fighting.

- Make sure your child plays on age-appropriate equipment. Equipment is specifically designed for ages two through five, and five through twelve.

- Children from two through five should not play on the following equipment: chain or cable walks, free-standing arch climbers or climbing equipment with flexible components, fulcrum seesaws, log rolls, long spiral slides (more than one turn), overhead rings, parallel bars, swinging gates, track rides, and vertical sliding poles.

- Do not allow your child to play on hot metal surfaces, such as sliding boards, or equipment with rust, chipping, splinters, cracks, or other signs of decay.

- Never dress children in scarves, or loose or stringed clothing, when they are going to be on playground equipment. The loose items can get caught on the equipment and strangle a child.

For more information, contact the National Program for Playground Safety at www.playgroundsafety.org, or (800) 554-7529.

Safe Schooling

Kids can find a lot of things to worry about at school. There's algebra, for example, and chemistry, biology, *Great Expectations*, bullies, and that awful stuff they serve in the cafeteria. However, some of the most serious threats to their safety lie in just getting to and from the school building each day. While we can't promise our children a safe world, we can take steps to minimize the risks.

Walking to School

Parents, more than 400 children between the ages of five and fourteen die each year after being struck by motor vehicles. Whether they are walking to school or to a friend's house, it is vital that your child knows some basic rules.

◆ To protect your child, walk with her to choose the most direct, safe route with the fewest streets to cross. **Keep in mind that the National SAFE KIDS Campaign recommends children ten and under never cross the street alone.**

◆ Select routes where as many youngsters as possible will merge at one place when crossing a hazardous street. It's usually more protected. If a shorter route is less safe, explain why it's not acceptable.

◆ Always use the "buddy system" when walking to and from school.

◆ Walk in well-lighted areas.

◆ Go straight to and from school — no loitering along the way.

◆ Cross at the corners. Stop at the curb. Listen and look left, right, and then left again before crossing.

- Also, look over your shoulder for vehicles that might make a turn. Keep looking in all directions while crossing.

- Do not go between parked cars.

- Do not assume that a crosswalk is automatically safe. *Be alert*!

- Cooperate with the police, school safety patrols, and adult crossing guards. Try to cross only at intersections where there's a crossing guard.

- Obey all traffic signals.

- *Walk* across the streets, don't run. Allow yourself plenty of time. Go only when the coast is clear.

- Face traffic when walking on roads without sidewalks.

- In bad weather, and when it is dark, wear something white or reflective and/or carry a light.

Riding the Bus

Remember: All school buses are surrounded by a ten-foot area called the "Danger Zone." In this area, it can be difficult for the driver to see you.

Parents, teach kids these National Safety Council rules for getting on and off the school bus:

- Leave home early enough to get to your bus stop on time.

- While you wait for the bus, stay away from traffic. Stand at least six feet back from the curb.

- Do not roughhouse or engage in other careless behavior.

- When the school bus approaches, line up away from the street or road.

- Wait until the bus has stopped and the door opens before you step onto the bus.

- Don't crowd your friends when getting on and off the bus.

- When you're on the bus, never put your head, hands, arms, or legs out the window.

- *Before stepping off the bus*, check and make sure that no cars are coming from the right.

- Take three "giant steps" away from the school bus after getting off — never walk next to the bus.

- Stay away from the rear wheels of the bus at all times.

- Don't pick up a dropped book or other object after exiting the bus. Get the driver's attention first.

- If you have to cross the street in front of the bus, walk at least ten feet ahead of the bus along the side of the road until you turn around and see the driver. *Make sure the driver can see you!* Wait for a signal from the driver before you cross the street. When the driver signals, walk across the street. Watch for traffic as you walk. Do not cross the centerline of the road until the driver signals that it's safe to keep walking.

At School

- Check playground equipment. Make sure it's anchored properly, and is at least six feet from fences and walls. Wood chips, pea gravel, or rubberized pads under the equipment should be at least twelve inches deep.

And, parents, about that bully: Confront bullying right away by keeping written records, and insist that schools protect children.

Abuse of Trust

Vince was thrilled when his son, Eric, was chosen to play on their community's select soccer team. Twelve-year-old Eric would receive excellent athletic training, play at the highest levels of competition, and learn valuable lessons that would stay with him into adulthood. Unfortunately, not all the lessons Eric learned playing soccer were positive. The team coach was caught abusing several of the boys and finished the season behind bars. Eric himself was unharmed, but his confidence in adults was badly shaken and he quit the sport.

Although studies vary, Prevent Child Abuse America supports the estimate that at least 20 percent of American women and 5 to 16 percent of American men experienced some form of sexual abuse as children. Generally, children are sexually abused by adults whom they or their families know, or by a relative. Children ages seven to thirteen are especially vulnerable.

What Parents Should Know

- ◆ No profile fits all offenders. However, be aware of people who:
  - treat children as property, by grabbing them or forcing attention and affection;
  - relate to children in a sexual or seductive manner;
  - use gifts and favors as their main way of relating to children;
  - entice children into their homes or into activities with them, or show excessive friendliness.
- ◆ Know your children's caretakers and check their references.
- ◆ Regarding special activities:
  - Make sure the organization does a background check on adult leaders.
  - See that adults supervise off-site travel.

- Be sure several adults of the same gender as the children are present when children use a locker room.
- Be cautious if an adult leader wants to spend time alone with your child for any reason.
- Talk to your child about how he or she likes the adult leader. If your child doesn't like the adult, or the activity, the dislike might be a signal of something more serious.
- ◆ Be wary of Internet contacts.

What Kids Should Know

- ◆ Give children clear and accurate information about sexual abuse. Teach them:
  - that most people are honest, and safe to interact with, but some people can be dangerous;
  - that it is *not* okay for an older person to touch or look at their private parts, and it is *not* okay for them to touch or look at anyone else's private parts;
  - the anatomical names of the private parts of their bodies (naiveté can make them vulnerable);
  - that they have the right to say *no* to a request for any inappropriate touch;
  - that they have a basic right to body privacy and ownership of their bodies;

- to always talk to adults about things that confuse or scare them;

- to tell you if they feel uncomfortable being alone with someone;

- that it's OK not to hug, touch, or kiss someone if they feel uncomfortable with that touch or person;

- to run away if someone tries to sexually abuse them;

- that when home alone, they shouldn't open the door or talk to unfamiliar callers on the phone;

- to accept gifts only if you approve;

- how to reach a responsible adult at all times;

- to always have a "buddy" when they play or go somewhere;

- not to play alone in deserted areas, or use public restrooms alone;

- never to get into or near a car with someone in it, unless they're with you or a trusted adult, and to never accept a ride from someone without first checking with you.

◆ Practice "what if...?" exercises at home, to prepare your child for dangerous situations by formulating appropriate responses.

◆ Explain the difference between "real love" (hugs) and "fake love" (inappropriate touching).

Handling Disclosures

Some signs of possible sexual abuse are: sudden changes in behavior (fears, hypersensitivity, compulsion, withdrawal, depression); disturbed sleeping patterns; fear of being left with a caretaker; dramatic problems at school; a child saying an adult is bothering him or her; a child unaccountably acquiring new toys or money.

◆ If your son or daughter tells you about confusing or sexual touches, *stop, listen, and believe.* Also:

- let your children know you love them and are very sorry it happened;

- tell them it's not their fault, and you're proud of them for having the courage to share this;

- then, get professional help for them.

For more information, contact Prevent Child Abuse America, (312) 663-3520, or visit www.preventchildabuse.org or affiliated state chapters.

Other organizations providing more specialized services include:

Childhelp USA, (800) 422-4453;
www.childhelpusa.org
a twenty-four-hour national child-abuse hotline offering crisis counseling and referrals.

VOICES in Action, (800) 786-4238;
www.voices-action.org
an international organization for adult survivors of childhood sexual abuse.

Summer Getaway

From the minute Tom and Debbie arrived at Disney World with their son, Michael, and his pal, David, they lost control of the day. Chalk it up to too much adrenaline and not enough planning. First, Debbie wore the wrong shoes — cute, but painful — and was hobbling from blisters in an hour. David's parents didn't say he was allergic to hot dogs, or that he sunburned easily. And then there was the two-hour episode when they all became separated from one another, and wandered aimlessly trying to link up, because they hadn't established a meeting place. Thank goodness they weren't on a real African cruise — they'd have ended up crocodile bait.

Whether it's a holiday with the kids or grandkids, or a long vacation, it's no time for safety to take a holiday.

Traveling with Kids

◆ Pack entertainment and snacks for children so the driver isn't distracted. Plan for extra rest stops.

◆ Take along a first-aid kit and book, and medication for motion sickness, nausea, diarrhea, and upset stomach.

◆ If the hotel doesn't have a sprinkler system, it doesn't deserve you — or anybody else. Find a safer place to rest.

◆ Ask for a room near exits on the lower floors. Keep the door locked.

◆ Familiarize yourself with your surroundings. Identify exits. Practice the fire escape route for your room with your family.

◆ Not all rooms are kid-ready. Check for problem areas, such as cords. Bring along socket covers and other devices you currently use around the house.

◆ Check the temperature of the hot water in your room to be sure it won't scald the kids.

◆ Keep poisonous and breakable products out of children's reach.

Summer Amusement

- Don't try to squeeze too many activities into one day. Pace yourself.

- Wear comfortable shoes with good traction. Dress in distinctive shirts or hats.

- Wear a wide-brimmed hat, sunglasses, and age-appropriate sunscreen.

- If your itinerary includes a theme park:
  - Make sure everyone knows the exact location of your car. Write it down for each child.
  - Obey all instructions regarding safety procedures, height, weight, age, etc. Don't be foolhardy.
  - Walk, don't run. Watch for slick surfaces and tripping hazards. Use handrails.
  - Note location of ride exits. Let children know where you will meet after a ride, or if they get lost.
  - It's best not to let children roam alone, even in the most well-supervised environments.
  - Don't force or tease a scared child onto a ride.

- Make sure there's one adult for every two children in your group.

- Children should know the full names of their parents and their home address. If you're out-of-town visitors, pin a piece of paper in their pocket with the name and address of your hotel or the relative you're staying with.

Water Parks

Water parks are a popular way to cool off, but basic water safety tips still apply.

- Be sure the area is well supervised before children enter the water, and keep your eye on them. Tell older kids to use the "buddy system."

- Stay in physical touch with toddlers at all times.

- If the child is not a good swimmer, use a Coast Guard-approved life jacket.

- Read all signs, and follow the directions. If you're not sure about something, ask questions.

- Don't dive and don't run.

- When you go to a new attraction, note that the water depth might be different, which can affect how a child uses the attraction.

- On water slides, go down face-up and feet-first. Don't count on being able to catch the kids at the end of the slide — sometimes the water is too deep to stand in.

- Wear sunscreen and drink lots of water.

- On "Lazy River" rides, ask for smaller inner tubes for the kids.

Protecting Teenage Workers

Yes, child labor laws have improved conditions for young workers, and employers are by and large more enlightened and trustworthy. **Nonetheless, the National Institute for Occupational Safety and Health finds that about 200,000 workers under the age of eighteen are injured each year, and 70,000 suffer injuries severe enough to require emergency room treatment.** Those alarming numbers can be reduced. Following the tips presented here can make work safer for your child.

Laws and Parental Rules of Thumb

As determined by the Secretary of Labor, teens below the age of eighteen cannot work in the following hazardous non-farm jobs: driving a motor vehicle or being an outside helper on a motor vehicle; manufacture and storage of explosives; slaughterhouses; jobs that require use of power-driven machines and cutters; radioactive operations; mining; logging and saw-milling; brick and tile manufacture; roofing, excavation, and demolition. For more facts, visit www.dol.gov/dol/esa/public/youth/tstour4.htm.

◆ Visit a school career center. Guidance counselors know what companies are good places to work.

◆ Go to the library and research a potential employer by reading articles and company profiles.

- If the employer is small and family-owned, ask for references.

- Forbid your teen to work late at night, including the weekend. Some safety advocates say teenagers shouldn't work after dark; others put the cutoff at 10 P.M., after which most violent incidents happen.

- Meet the co-workers and bosses. Be sure working conditions are safe, break areas are in visible places, and parking lots are lighted.

- Be sure your teenager receives thorough training about job hazards and how to prevent injuries.

- After a workday, ask about the day. Listen for anything that makes your teen nervous. It's important to ask tough follow-up questions.

- Take any concerns seriously.

- Be alert to possible fatigue. The combination of school, homework, and a job can result in the teen being less alert at work or when driving.

- Tell your son or daughter to call the police and you immediately if an attack occurs. Reassure them that it's OK to disobey a boss or lose a job if they are at risk.

- Talk over any concerns with management. If no action is taken, forbid your teen to work there — it's probably not a good company.

For Teens on the Road

- Have your parents take you to and from work.

- If parents aren't available, carpool with another reliable adult. Introduce that person to your parents and get his or her name, address, and phone number.

- If you drive yourself to work:
  - Keep the doors locked.
  - Never make eye contact with other drivers or make rude gestures.

- Have a security guard or trusted adult walk you to your car.
- Always check surroundings in a parking lot and under the car.
- Go back inside and tell an adult if you see or sense anything suspicious. If necessary, wait.

- On public transportation:
  - Sit near the driver. Report anything suspicious to the driver, who is trained to deal with such situations.
  - Don't talk to strangers.

Advice for the Young Worker

- Make eye contact with people coming into the workplace. Don't look down — it makes you look preoccupied and vulnerable.

- Get to know your co-workers. Check out anyone who seems suspicious. Ask others about the person. Note: The law prohibits employers from revealing confidential information, but court records are open.

- Be aware of your surroundings. Know where co-workers are.

- Do not go into secluded rooms alone. Find a "buddy" who always knows your whereabouts.

- Tell your parents or supervisor any rumors about someone's perverse or inappropriate behavior.

- If someone threatens you, or makes sexual innuendoes to you or a co-worker, report it immediately to a manager and your parents.

- If someone hurts you physically or sexually, call the police and your parents immediately, even if the boss tells you not to.

- Trust your instincts: if they say something is wrong, it probably is.

Don't Toy With Trouble

If you haven't seen the seasonal movie *A Christmas Story,* you're missing a treat, as well as a classic lesson in how *not* to give a child a dangerous gift. Ralphie has been warned for weeks that if he gets a BB gun for Christmas, he'll shoot his eye out. He gets the gun, Dad sends him off unsupervised to shoot it, and sure enough, Ralphie nearly shoots his eye out. But this is good-natured holiday fare, and our hero gets off easy. In real life, he might not have been so lucky.

According to the National SAFE KIDS Campaign, more than 100,000 children ages fourteen and under are treated in emergency rooms for toy-related injuries each year.

To keep the "happy" in your children's holidays:

Buy with Care

◆ Buy toys with safety in mind. Ask yourself:

• Will my child use this toy the way it was intended to be used?

• Is it chewable, breakable, detachable, flammable, or too noisy?

• Do the arms or legs of this doll pull off easily?

◆ Be sure the toy matches the age, skills, abilities and interest of each child.

Choking on balloons and pieces of balloons, small balls, small parts of toys, and tiny batteries, is the leading cause of toy-related deaths.

◆ Do not allow children under the age of six to blow up a balloon or be alone with one. **Balloons are the most dangerous "toy" for small children.**

◆ For children under the age of three, do not buy:

• toys with detachable parts small enough to fit inside a toilet-paper roll. A good rule of thumb: If a toy or part can slide through an empty toilet-paper roll, it's too small for young children;

• small toys that look, smell, or taste anything like food;

• toys with long ropes, chains, strings, or elastic bands that could encircle children's necks, especially if the toys will be placed inside a crib.

◆ Toys that *are* suitable for a child's first year include activity quilts, stuffed animals, soft dolls, and squeeze or squeaky toys. **Note**: Check to see that eyes, noses, ribbons, and buttons on dolls and teddy bears are securely fastened and cannot be bitten or chewed off. Better yet, buy toys that don't have them attached at all.

◆ Good toys for children between the ages of one and two are books, blocks, fit-together toys, larger balls, push-and-pull toys, and shape toys.

◆ For two-to-five-year-olds, consider nontoxic art supplies, books, videos, musical instruments, and outdoor toys, such as soccer balls.

◆ For additional suggestions, write the National SAFE KIDS Campaign, 1301 Pennsylvania Ave. NW, Suite 1000, Washington D.C. 20004 for their brochure on toys.

Buying for the Older Child

◆ If wheels (bikes, skates, skateboards) are on your gift list, include the necessary safety equipment (helmets, wrist guards, and knee and elbow pads).

◆ When purchasing toys for older children, consider the possibility that they might fall into the hands of younger children.

◆ Avoid propelled toys, such as toy darts and projectiles (and BB guns, until the child is old enough to take a gun-training course).

◆ Stay away from toys with rigid edges that can cut.

◆ Electric toys are for kids eight or older.

Storage

◆ To avoid injuries caused by toy-chest lids falling on children, buy a chest with a spring-loaded support that allows the lid to remain securely open.

◆ Children will also crawl into storage chests, so be sure all chests have air holes.

◆ Keep toys organized, with no little game pieces lying around. They can be tripping, choking, or poking hazards.

◆ Inspect toys regularly for safety.

Avoiding the Bad Bounce

*T*he *future looked bright for James. He was bright, athletic, and supported in all his endeavors by a loving family. When he asked for an outdoor trampoline to help him develop his gymnastic skills, the idea seemed to have merit. James and his companions spent many hours on the apparatus, twisting and bouncing and getting progressively more capable and daring. James wanted to develop a new skill that he'd seen an Olympic gymnast perform on television. With much confidence, but no*

professional training or adult supervision, he tried to execute the difficult maneuver. He almost succeeded, but missed the edge of the trampoline and crashed to the ground, hitting his head.

The future still looks bright for James, but now that he must use a wheelchair for the rest of his life, it looks considerably different.

The American Academy of Pediatrics recommends that parents "never purchase a home trampoline or allow children to use home trampolines," and that trampolines be banned from public schools. According to the U.S. Consumer Product Safety Commission (CPSC), trampoline injuries send almost 100,000 people to emergency rooms each year. As you might expect, most of them are children.

Given the potential dangers, here are some important considerations from the CPSC and others.

Look Before You Leap

◆ If you decide to buy a trampoline, some experts recommend you purchase one that is twenty-one inches high, or lower. Most injuries occur on full-size trampolines.

◆ Be sure anyone playing on the trampoline has first received proper instructions and guidelines for its safe use.

◆ Be sure the trampoline has shock-absorbing pads that completely cover the frame, hooks, and springs. The pads should be securely attached to the frame.

◆ Be sure the covering over the springs between the frame pad and the jumping bed is a color that contrasts with the color of the bed.

◆ Inspect a new trampoline carefully before using it, and check the condition of all parts every time you use it. Possible hazards include: punctures or holes worn in the bed; deterioration of the stitching in the bed; a sagging bed; ruptured springs; missing or insecurely attached frame pads; a bent or broken frame; and sharp protrusions on the frame or on the suspension system.

◆ Consider purchasing a net enclosure, which can help prevent injuries caused by falling off the trampoline.

◆ Don't use a ladder with the trampoline, because it provides unsupervised access to small children.

Spots and Spotters

◆ Always have adult supervision when children are present.

◆ Put the trampoline on a level surface and in a well-lighted area.

◆ Safe jumping requires a measured minimum of twenty-four feet from the floor to the ceiling. Few homes have this much indoor clearance.

◆ Keep trampolines fenced in and inaccessible to outsiders.

◆ If you use your trampoline outdoors at night, make sure lighting is ample and evenly distributed over the entire apparatus.

◆ Always have four "spotters" at ground level to break the fall of anyone who might tumble from the apparatus. Spotters should be located at the four sides of a rectangular trampoline, or around a circular trampoline. Their functions also include:

  • assuring that the jumper stays in the middle of the trampoline bed;

  • gently pushing the jumper back to the center of the bed if he or she comes too close to the springs;

  • telling the jumper to stop his routine if he appears out of control.

Once You're Airborne

◆ Learn the "Stop Bounce" before attempting other skills. The "Stop Bounce" is achieved by bending your knees and hips when your feet come in contact with the bed during the bouncing action.

◆ Don't get carried away. Keep your bounces low until you can control your position and consistently land in the middle of the trampoline.

◆ Save the complicated jumps for when you're under professional instruction at an accredited facility.

◆ Only one person should be performing on the trampoline at a time.

◆ Don't jump when you're tired or under the influence of alcohol or drugs.

◆ To avoid mat burns, wear socks, pants, and a shirt.

◆ Climb off the trampoline — don't jump off.

Information Sources

All articles have been reviewed by a Certified Safety Professional and Subject Matter Experts

AAA Foundation for Traffic Safety

ABC News

American Academy of Dermatology

American Academy of Orthopaedic Surgeons

American Academy of Pediatrics

American Association of Retired Persons

American Automobile Association

American Canoe Association

American College of Sports Medicine

American Council on Exercise

American Hiking Society

American Lung Association

American Lyme Disease Foundation

American Medical Equestrian Association

American Meteorological Society

American Optometric Association

American Red Cross

American Running and Fitness Association

American Speech-Language-Hearing Association

Arts, Crafts and Theater Safety

Arthritis Today Magazine

Association Of Home Appliance Manufacturers

ATV Safety Institute

Brain Injury Association

Cardinal Glennon Children's Hospital

Cellular Telecommunications Industry Association

Center to Prevent Handgun Violence

Centers for Disease Control and Prevention

Chesterfield Fire Protection District

Chesterfield Journal

Children's National Medical Center

City of Boulder, CO

Colorado Division of Wildlife

Consumer Reports

CRASH (Citizens for Reliable and Safe Highways)

Egleston Children's Hospital

Federal Bureau of Investigation

General Motors

Hand Tools Institute

Health Conservation Programs

Humane Society of the United States

Industrial Safety & Hygiene News

Institute for Preventative Sports Medicine

Insurance Institute for Highway Safety

International Hunter Education Association

Johns Hopkins Medical Letter

Juvenile Products Manufacturers Association

Laclede Gas

League of American Bicyclists

Logan College of Chiropractic

Los Angeles County Lifeguards

Massachusetts Registry of Motor Vehicles

MasterDrive

Mature Outlook Magazine

Michigan Department of Natural Resources

Missouri Botanical Gardens

Missouri Department of Conservation

Missouri Division of Highway Safety

Missouri State Highway Patrol

Missouri State Water Patrol

Modern Maturity magazine

Mothers Against Drunk Driving

National Association of Garage Door Manufacturers

National Committee to Prevent Child Abuse

National Council on Alcoholism & Drug Dependence

National Electrical Safety Foundation

National Fire Protection Association

National Food Safety Database

National Geographic magazine

National Highway Traffic Safety Administration

National Lead Information Center

National Paint & Coatings Association

National Program for Playground Safety

National PTA

National Rifle Association

National Safe Boating Council

National SAFE KIDS Campaign

National Safety Council

National Shooting Sports Foundation

National Ski Areas Association

National Sleep Foundation

National Spa and Pool Institute

National Spinal Cord Injury Association

National Weather Service

National Youth Sports Safety Foundation

Nutrition Action Health Letter

Ohio Sleep Medicine Institute

Operation Lifesaver

Outdoor Power Equipment Institute

Parade Magazine

Personal Watercraft Industry Association

Power Tool Institute

Prevent Blindness America

Recreation Vehicle Industry Association

Shriners Burns Institute

Sierra Club

Skin Cancer Foundation

St. Louis College of Pharmacy

St. Louis Metropolitan Police Department

St. Louis Post-Dispatch

St. Louis University Dept. of Occupational Therapy

State Farm Insurance

Texas Department of Public Safety

The New York Times

TIME magazine

Toy Manufacturers of America

U.S. Coast Guard

U.S. Consumer Product Safety Commission

U.S. Department of Agriculture

U.S. State Department

USA Today

U.S.A. Water Ski

Underwriters Laboratories

United States Golf Association

United States Lifesaving Association

University of Florida

University of Missouri

Utility Safety Magazine

Walking Magazine

Wall Street Journal

Index

Live Safely in a Dangerous World

Order Form

YES, I want _____ copies of *Live Safely in a Dangerous World* at $19.95 each   _____

Sales tax: Missouri residents: 6.575% ($1.31 per book)
Ohio residents: 6.25% ($1.25 per book)   _____

Shipping and handling:
First book: (please circle) USPS – $4.00, or UPS – $6.00; $2.00 each additional book   _____
International: $7.00 first book; $3.50 each additional book

Total   _____

Phone orders: Toll-free: (800) 247-6553 (Please have your credit card ready)

Fax orders: (419) 281-6883 (Send this form)

E-mail orders: order@bookmaster.com

Web site: http://www.atlasbooks.com/marktplc/00740.htm

Postal orders:
BookMasters, Inc.
P.O. Box 388
Ashland, OH 44805

Payment: ○ Check   ○ Credit card:
○ MasterCard   ○ VISA   ○ American Express   ○ Discover

Card Number _____ Expiration Date _____

Signature _____

Name: _____

Address: _____

_____

_____

City/State/Zip: _____

Phone: _____

E-mail: _____